The *Tilted Arc* Controversy

The *Tilted Arc* Controversy

dangerous precedent?

Harriet F. Senie

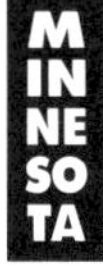

University of Minnesota Press Minneapolis / London

Contents

Illustrations

All works are by Richard Serra unless otherwise noted.

Preface

> Spectacle is the best means by which an official story is formed and is a superior mechanism for guaranteeing its longevity.
>
> **—Toni Morrison**

The issues in a public art controversy are always the same. You could name them now: It isn't art. It's an imposition of elitist taste. It's a waste of money. It's dangerous. What changes is the art, and sometimes response is so intense that it creates the illusion that the art under attack is somehow different, that this controversy is really only about the particular object in front of our eyes. The passionate arguments surrounding Richard Serra's *Tilted Arc* were like that.

In 1981 Federal Plaza in lower Manhattan was an open space framed by two nondescript government office buildings (Figure 1). Later singled out as one of the worst public spaces in New York, it was defined by a curvilinear pattern in the pavement and an inoperative fountain. There were no plantings and no place to sit except the rim of an empty pool. Enter *Tilted Arc,* commissioned by the General Services Administration (GSA) under a newly revived program that allocated for art a percentage of the construction costs of each federal building. *Tilted Arc,* a ten-foot-high, 120-foot-long sculpture of Cor-Ten self-rusting steel by Richard Serra (Figure 2), took employees by surprise. A chief judge of the U.S. Court of International Trade at Federal Plaza immediately began complaining to the head of GSA, an employee of the Army Corps of Engineers started a petition to have the work removed, and local art critics in the *New York Times* and *Village Voice* called *Tilted Arc* the worst public sculpture around, an indication of everything that was wrong with contemporary public art. This initial flurry of opposition had subsided by 1984, when William Diamond was appointed GSA regional administrator in the New York office.

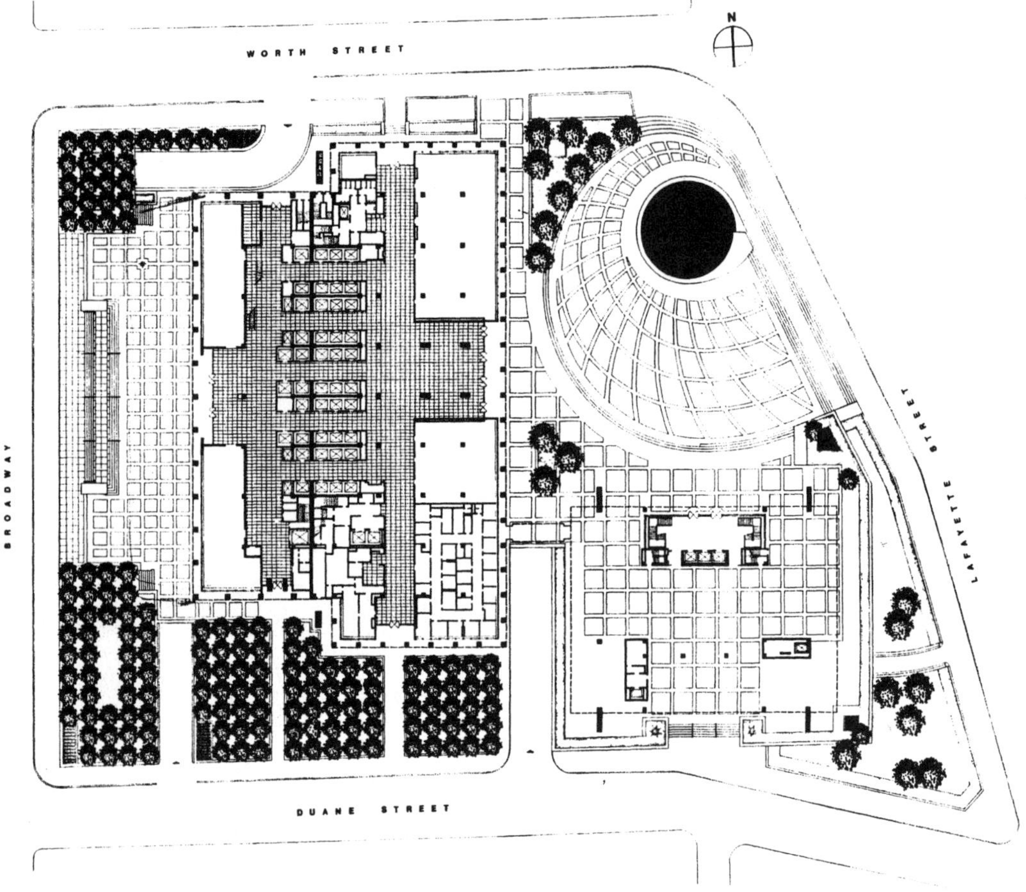

Figure 1. Federal Plaza site before *Tilted Arc,* plan, no date, New York City. Courtesy of the General Services Administration.

A graduate of Columbia Law School and a career, Republican-appointed, government official, Diamond launched a campaign to rid Federal Plaza of the sculpture. The widely publicized three-day public hearing he staged in March 1985 attracted an international audience to this local issue, and the *Tilted Arc* controversy became a spectacle of the 1980s. Although the overwhelming majority who testified at the hearing favored keeping the sculpture, Diamond persisted. After a panel of art professionals chaired by labor mediator Theodore Kheel in 1987 failed to approve any suitable alternative site, and after Serra had exhausted all legal remedies, Diamond finally succeeded in 1989 in having *Tilted Arc* removed, in pieces, to a warehouse in Brooklyn.

Tilted Arc was installed the year Ronald Reagan was first inaugurated president, and it was removed eight years later, the year the Berlin Wall fell. Like the destruction of most public art historically, it reflected a shift of political power and cultural values. Reagan's widespread dismantling of federal social programs, along with selective tax cuts and much corporate deregulation, created an ever widening chasm between rich

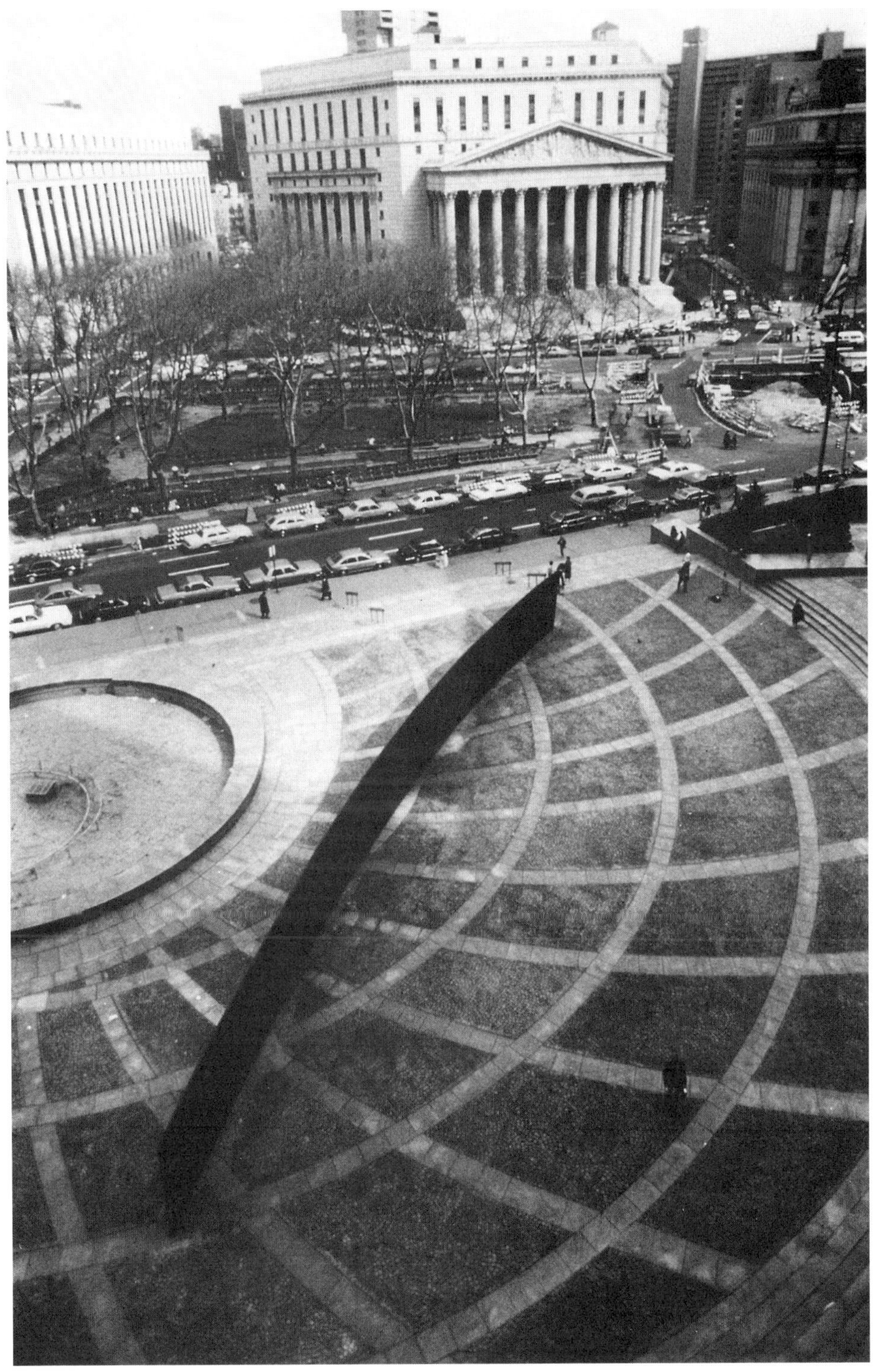

Figure 2. Richard Serra, *Tilted Arc,* 1981, New York City. Photograph by Anne Chauvet; courtesy of Richard Serra.

and poor and, for many in the middle class, rendered expectations of upward mobility futile. The American dream, it seemed, had turned to myth, and for many, daily life in New York had become an experience of increasing irritation or worse.

As conventional wisdom would have it, he who frames an issue usually wins. Diamond, at the hearing and elsewhere, defined what became the official narrative of the *Tilted Arc* controversy: the public versus art, with the sculpture pitted against public opinion and the free use of the plaza. Indeed, Serra's sculpture seemed to divide an open space in a city having precious little of it. And like public art in general, it both focused and reflected local problems. By appearing to threaten freedom of movement, *Tilted Arc* intensified a sense of victimization at Federal Plaza, with its ever worsening working conditions for government employees.

As the controversy persisted, a few blocks away on Wall Street the nation's economy peaked and began unraveling. As scandal after scandal came to light in local and national government, it seemed as if established controls had ceased to function.[1] At Federal Plaza, *Tilted Arc* reversed all expectations of art by controlling the viewer by virtue of its size and sweep. There was no way to avoid it; one became, willingly or not, a participant (not a spectator) in a city where staying uninvolved was perceived as the safest personal strategy, the preferred way to negotiate a public space.

The actual events of *Tilted Arc*'s installation (ten years after the opening of the building, yet without any public preparation), the way it suddenly blocked existing sight lines, and the strong visceral reaction of feeling threatened by the tilt of the arc, typical of Serra's work, were real enough. But in the "civic center" of lower Manhattan, representing the federal presence in New York, *Tilted Arc* gathered a disproportionate rage. The potency of its symbolic narrative of the public versus art revealed a hostility that took many by surprise. Obscured by several decades of government funding for art and what appeared to be art's increased popularity (as evidenced in more museums and increased museum attendance), the art world in the personification of Richard Serra was suddenly, in one fell swoop it seemed, marginalized and demonized.

As a group, artists seem to inhabit a world apart, perceived as privileged yet often reviled. And art is treated in our culture as peripheral, an exclusive form of entertainment or a hobby. In the news only when it is the object of controversy or when huge sums of money are involved (at auctions or in thefts), art is nevertheless seen as separate from money (as if somehow above it). A unique product without fixed prices, its relationship to business is always masked. Museums no longer sell art directly, but a museum exhibition will double an artist's prices. Museum gift shops, though never in the galleries, are often located so close to them that one can hear the cash registers ringing.

And elsewhere the art world appears to do business invisibly. Contemporary galleries create a pristine atmosphere (bare, like Cistercian monasteries; their employees dressed in black). All visual attention is focused on the objects displayed without price tags (literally priceless); a discrete red dot next to the label is the gallery version of a "sold" sign. Although by law a price list must be available at the desk, an exhibition may be sold out well before it opens. Important customers (private collectors and museum curators) are called ahead of time and offered the opportunity to buy. There is widespread suspicion that not everyone is quoted the same price. News of exhibitions, ads, and validating critical reviews appear in art magazines and special sections of newspapers. All this, when coupled with the widespread belief that making art is not work, fosters an aura of elitism and exclusivity, prompting deep resentment.

The *Tilted Arc* controversy was used to rehash a well-established story line that only furthered the cultural divide: Abstract art alienates the public. Typical of our time, when publicity seems to determine public issues, the controversy, rather than the sculpture, has survived. It continues to be discussed intensely, usually in terms of right and wrong, usually with participants "taking sides." But this divisive frame creates a closed loop constantly reinforcing the furor it evokes. As so often during the 1980s, a controversy with apparent winners and losers, an opportunity to vent anger, a spectacle that validated existing prejudices were the preferred avenues of address.

The aim of this book is to reframe the controversy. It begins with a brief history of public art patronage in the United States and of Serra's early career, followed by a detailed account of the GSA commission, which was often mis- or only partially reported in the press. Although public opinion was often invoked, it was never documented. Here public opinion is gauged from testimony and fliers pertaining to Diamond's hearing, letters to the GSA, television and newspaper coverage, and critical opinion expressed in various professional journals. The controversy is then reframed within the shifting paradigms in art, public art, public space, and public policy that characterized the 1980s. Each section addresses the controversy from a different perspective.

Art

Public art is not usually discussed as art, and Serra's work is not easily understood even in an art context. Seen both as minimal and postminimal, it has thus far been restricted to formalist and phenomenological readings. In a postmodern and multicultural art world, it was seen as demonstrating not only the decline of prescriptive modernism (especially abstraction) but the malevolence of the white male artists who defined it. However, by considering biographical elements, long denied relevance in interpreting abstract art, a different understanding of Serra's work and this complex sculpture emerges.

Public Art

Although viewed as part of the art world, public art operates outside the gallery system. It is thus a peripheral category in an already marginalized arena. It cannot be shown in museums except by proxy (drawings, models, photographs). And it functions differently economically: It doesn't generate revenue within the art business. If it is commissioned directly from the artist, there may be no fee for the gallery. There are few ads and therefore fewer reviews. (Here *Tilted Arc* was an anomaly, widely discussed as a result of the controversy.) Presumably, public art cannot be resold. Often artists end up spending their own money to supplement allocated funds. In the evolution of contemporary public art, *Tilted Arc,* even at the time of its commission, represented something of an old order, considered less critically viable than work that addressed public use and interaction. But Serra's sculpture was in no way a typical work of modern public art that might be easily anthropomorphized into a civic emblem or adopted as a corporate logo. *Tilted Arc,* with its sweeping form and precipitous tilt, could not be "used" except as a powerful art experience, one that was problematic in the already bleak urban context of its public space.

Public Space

Federal Plaza was typical of the open spaces that had proliferated in New York since the 1961 zoning ordinance that encouraged their development: an empty forecourt in front of a building.[2] As many of these so-called urban plazas came to be used for drug trafficking and were increasingly inhabited by the homeless, they were eventually deemed a failure. Later zoning encouraged a particularized rather than universal approach, valuing public use rather than open space, often in a more easily patrolled interior setting with commercial "amenities." In the media *Tilted Arc* was blamed both for not improving Federal Plaza and for rendering it useless. This criticism reflected an often unstated expectation that public art should function as urban renewal. In the postmodern art world, public art was attacked by some for not clearly addressing larger problems in the public sphere in a period of late capitalism.

Public Policy

From the start of the decade, arts funding was challenged at the highest federal level, and by the decade's end the very survival of the National Endowment for the Arts (NEA) was in question. *Tilted Arc* was caught in bureaucratic struggles both at the GSA, which commissioned it, and at the NEA, which appointed its selection panel. The controversy revealed problems in the public art process and a potentially serious gap in a legal system that appears to offer only limited protection for art, especially abstract art perceived as having no content.

As these various frames reveal, the controversy surrounding *Tilted Arc* was by no means simple or one-dimensional, but the actual issues and the diversity of responses were buried under an avalanche of antagonism. Since the 1980s, Serra's work has evolved, the so-called culture wars erupted, and the controversy has been variously historicized. It has been cited as a landmark in the history of recent public art in basic art history texts and in books on contemporary art, censorship, and public policy. Although no single interpretation pertains, the polarizing "art versus the public" narrative remains.

Reframing the controversy inevitably leads to a certain amount of repetition. Serra's work is discussed in the introduction, in the story, and in a section on the artist's work after the creation of *Tilted Arc.* The selection process for public art is considered in both the section on public art and the one on public policy. Issues raised at the hearing are analyzed in the chapter on public opinion and revisited in the chapter on the historicized controversy. The book is intended to be read as a whole with issues (re)considered from a variety of perspectives. But the various context sections may stand alone in terms of both what they contribute to and what they omit from an understanding of the controversy.

At times an interpretation of Serra's work, at times a reflection of the politics and policies of the 1980s, this book, like the evolution of the controversy, interweaves various narratives, both to offer a broader perspective and to present different contexts for considering its various implications. By reframing the controversy, I hope to replace the rage it evoked with a more useful dialogue about the nature of controversy and the place of public art in our culture. Toward that end, I intend to leave the reader with pertinent questions rather than definitive answers.

Acknowledgments

Over the past decade I have had the benefit of numerous exchanges with individuals directly and indirectly involved with the *Tilted Arc* controversy. Many people responded to my previous publications on the subject (a profile of Richard Serra published in *Artnews* in March 1984; the Public Art Fund Newsletter, Summer 1985; "Richard Serra's *Tilted Arc:* Art and Non-Art Issues," *Art Journal,* Winter 1989) and discussed the issues with me at various symposia, professional meetings, and hearings. My students in seminars on public art at the City College and at the Graduate Center, City University of New York (CUNY), have also made valuable contributions. A PSC-CUNY research grant in 1992 enabled me to study several of Serra's sculptures in France and Germany, and a sabbatical in 1997 provided valuable time to synthesize the material.

Ongoing conversations with various public art administrators and curators over the years have greatly informed my thinking. My thanks to Sandra Bloodworth, Jim Clark, Charlotte Cohen, Jenny Dixon, Tom Eccles, Wendy Feuer, Tom Finkelpearl, Patricia Fuller, Pallas Lombardi, and Anne Pasternak. I also benefited from the expertise of several key individuals at the General Services Administration (GSA): The late Don Thalacker, director of the Art-in-Architecture program when Serra was awarded the commission, was a model of integrity and commitment; Marilyn Farley's first-hand insights into its workings were invaluable. I also wish to thank Dale Lanzone, director of the Arts and Historic Preservation program from 1988 to 1996, and Susan Harrison for providing useful information and access to documents. Crucial insight into the workings of GSA was provided by Terry Golden, who was its chief administrator from 1985 to 1988. William Caine was of immeasurable assistance with information on recent GSA policy. At the National Endowment for the Arts (NEA), I am grateful to Michael Faubion, former assistant director of the Visual Arts program, for his comments and insights and to Richard Andrews, director of the Visual Arts program from 1985 to 1987, for his recollections and valuable perspective.

Barbara Hoffman's articles and comments were crucial to my understanding of the legal issues involved, as were discussions with Jack Guthman and Jean Reed Haynes. A shortened version of this portion of the manuscript was published in *Public Art Review*, Fall 1994.

My thanks to Stanislaus von Moos for the opportunity to present portions of this book to a seminar he was teaching at Princeton University in spring 1997 and as a lecture in the series KunstBauKunst sponsored by the Schweizerisches Institut für Kunstwissenschaft in Zurich in January 1988. My thanks also to those who provided valuable commentary on various portions of the manuscript: Michael Brenson, Wendy Feuer, and Laurie Wilson; and my deepest appreciation for those who read it in its entirety at various junctures in its development: Judith Chiti, Lise Kjaer, Michael Kwartler, Burt Roberts, Elke Solomon, and Sally Webster. A special thanks to my mother, Gerda Freitag, for her translations of various German texts, and to James Romaine for some crucial fact checking at the end of the project; to my editor at the University of Minnesota Press, Jennifer Moore; and to copy editor Kathy Delfosse.

I wish to express my deepest appreciation to Richard Serra for his cooperation and willingness to discuss difficult issues and to Trina McKeever for her assistance with photographs and much else.

Prologue

When *Tilted Arc* was commissioned in 1979, strong federal support for art had been in place for little over a decade and was already beginning to be questioned. The first phase of the public art revival of the late sixties appeared to be drawing to a close, and Richard Serra was considered an important younger artist working in ways that expanded definitions of modern sculpture. Enjoying the patronage of important dealers and museums in the United States and Europe, he had already begun a career in public art, and several of his commissions were aborted or re-sited or became the object, at least for a time, of bitter controversy. In almost every way, the *Tilted Arc* controversy, if not prefigured, was certainly predictable.

Public Art Patronage in the United States

> Democracies alone can afford to permit differences of opinion, even in aesthetic matters.
>
> **—Holger Cahill**

Although public art might seem to be the ideal art form for a democratic society, that has hardly been the case. From this country's start, federal public art patronage has been fraught with problems. The issues raised by the *Tilted Arc* controversy were remarkably similar to those surrounding Horatio Greenough's *George Washington* (1832–41), a seated seminude figure in classical dress, commissioned for the Capitol rotunda in Washington, D.C., to celebrate the centennial of the first president's birth.[1]

Both Greenough and Serra had strong support in the art world, were the recipients of prestigious commissions intended for federal property, and worked in a style that was misunderstood and criticized by large segments of the public for whom these works were ostensibly intended. Both sculptures were initially the butt of memorable insults (*George Washington* was dubbed "Venus of the bath" and *Tilted Arc* was called "the Berlin Wall of Foley Square"). Both were vandalized by graffiti and were eventually removed from their original sites (Greenough's first to the Capitol grounds and later to the entrance hall of the Museum of History and Technology of the Smithsonian Institution in Washington, D.C.; Serra's initially to a warehouse in Brooklyn, New York, and subsequently to a GSA storage area in Middle River, Maryland, outside Baltimore). More significantly, both precipitated discussions of art on a national scale and remain historicized as examples of public art disasters.[2]

Other works, like the Washington Monument and the New York Public Library lions, now an integral part of their urbanscapes and completely identified with their sites, were once the subject of bitter controversy.[3] Modern and contemporary art, particularly public art, seem to rest uneasy in the United States. There has never been a consistent pattern of public support for art in this country. Related to European practices associated with the monarchy or the church, official patronage was considered suspect in the new republic.[4] Although income-tax policies encouraged private support of the arts, it was not until the 1930s that an institutionalized system for direct federal funding was established. At that time, in response to the national economic crisis of the Great Depression, the United States embarked on the largest public art program in the world.[5] From 1935 to 1943, under various federal departments, artists were employed (like other workers) both to make art and to create works for specific government buildings.

The Works Progress Administration Federal Art Project (WPA/FAP), created in 1934 and supervised by Holger Cahill, was a wide-ranging relief program for artists. It served as a precedent for many later programs of the NEA. The Treasury Department's Section of Painting and Sculpture (later the Section of Fine Arts, known as Section), also established in 1934 and directed by Edward Bruce, commissioned art directly for federal buildings by allocating 1 percent of construction costs.[6] Terminated in 1943 because of the war effort, this program served as a funding model for the GSA's Art-in-Architecture program, created twenty years later, which commissioned Serra in 1979 to create a sculpture for Federal Plaza.

Both the Section and GSA programs, unlike the WPA/FAP and the NEA, commissioned art directly, but there were substantial differences between them, both in impetus and in the type of art commissioned. Although both programs were based on the premise that art was a desirable addition to architecture, the New Deal programs were part of the total government relief program directed at individuals, while the GSA program was part of a larger urban renewal effort directed at the deteriorating conditions of U.S. cities.

Section art commissions were largely determined by anonymous local competitions with the federal office having the final say. Both famous and lesser-known artists working in a variety of representational styles were selected by this time-consuming and expensive method. The GSA's Art-in-Architecture program was more centralized and aimed to commission permanent art from major national artists. Until *Tilted Arc* and for a brief time thereafter, selection panels were appointed by the NEA.

During the New Deal only a few large-scale sculptures were commissioned, mostly by artists already on relief hired by the WPA/FAP. Sculpture also accounted for only a small portion of Section art because its materials, labor, and installation costs were much more expensive than those of painting.[7] Then, too, the narrative subjects considered suitable for government buildings were more easily depicted in murals. Of the 300 sculpture commissions (out of a total of 1,400 commissions), most were for small reliefs.

Compared to the New Deal art programs, the GSA Art-in-Architecture program commissioned a large percentage of freestanding sculptures of monumental scale. By the early 1960s, stone buildings that had once provided a surface for relief sculptures had been largely replaced by modern structures with no place for art, sculpture had become as important a medium for contemporary art as painting, and abstraction had replaced the neoclassical and moderne figurative conventions favored in earlier decades.

After World War II put an end to federal funding, the subsequent McCarthy hearings of the 1950s, investigating the allegations of communist affiliation lodged against many cultural figures, made artists and politicians alike wary of government association with the arts. There was still apprehension in the sixties that a federal arts agency might appear to be setting a national art policy, violating the right to freedom of expression. The NEA and GSA public art programs emerged gradually under the subsequent administrations of Presidents John F. Kennedy and Lyndon Johnson, reaching full support under President Richard Nixon.[8] Once a solid pattern of funding had been established, concern shifted to an equitable national distribution. Support for mainstream art and art institutions in urban centers had to be balanced with encouragement for regional community-based art.[9]

The Public Art Revival of the Late 1960s

A national public sculpture revival began in the late 1960s, a decade before *Tilted Arc* was commissioned, reflecting a new focus on the livability of cities. The Great Society Task Force and the Department of Housing and Urban Development were created in 1964 and 1965, respectively, and the Model Cities Act was passed in 1966.[10] The NEA's Art in Public Places program was created in 1967, two years after the Endowment itself.

The public sculpture revival began with the placement of large-scale sculpture by already world-famous artists in conjunction with corporate architecture and urban renewal projects. By mid-decade plans were underway to situate works by Pablo Picasso, Henry Moore, and Alexander Calder in prominent public spaces around the

A Calder sculpture was also the first work commissioned by the GSA after its Art-in-Architecture program was reactivated in 1972. Championed by one of the building architects in Chicago, Carter Manny Jr. of C. F. Murphy Associates (Manny had also been involved with the Chicago Picasso), Calder's *Flamingo* was installed in 1973 at Chicago's Federal Plaza in front of a building designed by Mies van der Rohe.

Six years later, when *Tilted Arc* was commissioned, the GSA's practice of choosing large-scale, mostly abstract work for new federal construction was well established. Commissions had been awarded to well-known sculptors such as Mark di Suvero, Louise Nevelson, Isamu Noguchi, Claes Oldenburg, George Rickey, George Sugarman, and Tony Smith.[15] While historical models of the statue in the square fulfilled a commemorative function, their latter-day incarnations were monumental in scale only and expressed an aesthetic largely unfamiliar and often unfathomable to a significant segment of its audience.[16]

Although Serra conceived his site-specific sculpture in antithesis to then recent public art that was criticized for having no relationship to its site and for serving a merely decorative function, *Tilted Arc* was later seen as marking the end of an era of public art defined by abstract object sculpture, referred to disparagingly as "plop art." In the absence of any recognizable meaning relevant either to the public or the site, this type of public sculpture came to be seen as the embodiment of the presumptuous elitism of the art world.

Richard Serra before *Tilted Arc*

Richard Serra, generally recognized in the art world as one of the most important sculptors of the twentieth century, was born in San Francisco in 1939, the middle son of a Spanish factory-worker father and a Russian-Jewish mother who was more than a Sunday painter and who often took him to museums. He was encouraged by his parents to draw (something his two brothers did not do). Art books were readily available, so early on he "could identify paintings as well as most kids could identify cars."[17] As a child he was also greatly impressed with the launching of ships. A combination of influences from the world of work and the world of art characterize much of his subsequent work.

Serra studied at the Berkeley and Santa Barbara campuses of the University of California, earning an undergraduate degree in English literature in 1961. While in college, Serra worked in steel mills to support himself; later he came to think of steel mills as his studio. He graduated from Yale University in 1964 with an M.F.A., along with Chuck Close, Rackstraw Downes, Janet Fish, Nancy Graves (to whom Serra was briefly married), and Brice Marden, among others.

The recipient of a Yale traveling fellowship, after graduation Serra went to Europe for the first time, visiting Paris because he had "a great respect for Cezanne and Brancusi." The following year he went to Italy on a Fulbright scholarship. In his first one-person exhibition in 1966, at the Galleria La Salita in Rome, Serra constructed habitats of found objects and dead animals, work he feels had an important influence on the subsequent development of arte povera.[18]

Settling in New York in 1966, Serra found a hybrid art world that he later described as follows:

> The predominant languages at the time in movement-conscious New York were Pop and Minimal Art, Abstract Expressionism being on the decline. . . . Stella and Judd were already creating structures which were not encumbered by the mythological, emotional, subjective content of Abstract Expressionism. Pop Art, which was in full swing, was a rehash of Cubism with generic American content overlaying the underlying traditional grid. It seemed very much about a commercial need to establish a new market and a new clientele. Pop Art was not my concern—with the exception of Oldenburg's plaster pieces from *Store Days.* Unlike the minimalists Oldenburg had not distanced himself from a direct involvement with material (hand-manipulation) and his use of gravity as a building component affected me. It coincided with Smithson's interest in entropy.[19]

Serra's concerns were shared by composer Philip Glass (whom he had met in Paris); artists such as Michael Heizer, Eva Hesse, Bruce Nauman, and Michael Snow; and filmmaker and choreographer Joan Jonas (at one time married to Serra). What linked this group, according to Serra, "was that everybody was investigating the logic of the material and its potential for personal extension—be it sound, lead, film, body, whatever."[20]

Serra defined his approach to making art with his *Verb List* of 1967–68. Using eighty-four transitive verbs and twenty-four phrases, Serra identified the various processes and constraints that interested him. The verbs begin: "to roll, to crease, to fold, to store, to bend, to shorten, to twist," indicating a variety of possible physical actions. These are followed by phrases "of tension, of gravity, of entropy, of nature . . . of location, of context, of time," the factors that determine or control the form of the work.

Serra's splash pieces of 1968–69 combined abstract expressionist gesture with industrial materials. Wearing a gas mask, he flung molten lead into the corners of various spaces including Jasper Johns's studio, Leo Castelli's warehouse, and the Whitney Museum of American Art.[21] In other pieces, such as *Tearing Lead from 1:00 to 1:47* (1968) and *Cutting Device: Base Plate Measure* (1969), Serra either disbursed his material horizontally in apparently random patterns or stacked it vertically. The implicit threat of imminent collapse inherent in propped or stacked pieces such as *One-Ton Prop (House of Cards)* (Figure 5), also of 1969, created a sense of precariousness, drama, and tension. These monumental balancing acts were precursors of the large outdoor pieces of the following decade, pieces that appeared even more dangerous outside the implicit safety of guarded museum spaces.

Serra's art world success began almost as soon as he settled in New York; he has always been represented by blue-chip galleries. Beginning in 1969 Serra was with Leo

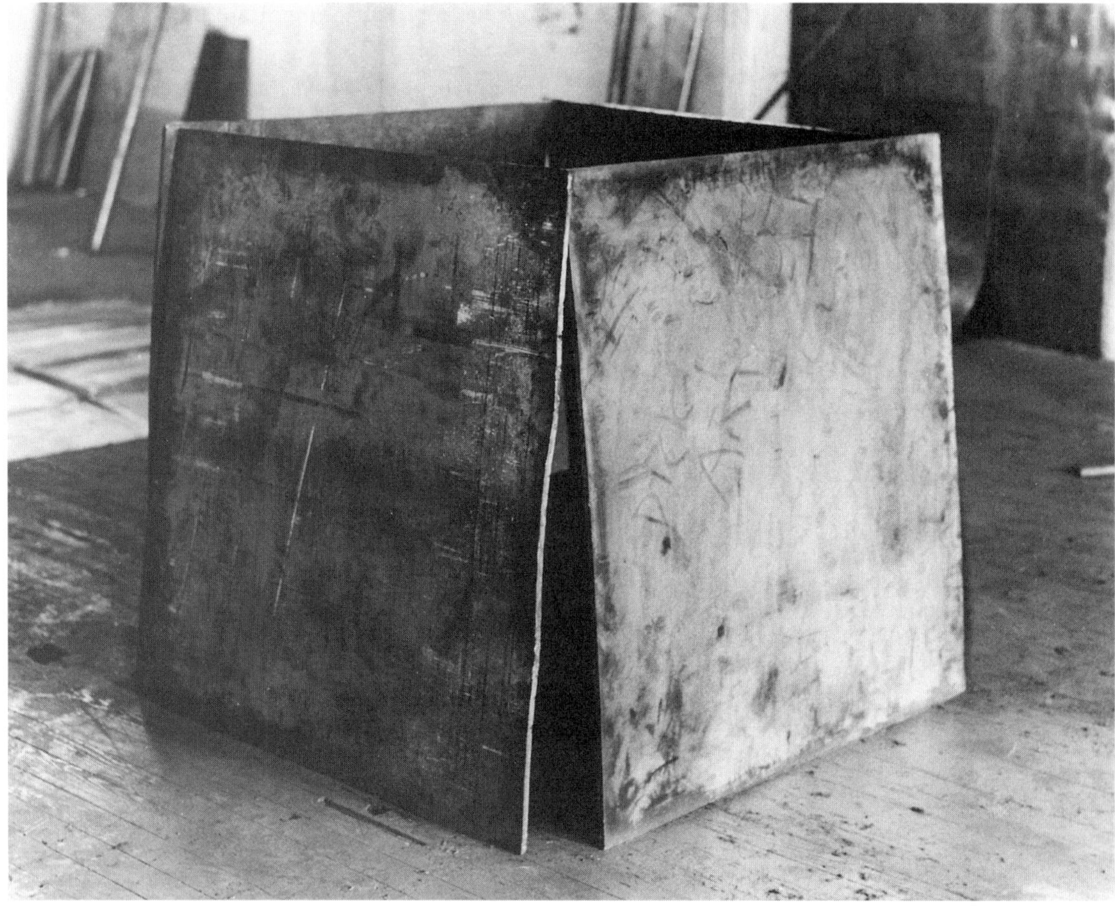

Figure 5. Richard Serra, *One-Ton Prop (House of Cards),* 1969, New York, Museum of Modern Art. Photograph by Peter Moore; courtesy of Richard Serra.

Castelli, and a year later he was also affiliated with Joseph Helman.[22] During the 1970s Serra exhibited regularly in New York, California, and Europe, especially Germany. He had one-person exhibitions at the Stedelijk Museum in Amsterdam (1977); the Museum of Modern Art in Oxford, England (1978); the Staatliche Kunsthalle in Baden-Baden, West Germany (1979); and the Hudson River Museum in Yonkers, New York (1980). His first retrospective in the United States was held at the Museum of Modern Art in New York in 1986.

Coincident with his museum and gallery art, outdoor sites became important in Serra's work after 1970.[23] He helped Robert Smithson stake out *Spiral Jetty* (1970) in the Great Salt Lake in Utah, thereby participating in the creation of the piece that came to epitomize earthworks.[24] He traveled to Japan to see the Zen gardens at Kyoto and later visited Michael Heizer's huge earth sculpture *Double Negative* (1969–70) near Overton, Nevada.[25] These various influences were evident in Serra's own outdoor pieces begun shortly thereafter.

Sculptures in the Landscape

Serra's first large-scale sculpture in a landscape site was commissioned by Emily and Joseph Pulitzer Jr., important collectors in St. Louis. *Pulitzer Piece: Stepped Elevation* (1970–71) consisted of three Cor-Ten steel plates, each five feet high and two inches thick, in lengths ranging from 40 feet, 3 inches, to 50 feet, 7 inches, strategically placed in a 450-foot-square area (Figure 6). Serra wanted the piece to incorporate elements of time:

> All of the landscape pieces involved anticipation and reflection and walking and experiencing the time of the landscape. The pieces acted as barometers or viewing edges within the landscape. The landscape work reopened the more structural pieces and defined new omnidirectional axial radii for there were many ways of entering into, through, and around. At that point, the basic content changed from a discrete

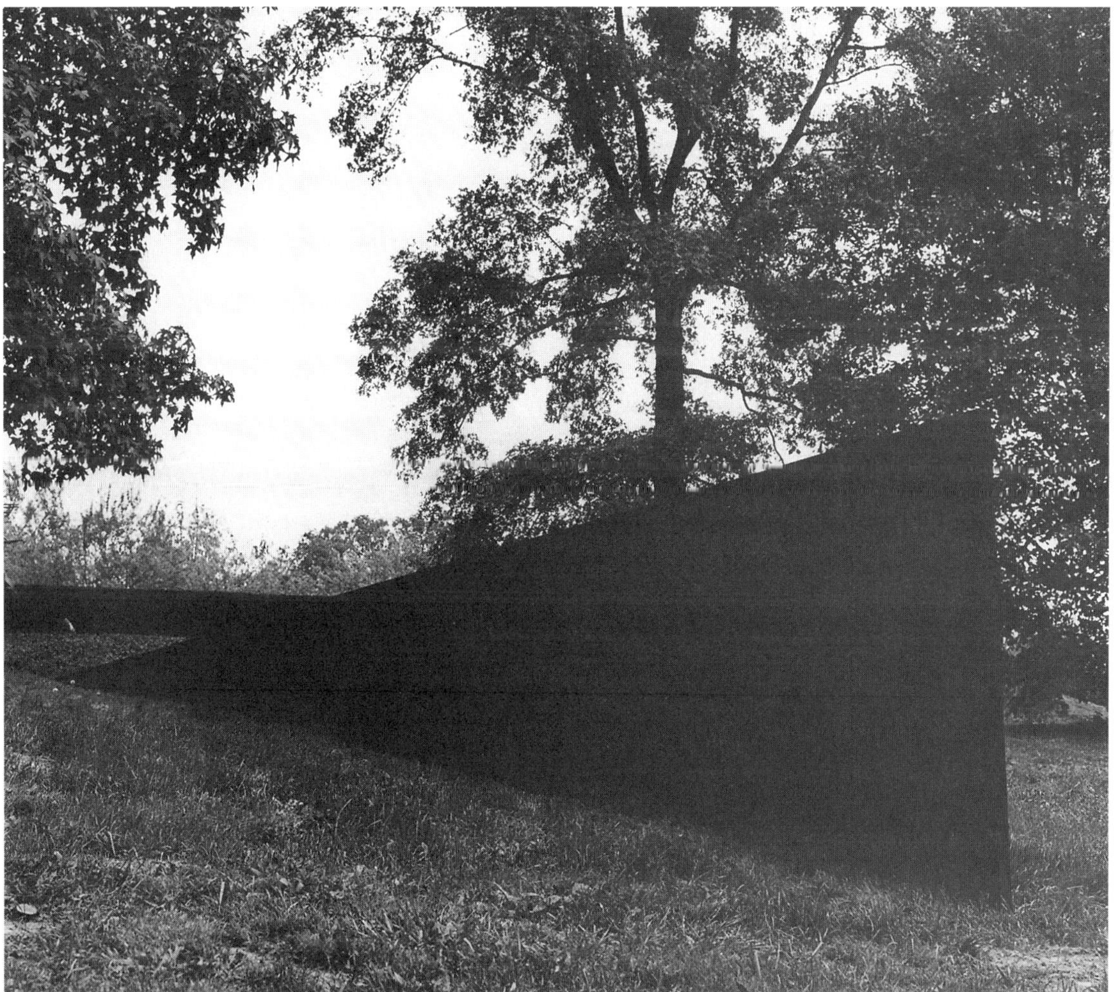

Figure 6. Richard Serra, *Pulitzer Piece: Stepped Elevation,* 1970–71, St. Louis, Missouri, collection of Emily Rauh Pulitzer. Photograph by Shunk-Keder; courtesy of Richard Serra.

> object in the round to walking in time, which has to do with anticipation and reflection. It is a different concept of organizing space.[26]

This piece was an important influence on Maya Lin's creation of the Vietnam Veterans Memorial (Figure 7) a decade later, when she was an architecture student at Yale and Serra was teaching there.

Re-Sited Commissions

During the 1970s Serra also began to create vertical structures for outdoor sites. *Sight Point,* composed of three steel plates each measuring 40 feet × 10 feet × 2 ½ inches, was intended for the Center of the Arts designed by Kevin Roche for Wesleyan University in Middletown, Connecticut. According to school officials, although the building committee invited Serra to make a model, financial backing did not materialize, partly due to overall budget constraints and perhaps also partly due to a lack of appreciation for the sculpture.[27] According to Serra, however, he won a competition in 1971 only to be rejected by the university's architect because the model was "too large and too close to the campus's historical building."[28]

In any event, *Sight Point* was built a few years later in 1975 for the Stedelijk Museum in Amsterdam; it was sited in the only available space, a rear court (Figure 8).

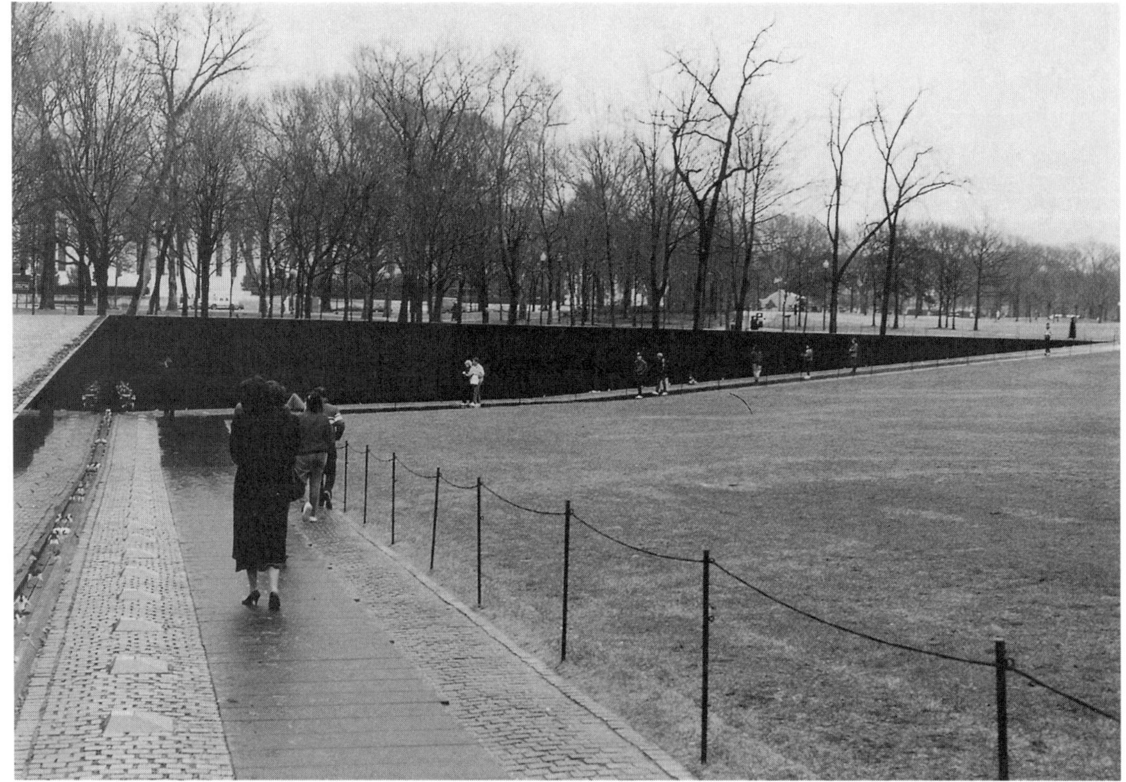

Figure 7. Maya Lin, Vietnam Veterans Memorial, 1981, Washington, D.C. Photograph courtesy of Annie Shaver-Crandell.

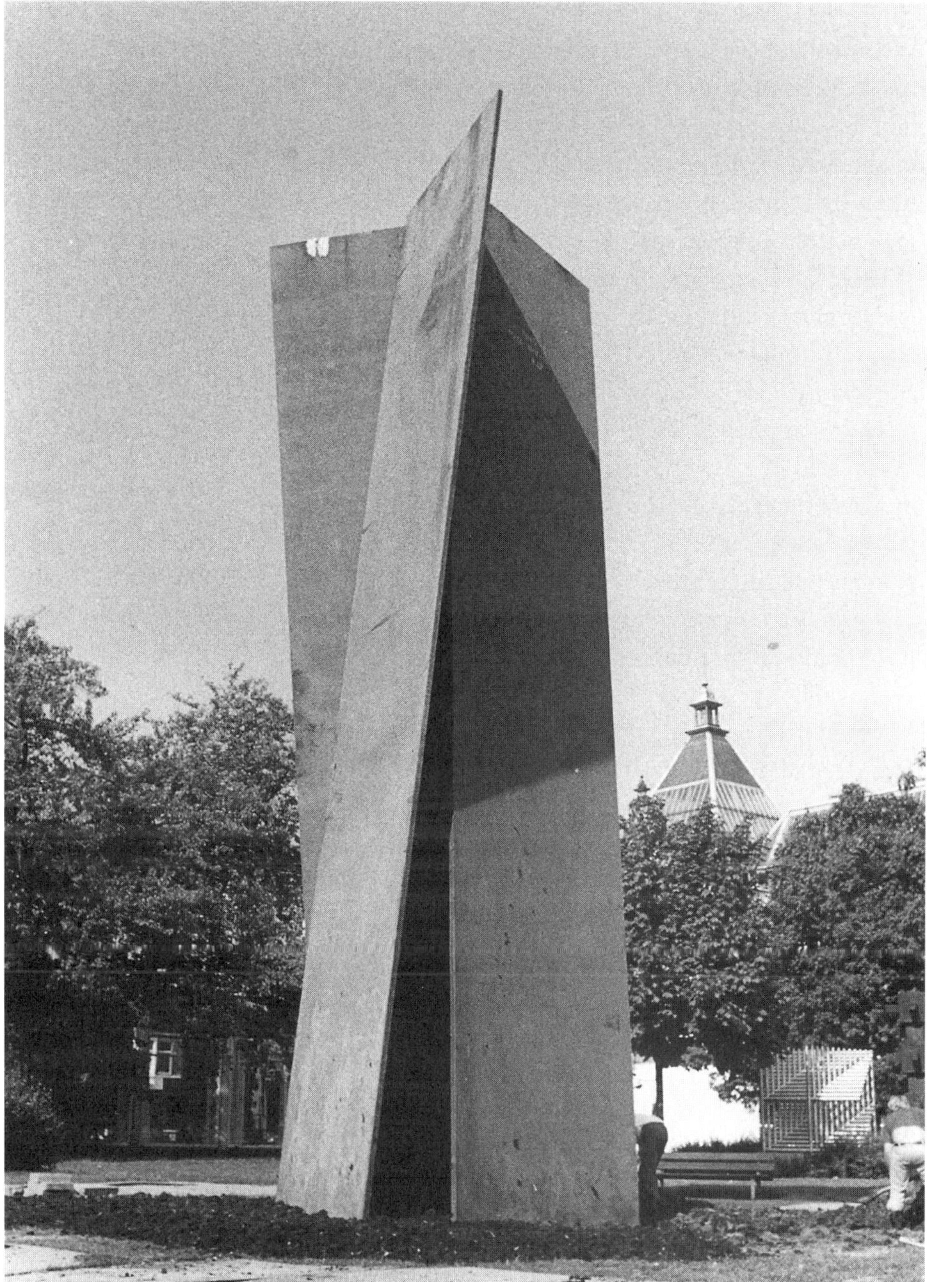

Figure 8. Richard Serra, *Sight Point,* 1971–75, Amsterdam, Stedelijk Museum. Courtesy of Richard Serra.

As a result of this change in location, Serra felt that the piece "lost all relationship to a pattern of circulation, which was a major determinate for its original location at Wesleyan."[29] This was the first time Serra allowed a piece intended for one site to be installed in another.

Other Controversies

What would have been Serra's first federal commission was aborted because of an irresolvable conflict with the architect of the proposed site, Robert Venturi. The fourteen-million-dollar project to revitalize the twenty-one blocks of Pennsylvania Avenue between the Capitol and the White House included two major public areas, a park and a plaza. Ira Licht, then head of the Art in Public Places program for the NEA and later a member of the panel that selected Serra for the GSA commission at Federal Plaza, called it "the biggest opportunity for an artist since the Washington Monument."[30]

After screening nearly one hundred possible artists, an NEA-appointed panel, acting as consultants to the Pennsylvania Avenue Development Corporation (PADC), a federal agency funded in 1977, recommended a shortlist of five.[31] Serra, who had recently completed a large vertical piece for Documenta 6 (the international art exhibition held in Kassel, Germany, every five years), saw the Washington project as an opportunity to expand the possibilities of working with a specific site. His initial idea was "an attempt to complete L'Enfant's original plan for the city and serve as a subpause before you get to the end of Pennsylvania Avenue. . . . probably something one can walk into, through and around but unlike the piece at Documenta 6, it will focus not upon itself, but upon the site and the vista down Pennsylvania Avenue." Serra's proposal, however, conflicted with the architect's concept of the project.

Venturi envisioned two pylons framing the site (later he added flags on top), an idea the sculptor felt was both an appropriation of his visual language and totally inappropriate for the site. According to Serra, the architect asked him to build either the pylons or a two-part piece in which he could frame the Treasury Building. Calling Venturi's idea Hitlerian, Serra showed images of pylons installed in Berlin, Nuremberg, and Dresden. J. Carter Brown, a member of the advisory group and at the time director of the National Gallery of Art and head of the Fine Arts Commission, reported that there was "an extraordinary amount of consensus that the Venturi proposal was better," and Serra was directed to work with Venturi's solution.[32] According to the sculptor, he was threatened that if he refused he would never get another commission in the United States.

A few years later, Serra was still angry and adamant:

> I think this can go back to Abyssinia or you can come right to Albert Speer and frame Nuremburg, but the notion of that kind of bracketing has all of those overtones and it really doesn't matter if you put an eagle, a swastika, or the American flag on top. You wouldn't ask Brancusi or Rodin to do that. . . . It's not the nature of my work to reassert ideological values of government. The value of my art isn't other values—it's contained within the structure of the work.[33]

The controversies surrounding Serra's work were not limited to the United States. The sculpture Serra made for Documenta 6, just prior to the aborted PADC project, was eventually renamed *Terminal* (Figure 9) and installed in 1977 in Bochum, where it became the center of a controversy that in many ways prefigured the one

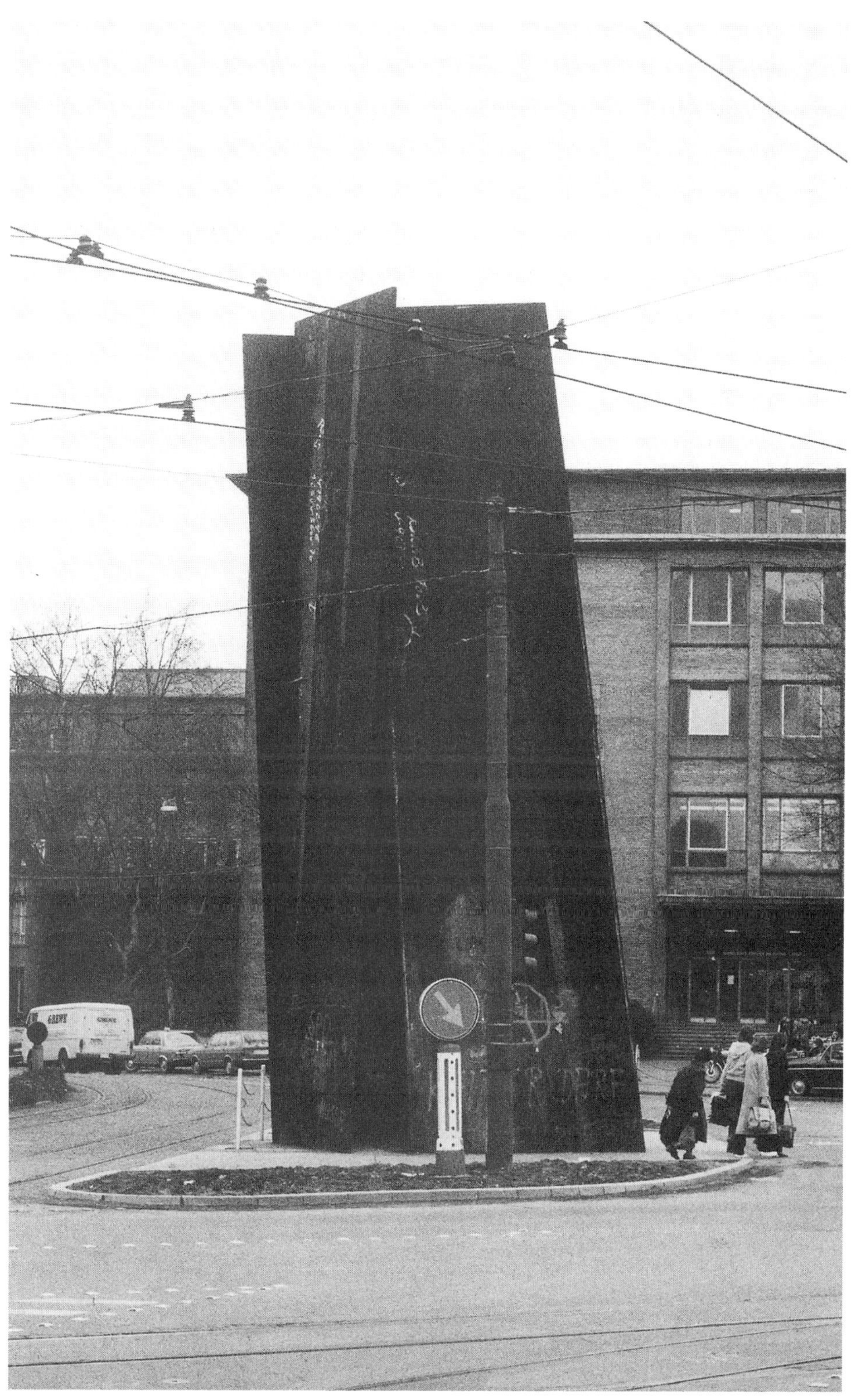

Figure 9. Richard Serra, *Terminal,* 1977, Bochum, Germany. Photograph by Alexander von Berswordt-Wallrabe; courtesy of Richard Serra.

surrounding *Tilted Arc.* Composed of four trapezoidal Cor-Ten steel plates, each measuring 41 feet × 12 feet × 9 feet × 2 ½ inches, leaning together like a house of cards, the sculpture recalled Serra's earlier sculpture *One-Ton Prop (House of Cards)* (Figure 5). While the sculpture was on display in Kassel, the exterior surfaces of the plates were covered with graffiti and used as a bulletin board by artists demonstrating nearby.[34]

After Documenta 6 Serra was offered three options for a permanent site: one in Kassel, one next to Cologne Cathedral, and the Bochum site on a traffic island near the train station. He rejected the first two because they "were picture-postcard sites that suggested conventional public sculpture."[35] The purchase of the sculpture from Serra's European dealer, Alexander von Berswordt-Wallrabe, owner of Galerie m,[36] became an issue in local politics when the Democratic Socialist Party (SPD) supported it, relating the material to the Bochum steel industry, and the Union of Christian Democrats (CDU) opposed it, objecting, among other things, to the rust.[37]

Issues of cost, location, aesthetics, and a seemingly undemocratic selection process were also raised, as they later were in the *Tilted Arc* controversy. Both sculptures became the focus of widespread media coverage and were vandalized with graffiti.[38] However, in Bochum the controversy died down and the sculpture was eventually even used as a civic emblem. At the annual carnival in 1981, the year *Tilted Arc* was installed, the Bochum city traffic association handed out beer mugs with a golden image of *Terminal.*[39]

Another of Serra's vertical sculptures, *T.W.U.,* also the object of verbal and physical attack, eventually found a permanent site in Germany. The title refers to the Transport Workers Union because Serra completed the sculpture the day the workers ended a strike. His identification with workers is also reflected in the film *Steelmill/ Stahlwerk,* which he made in Germany with Clara Weyergraf in 1979.[40]

In 1980 *T.W.U.* was installed as a temporary piece on a triangle in downtown Manhattan near both Serra's home and Federal Plaza (Figures 10, 11). Serra thought the sculpture, composed of three Cor-Ten steel plates each measuring 36 feet × 12 feet × 2 ¾ inches, less complicated than *Terminal* since its structure was more easily discernable to the eye:

> In *Terminal* you're enclosed in a nine foot by nine foot shaft looking up and out of a square opening forty feet above. The work consists of four trapezoidal plates tilting on their axes. Walking around it, you have no idea of the character of the enclosed space, whereas from inside there is no possibility of determining the outside structure. That's different from *T.W.U.,* where after any prolonged viewing, the structure of the work is definable.[41]

T.W.U., like *Terminal,* was sponsored by Serra's German dealer. Installed in New York (with support from the Public Art Fund, a local, privately funded organization) a year after *Tilted Arc* was commissioned, it became an immediate target for splattered

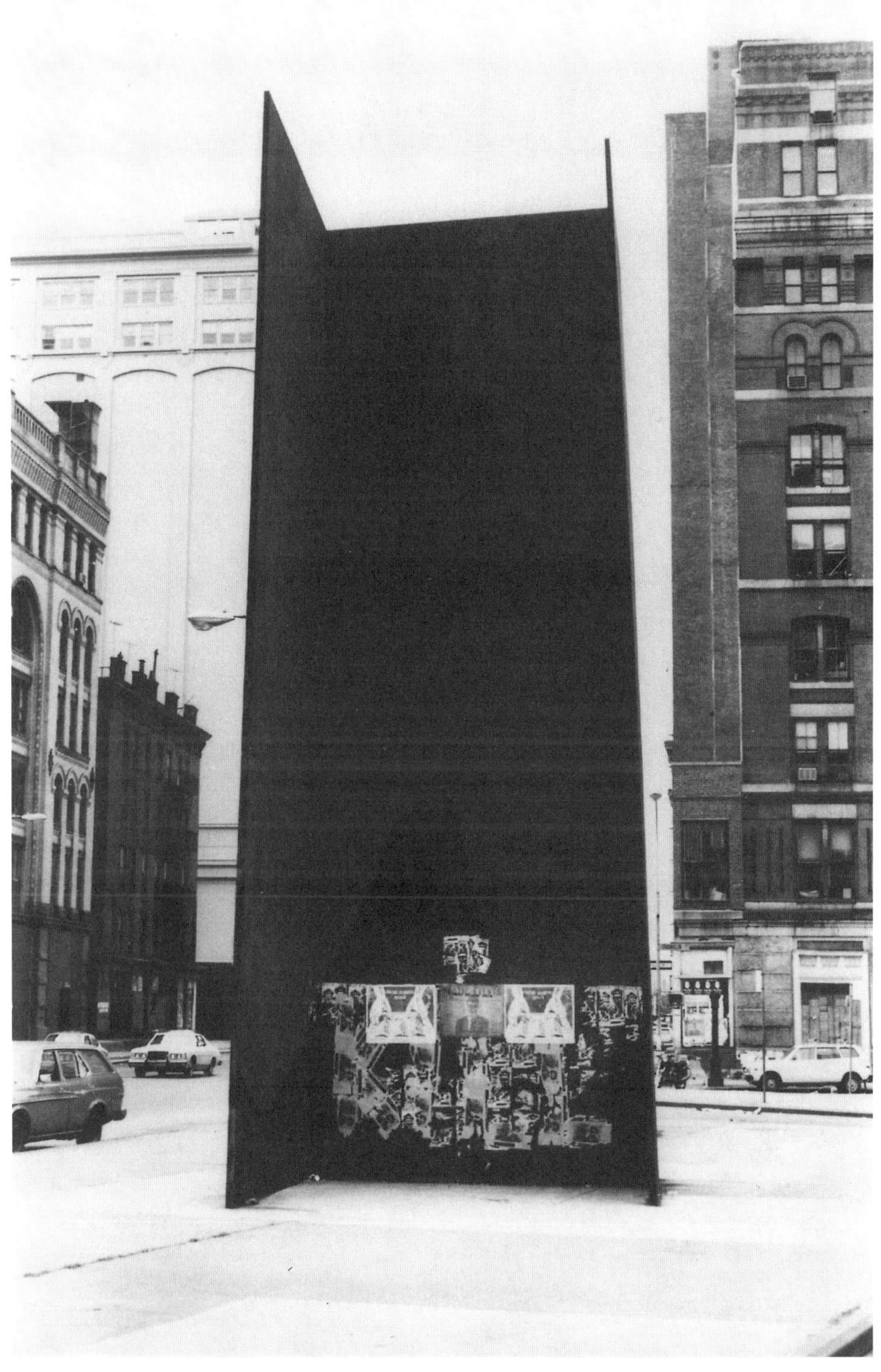

Figure 10. Richard Serra, *T.W.U.*, 1980, installed in New York City. Photograph by Earl Ripling; courtesy of Richard Serra.

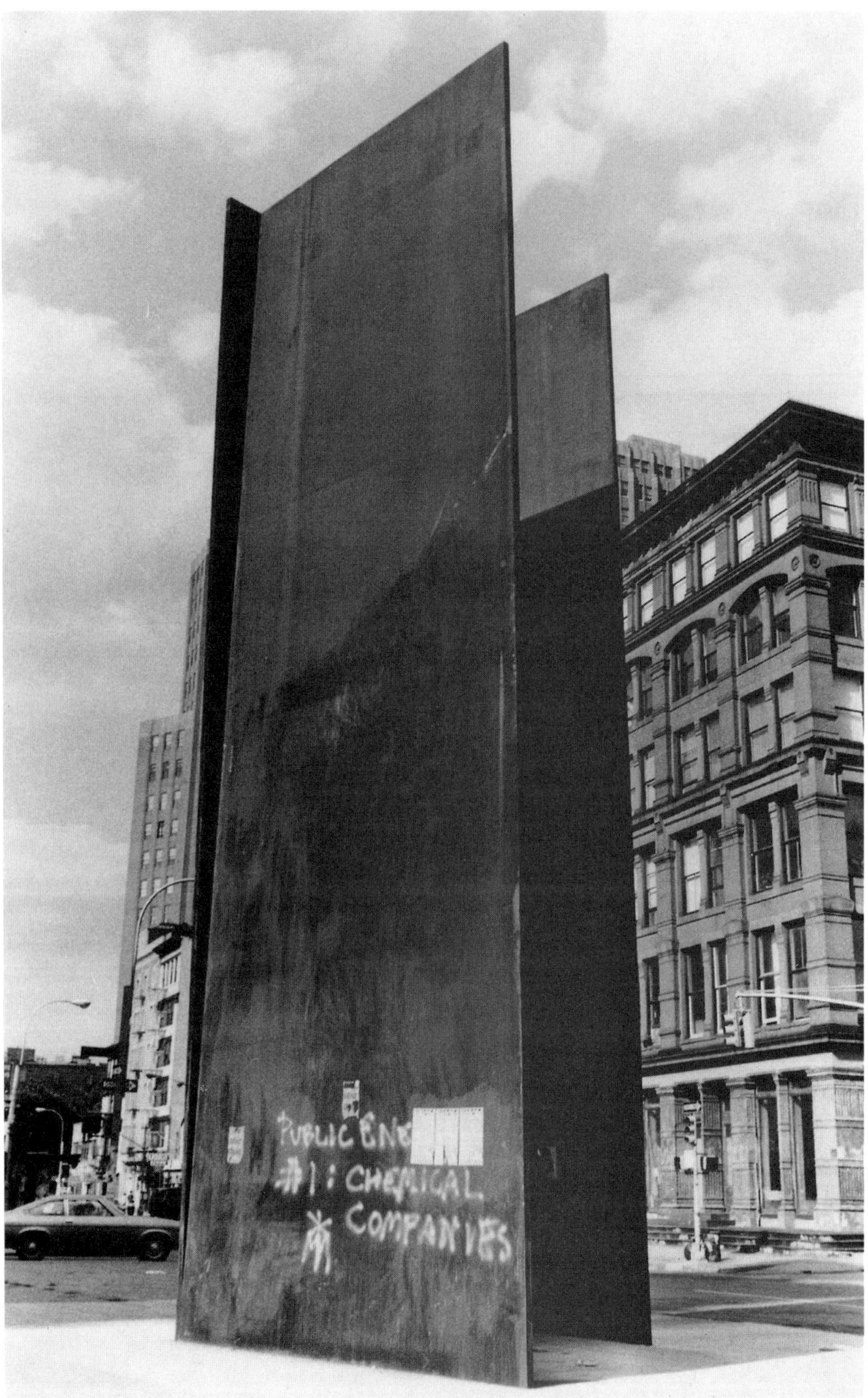

Figure 11. Richard Serra, *T.W.U.*, 1980, installed in New York City. Photograph by Earl Ripling; courtesy of Richard Serra.

eggs and paint. In 1981 David Hammons, an artist known for work that addresses African American racial issues, used it as the backdrop for two performance pieces. *Shoetree* consisted of slinging twenty-five pairs of shoes on strings over the top of the sculpture. In *Pissed Off* Hammons urinated on *T.W.U.* and, judging from a series of photographs taken by Dawoud Bey, was nearly arrested.[42]

After attempts to find a permanent site for the sculpture failed, it was exhibited in 1989 at the Deichterhollen in Hamburg in front of an art building adjacent to the train tracks, and it was subsequently bought by the city (Figure 12). At the time, Serra preferred vertical pieces for urban sites because he felt they corresponded better to the scale and shape of their architectural environment.[43]

Precursor to *Tilted Arc*

St. John's Rotary Arc (Figures 13, 14), installed in lower Manhattan in 1980 at the same time as *T.W.U.*, marked a new direction in Serra's work. Both in form and in location it was closer to *Tilted Arc*. An arc of Cor-Ten steel measuring 200 feet × 12 feet × 2 ½ inches, it was created for a circular space at the exit of the Holland Tunnel, a previously empty site owned by the Port Authority of New York. Seen primarily

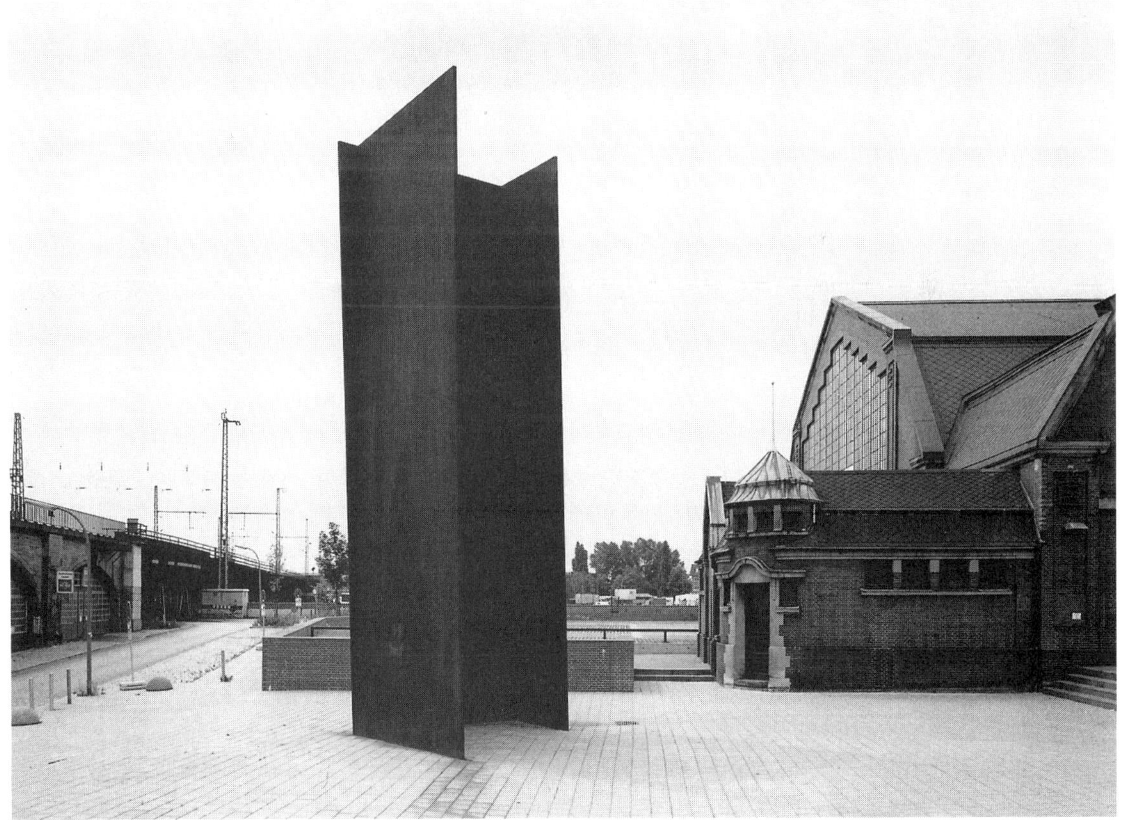

Figure 12. Richard Serra, *T.W.U.*, 1980, installed in Deichtorhallen, Hamburg, Germany. Courtesy of Richard Serra.

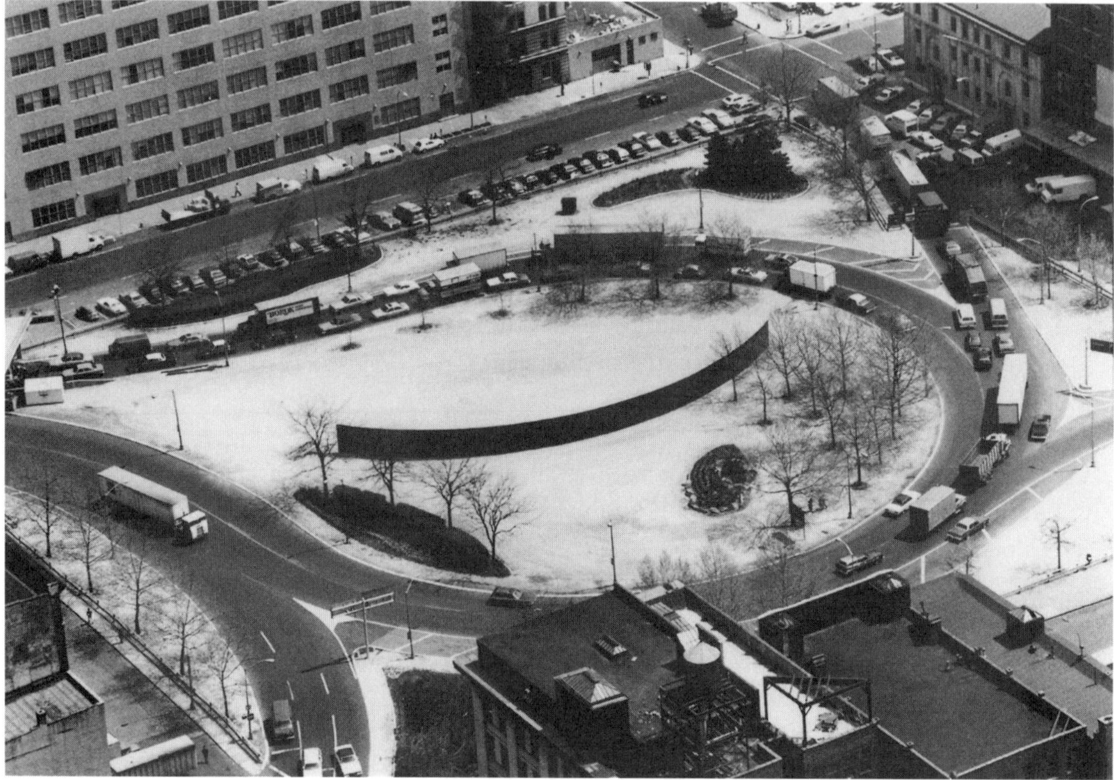

Figure 13. Richard Serra, *St. John's Rotary Arc,* 1980, installed at Holland Tunnel exit, New York City. Photograph by Tom Bills; courtesy of Richard Serra.

from moving vehicles driving by a site rarely used by pedestrians, the sculpture literally did not get in anyone's way.

Serra liked the Holland Tunnel site, as he did the Bochum location, because it had "no romantic, historic, architectural, esthetic or picturesque pretensions; no commercial or symbolic references."[44] While watching the installation of the sculpture, Serra got the idea of a tilted arc for Federal Plaza. An arc like *St. John's Rotary Arc,* he felt, would have created an ensemble with the existing inoperative circular fountain. And a vertical enclosure like *T.W.U.* would not have provided the kind of volume he wanted.

In 1981 Serra exhibited *Slice,* an arc of Cor-Ten steel measuring 10 feet × 124 feet, 6 inches × 1 ½ inches (Figure 15), at the Leo Castelli Gallery in New York, which had also sponsored *St. John's Rotary Arc.* Eliciting negative critical responses similar to those that later greeted *Tilted Arc,* it was called "a curved Berlin Wall" and "a truly hostile piece of art" by Kim Levin in the *Village Voice,* and Elizabeth Frank complained in *Art in America* that "the arc, by taking command of the gallery space as a physical environment, confounded it utterly as a social one" and that "the piece's physical power was undermined by its conceptual belligerence."[45]

Clearly, when the NEA panel recommended Serra and the GSA proceeded to

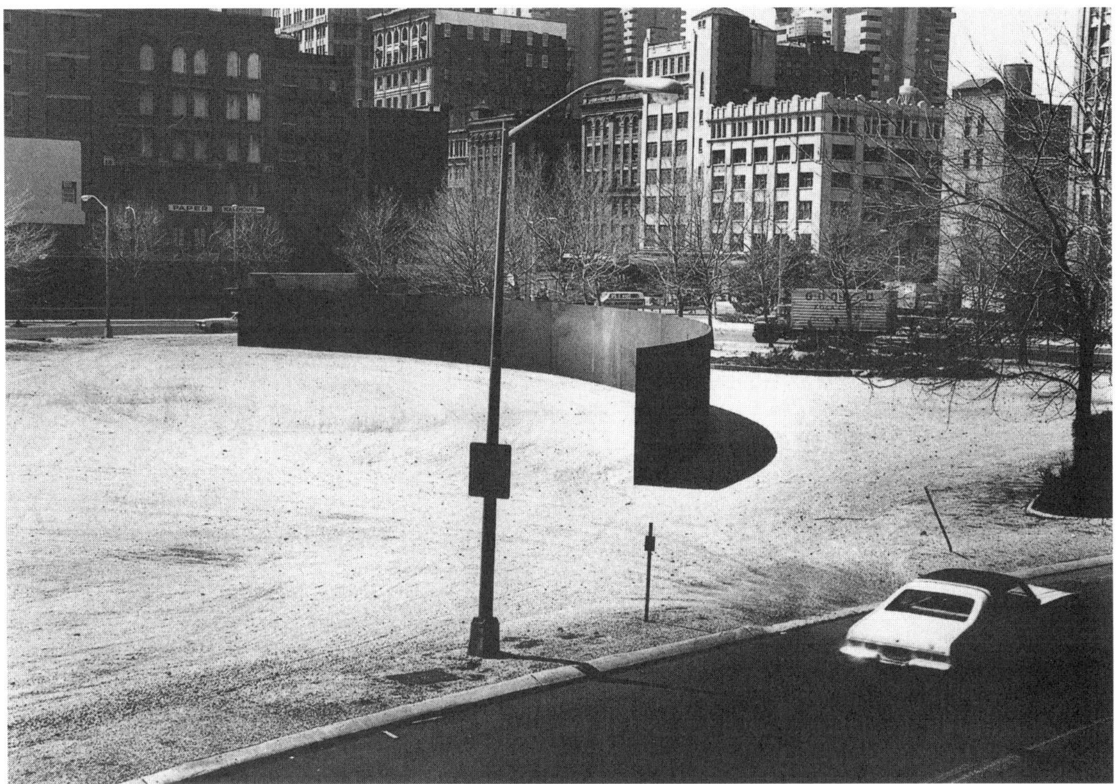

Figure 14. Richard Serra, *St. John's Rotary Arc,* 1980, installed at Holland Tunnel exit, New York City. Photograph by Gwenn Thomas; courtesy of Richard Serra.

commission him to make a sculpture for Federal Plaza in 1979, and certainly by the time they approved his work for installation in 1981, he was a known artist with a history of controversy surrounding his public pieces. Both the nature of his sculpture and the public and critical responses to it were familiar to those involved. What, then, led them to proceed with this choice?

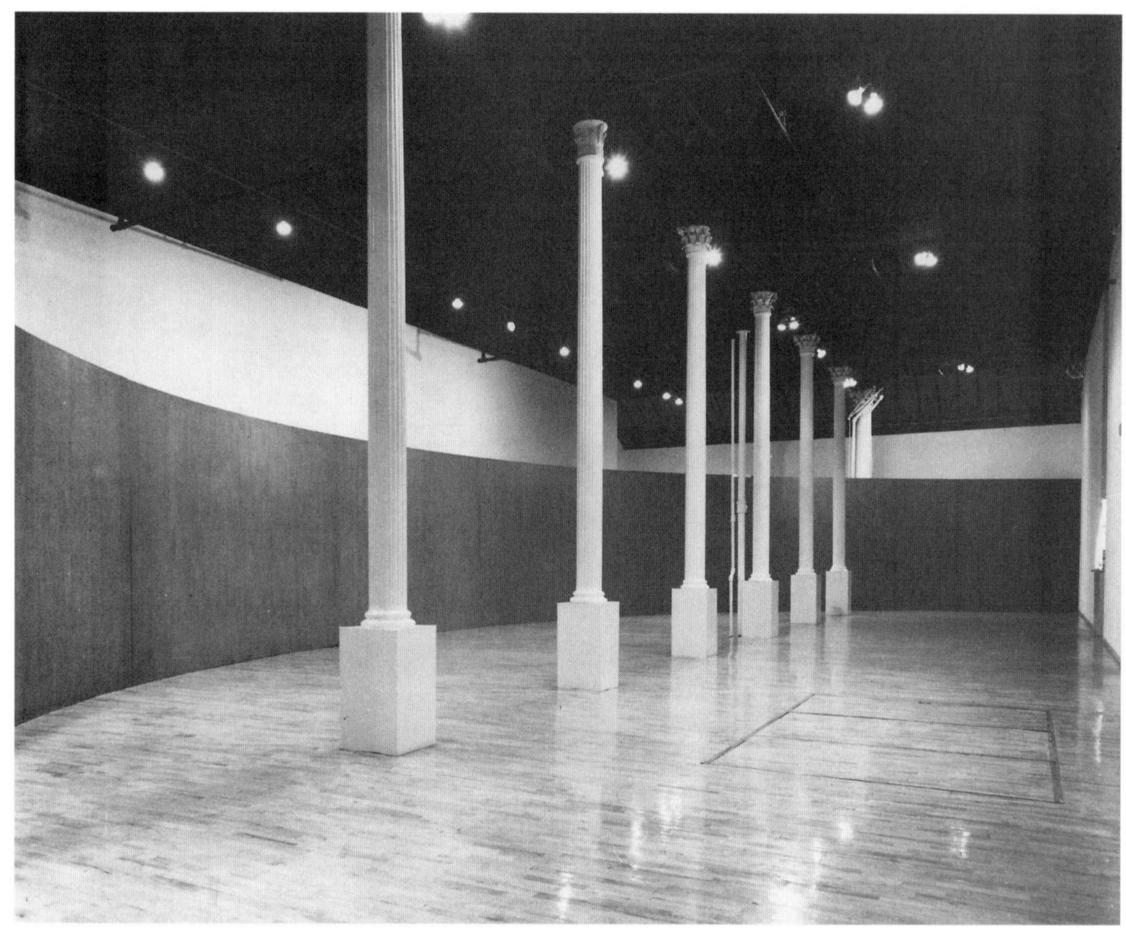

Figure 15. Richard Serra, *Slice,* 1981, installed at Leo Castelli Gallery, New York City. Photograph by Bevan Davies; courtesy of Richard Serra.

1. Commission, Installation, Removal

> A combination of two critical elements is required for art controversies to erupt: there must be a sense that values have been threatened, and power must be mobilized in response to do something about it.
>
> **—Steven C. Dubin**

The Commission

Throughout 1979 the GSA was plagued by scandals of corruption involving kickbacks from private contractors. The agency spent approximately five billion dollars annually as the federal government's purchasing agent but was reportedly losing millions each year to theft and corruption. After numerous fraud trials several GSA employees received jail sentences.[1] Art seems to have been the least of the GSA's problems.

When Richard Serra was commissioned to create a sculpture for Federal Plaza in 1979, Donald Thalacker, the head of the GSA's Art-in-Architecture program, had just finished writing a book documenting the program's accomplishments.[2] Jay Solomon, appointed by President Jimmy Carter in 1977 as GSA administrator, was a staunch supporter of the Art-in-Architecture program. And the support for art of the then vice president's wife, Joan Mondale, was so well known that she was often referred to as "Joan of Art." When Jay Solomon left office in 1979, President Carter replaced him with Rear Admiral Roland G. Freeman III, who finally and apparently under some pressure approved *Tilted Arc* for Federal Plaza.[3]

According to established agency procedure, the commissioning process began on the recommendation by the building architect that sculpture be included in the plaza.[4] At Federal Plaza three architectural firms were involved: Kahn and Jacobs; Alfred Easton Poor; and Eggers and Higgins. When construction of the U.S. Court of International Trade (Customs Court) and Jacob K. Javits Federal Office Building was completed in 1968, four works of art were planned for the two buildings. An eagle in the lobby and a mosaic wall on the south side were commissioned for the Court of International Trade. A sculpture by Robert Cronbach in the plaza fountain and a United States seal for the lobby by Sally Ann Carr were planned for the Federal Building but were not commissioned.

In 1973 Alfred Easton Poor recommended "an abstract sculpture of steel or bronze matching the color of the metal at the front entrance of the building [on the plaza]. It should be 30′ to 35′ high and 8′ to 10′ at its widest point. The sculpture should be on a substantial granite base. He suggested that Alexander Caulder [sic] do the work."[5] After Calder's death (in 1976), the architect recommended "an abstract sculpture by an artist of similar rank and importance." In 1977 Poor complained to Thalacker that he was still waiting for a response to his proposal. That year GSA commissioning policies for art were changed to include "art experts," preferably from the local community. In 1978 selection procedures were amended again. This time the procedures specified that at least one of the panelists be an "expert in contemporary art and be from the area of the art project."

Ten years had elapsed between the completion of the building and the commission of a sculpture. The NEA-appointed selection panel consisted of Suzanne Delehanty, then director of the Neuberger Museum at SUNY, Purchase; Ira Licht, then director of the Lowe Museum at the University of Miami; and Robert Pincus-Witten, a New York art critic and art historian. Both Delehanty and Licht had served previously on GSA selection panels. Licht had been director of the NEA's Visual Arts program during Serra's confrontation with Venturi and the PADC, and Pincus-Witten had written extensively about Serra.[6] Joseph Colt represented the project architects and participated as a nonvoting member of the panel.

On July 20, 1979, the selection panel met at Federal Plaza in New York. Some initially questioned whether the "highly architected" site needed sculpture.[7] They reviewed slides of the work of nearly fifty artists and debated whether it would be better to select a prominent figure of the 1960s or an important younger artist. Delehanty pointed out that New York had not had a commission of important recent art. Pincus-Witten argued that this was a major site with an incredible audience and that the commission should be bold, not conservative. The most compelling considerations, frequently reiterated, were the quality of the art and its appropriateness for the site. This had been the rationale for selecting artists for public art projects for quite some time.

Each of the panel members spoke in favor of certain artists. Colt, the architect's representative, initially favored Ronald Bladen, Christopher Wilmarth, and Nancy Holt; on the second ballot he voted for Holt, Robert Irwin, and Bladen. The six artists forwarded to the GSA and ranked in order of preference were Robert Irwin, Richard Serra, Donald Judd, Robert Rauschenberg, Ronald Bladen, and Ellsworth Kelly. The panel's first choice, Irwin, was eliminated because he had already accepted a GSA commission for the recently renovated Old Post Office building on Pennsylvania Avenue in

Washington, D.C., which housed, among other things, the offices of the NEA and the National Endowment for the Humanities (NEH). A California artist known for his interest in light, Irwin created a transparent hanging piece for the atrium. Serra, a substantially different kind of sculptor, thus became the panel's first choice by default.

On August 16, 1979, the GSA design-review panel—consisting of David Dibner, assistant commissioner for design and construction; Walter Roth, director of the Art-in-Architecture program and of historic preservation; and Karel Yasko, counselor for the program—followed the selection panel and recommended Serra. He was approved by GSA Administrator Freeman on August 31, 1979.

The following year, on March 3, Serra presented his proposal for *Tilted Arc* to the GSA design-review panel whose voting members were Mike Marshall (commissioner of Public Building Services), David Dibner, and Karel Yasko. Notes taken by an Art-in-Architecture staff member indicated that "Mr. Marshall doesn't like it!" Yasko observed that "John Q. Public will call it a wall." And Dibner saw the "symbolism as a barrier."[8] The presentation did not go smoothly.

Serra, known to have a temper and embittered by his recent experience with Venturi and the PADC commission, exploded. Julia Brown, coordinator of the project at GSA, calmed the artist and tried to protect the project. Administrator Freeman was brought in and actually saved the proposal. Reportedly, as an engineer and admiral, Freeman was impressed both with the shiplike references and the design's technical expertise.[9] Later he denied this and alleged that Joan Mondale had twisted his arm to approve it. In 1985 he remembered events this way:

> There was complete disagreement with putting [the sculpture] up there. I disagreed with it, too. But I was caught in a political problem, and that's what the decision was made on. I had enough darn problems. I was trying to clean house at GSA and I didn't need this. . . . I had the NEA recommending something, and there were strong feelings on the part of a lot of people that Mr. Serra did good work. I thought it was a piece of junk. I have never agreed with rusty metal. I was a flag officer and I *hate* rust! It's something that just doesn't appeal to me.[10]

According to a reconstruction of events prepared in 1985 for Frank Hodsoll, then director of the NEA, by Richard Andrews, director of the Visual Arts program, the design-review committee was divided but negative about Serra's sculpture. Freeman "gave a conditional approval at that time, conditional on the resolution of the technical questions such as wind load, waterproofing of the plaza, etc." If contact with the White House occurred, the report speculated, it occurred during the conditional-approval period out of "a desire to inform or alert the Vice President's office since the artwork was likely to be controversial and that office had been supportive of the GSA Art-in-Architecture program."[11]

Nevertheless, despite strong personal reservations, key members of the GSA staff approved Serra's design. At the time this apparently seemed like the course of least resistance.

The Artistic Evolution of *Tilted Arc*

In an interview with art critic Douglas Crimp published in 1980, a year after the GSA commission but before the piece was installed, Serra stated,

> The Federal Building site didn't interest me at first. It's a "pedestal site" in front of a public building. There is a fountain on the plaza, [and] normally you would expect a sculpture next to the fountain, so that the ensemble would embellish the building. I've found a way to dislocate or alter the decorative function of the plaza and actively bring people into the sculpture's context. I plan to build a piece that's 120 feet long in a semi-circular plaza. It will cross the entire space, blocking the view from the street to the courthouse and vice versa. It will be twelve feet high and tilt one foot toward the Federal Building and Courthouse. It will be a very slow arc that will encompass the people who walk on the plaza in its volume.

When Crimp questioned whether his intention was to block the existing views, Serra replied,

> No. The intention is to bring the viewer into the sculpture. The placement of the sculpture will change the space of the plaza. After the piece is created, the space will be understood primarily as a function of the sculpture.[12]

Serra saw Federal Plaza as representing the American justice system, and he did not want his piece to become its symbol.[13] He was convinced that art had to be oppositional to maintain its integrity:

> It's really the obligation of the sculptor to define sculpture, not to be defined by the power structure that asks you, that while you put your sculpture up, to please make this place more beautiful. I find that a totally false notion, because their notion of beauty and my notion of . . . sculpture are always, invariably, at opposite ends.[14]

At the time Serra created *Tilted Arc* he was just beginning to work with curved pieces. He had recently completed *St. John's Rotary Arc* for a nearby site in lower Manhattan and was developing a new piece consisting of two curved arcs *(Clara-Clara)* for a retrospective of his work scheduled for 1983 at the Beaubourg in Paris. At Federal Plaza he was exploring the difference between tilting a plane or using a section of a cone. As always, he worked toward his formal solution in a hands-on way:

> *Tilted Arc* is a rectilinear plate which has been bent one foot over its elevation. It was then impaled into the ground at both ends so that the middle section rides flush with the ground. When you bend the plate without cutting, the fact that the middle is riding continuously along the ground means that the top will crown so that the piece rises into the center. One way of achieving the same effect without the crown, without having to impale the work into the ground, would be to cut the plate. You would have to cut it on the bottom and top and then bend it. Following this procedure what you end up making is a section of a cone. If you cut the section of a cone and

> invert it one way, it would act like the lip of a frying pan and if you invert that same piece, then it works as a flower pot upside down. The conclusion of dealing with a conical shape is the piece in Paris *[Clara-Clara]* where you have one section of a cone leaning away from you and an inversion of that section leaning toward you. When these pieces are placed in juxtaposition next to each other, you have a parallel tilt in the center.[15]

Serra often works on several projects simultaneously. While each piece is conceived in relation to its intended site, it also marks a point in his artistic evolution. Serra developed *Tilted Arc* much as he did his other site-specific sculptures. Working from the site and photographs, he initially experimented with small-scale models built in a sandbox in his nearby studio and repeatedly tested his ideas in the actual space:

> The longest part [of the process] is the period when I acquaint myself with the site. Seldom do you come up with a way of dealing with the site upon arrival. That usually becomes where you formulate the piece, and often it's a process of going to the site, working from photographs, working from models, going away from the site, building models, coming back and testing them against what you thought was a commensurate experience and finding out it was different, and then changing the project.[16]

When he felt he had the right solution for Federal Plaza, he put up ten-foot-tall poles at the site and staked out the curve of the arc with strings, making certain that it accomplished his artistic intentions and did not interfere with the paths of pedestrian traffic. Then he submitted his proposal to the GSA.

For the next two years, Serra, working with engineer Malcolm Graff, addressed GSA concerns about traffic flow, drainage, lighting, and wind and weight loads.[17] At one point in February 1981, GSA Assistant Commissioner for Design and Construction Dibner instructed the Art-in-Architecture program to stall the installation of the sculpture until late summer, after President Reagan's budget and tax cuts had been passed.[18] Subsequently, when protests began, the GSA wanted to speed up the installation and finish it within thirty days rather than in the three months allowed by contract. This time the contract held.

Initial Responses

Serra recalled, "The cries of protest began as the piece was under construction so the workers [putting up the sculpture] out there were getting a lot of heat. People, namely judges, who were a little incensed were flaming the fuel of the populists." In spite of this initial negative public response and his prior experience, Serra was surprised by the vehement opposition to the piece:

> When the first protests actually began coming, I was in Germany and I came back to New York and I saw the piece again and, without being too naive, I didn't understand quite what all the commotion was about. I mean, I thought I was being scapegoated

> for something. Certainly the piece has its presence, but it also has a kind of lyricism, and I was really wondering what they were talking about in terms of aggression because the piece has a very lyrical line to it.[19]

After *Tilted Arc* was dedicated on July 16, 1981, Richard Serra was invited by the NEA to the White House and congratulated by President Reagan on his "contribution to the cultural heritage of the United States."[20] Concurrently, nearly from the moment of its installation, Edward D. Re, chief judge of the U.S. Court of International Trade located at Federal Plaza, began complaining about the sculpture. In a letter to the GSA in Washington dated July 27, he protested that the sculpture was an architectural barrier that destroyed the spaciousness and use of the plaza.

On August 7, in an article in the *New York Times,* art critic Grace Glueck called *Tilted Arc* "an awkward bullying piece that may conceivably be the ugliest outdoor work of art in the city."[21] Judge Re quoted Glueck in his next letter to the GSA on August 18 and asked for procedures "for the purpose of preventing its being permanently affixed to the plaza [it already was], and its ultimate removal."[22]

GSA Administrator Gerald P. Carmen did not reply until the following month, when he received two petitions from federal employees working in and around Federal Plaza requesting the removal of the sculpture. One petition, signed by 1,000 employees of the Department of Housing and Urban Development, complained that the sculpture blocked the main doorways, making access "awkward and confusing," and that it "brutally destroy[ed] the plaza's vistas and amenities" and cast "an ominous and threatening shadow." Another petition, with 300 signatures, circulated by the Environmental Protection Agency, protested the use of taxpayers' money for "ripping up the plaza," the "blocked views and disruption of foot-traffic patterns," and the sculpture's potential as a "graffiti-catcher."

Charles LeDuc, assistant regional administrator in New York for public buildings services, was not overly concerned: "There are approximately 10,000 employees in the building and if you have 1,300 signatures against it, there could possibly be 1,300 people who favored it. We wouldn't consider removing the work; we see no need to."[23] However, the petitions prompted a response from Washington. GSA Administrator Carmen assured Judge Re that on his next trip to New York he would look at the sculpture and finally address the judge's concerns.[24] During these initial stages of the controversy, Judge Re continued to write to the GSA, and the building's architectural firms began complaining (incorrectly) that they had not been consulted.

In 1982, presumably in response to complaints about *Tilted Arc,* the GSA issued a directive to involve a cross-section of local citizens and building occupants at the earliest stages of commissioning art. However, this procedure was neither clearly defined (as to how many individuals were to be involved or how they were to be chosen) nor formalized. Although not part of the official selection process at the time of the Serra commission, the absence of community representatives was later cited by GSA administrators as a major factor in the *Tilted Arc* controversy.[25]

For most of 1982 and all of 1983 nothing further happened. Although the GSA regional office in New York contacted Serra to ask how graffiti on the sculpture should be removed, it seemed for a time as if the initial flurry of objections, a common occurrence in public art, was indeed over. Then, in 1984, William Diamond was appointed GSA regional administrator in New York and complaints about the sculpture were orchestrated into a full-scale attack.

The Public Hearing

> Decisions made as part of power confrontations will be made in favor of the side with the most power, and the so-called guidelines or criteria that are ostensibly the basis for decisions will be bent and twisted, often out of possible recognition, during the process.
>
> **—John J. Costonis**

The local conflict became an international spectacle with the so-called public hearing chaired by Diamond in New York. Judge Re's complaints had been restricted to agency correspondence and informal meetings; Diamond's approach was more aggressive and public. He began by asking the Art-in-Architecture program for a procedure to remove the sculpture.

There are two accounts of what transpired at the meeting in Diamond's office on November 16, 1984.[26] According to Marilyn Farley of the Art-in-Architecture program, Diamond was informed that there was no precedent for what would in any event be "a long, drawn out, complex process," and he, in turn, both suggested and insisted on a public hearing. Paul Chistolini in Diamond's office (subsequently appointed to serve on the hearing panel) attributes the suggestion for a public forum to Farley. Since Diamond was determined to proceed, and since the Art-in-Architecture program was unlikely to initiate a process of removal without a policy in place, Farley's account is more plausible.

On December 5, 1984, Diamond instructed Chistolini to advertise a public hearing scheduled for February 1, 1985.[27] He also ordered a cost estimate for removal (approximately $86,000 to remove *Tilted Arc,* restore the plaza, and reinstall the sculpture within one hundred miles of New York City). Concurrently, Diamond sent letters to a number of art institutions, including the Museum of Modern Art and the Cooper-Hewitt Museum, asking if they would be interested in taking the sculpture.[28] The Storm King Art Center in Mountainville, New York, expressed an interest until they learned that Serra had not been consulted.

On December 13 Diamond met with Donald Thalacker in Washington. According to Thalacker, Diamond praised the program, and stated that *Tilted Arc* would never be removed simply on the basis of whether people liked or disliked it and that in any case it would be removed only if there were a more suitable and appropriate location. Insisting on his impartiality, he asked for Thalacker's support for the public hearing set for February 1, 1985. Thalacker in turn requested that the hearing be postponed, since on January 30, 1985, the Art-in-Architecture program was scheduled to receive a presidential award praising its courage in supporting "many stimulating and often controversial works of art in federal facilities across the nation."

On December 29 Diamond was quoted in the *New York Times:* "I want to make it very clear that this is not an attack on the esthetics of the artist. . . . What we're deeply concerned about is the fact that this piece, for three and a half years, has made it impossible for the public and Federal community to use the Plaza."[29] In response, Serra asked Diamond if it would be possible to organize an educational forum allowing him "to explain his art and its function to people in the Federal Office Buildings."[30] Diamond refused.

Notices of the so-called hearing, then slated for March 6, 7, and 8, 1985, appeared in the *New York Times* and the *Village Voice* on December 23, 1984, and again on January 1, 1985. Diamond sent out more than a thousand letters stating, "The purpose of the hearing is to decide whether or not the art work known as *Tilted Arc* currently on the east plaza of the Jacob K. Javits Federal Building in Manhattan should be relocated to increase public use of the plaza."[31] By the end of February, Serra, marshaling the forces of the art world, put out an extensive mailing requesting supporters to speak on his behalf and to submit a written statement to Diamond.

Prior to the hearing the GSA regional office also posted fliers (in English and Chinese) in the federal buildings and surrounding areas. The fliers featured a town crier in revolutionary dress calling for the public to SPEAK OUT! (Figure 16). The hearing, it stated, would consider "ways to more fully utilize the plaza on the Lafayette Street side of this building. This could include the relocation of the large metal sculpture known as the '*Tilted Arc.*'" The last sentence, "We would like to hear from you," was followed by a number to call to arrange to *"speak out."*

Diamond also had petitions and form letters placed in the lobby of the federal building. The petition titled "For Relocation" stated, "We the undersigned feel the artwork called *Tilted Arc* is an obstruction to the plaza and should be removed to a more suitable location. The individuals whose names are listed with an asterisk find no artistic merit in the Serra artwork."[32] The other petition "Against Relocation," provided no opportunity for its signers to offer an aesthetic judgment. Artistic merit was later omitted from any argument and was proclaimed irrelevant, since arguing on the basis of aesthetic judgment would have weakened the GSA's case legally by raising First Amendment issues.

In the form letters addressed to Diamond, the undersigned stated, "I would like to express my opinion on the use of the plaza and more specifically the relocation of the artwork known as 'Tilted Arc.'" They then voted for or against the relocation of the sculpture by checking the appropriate box. The box marked "I am for" preceded that marked "I am against." At the bottom there was space for comments, a signature, and the name of the respondent's agency.[33] At the hearing Diamond referred to these simply as letters, implying they were spontaneous, individual responses.

Diamond chaired the hearing and appointed the four panel members who

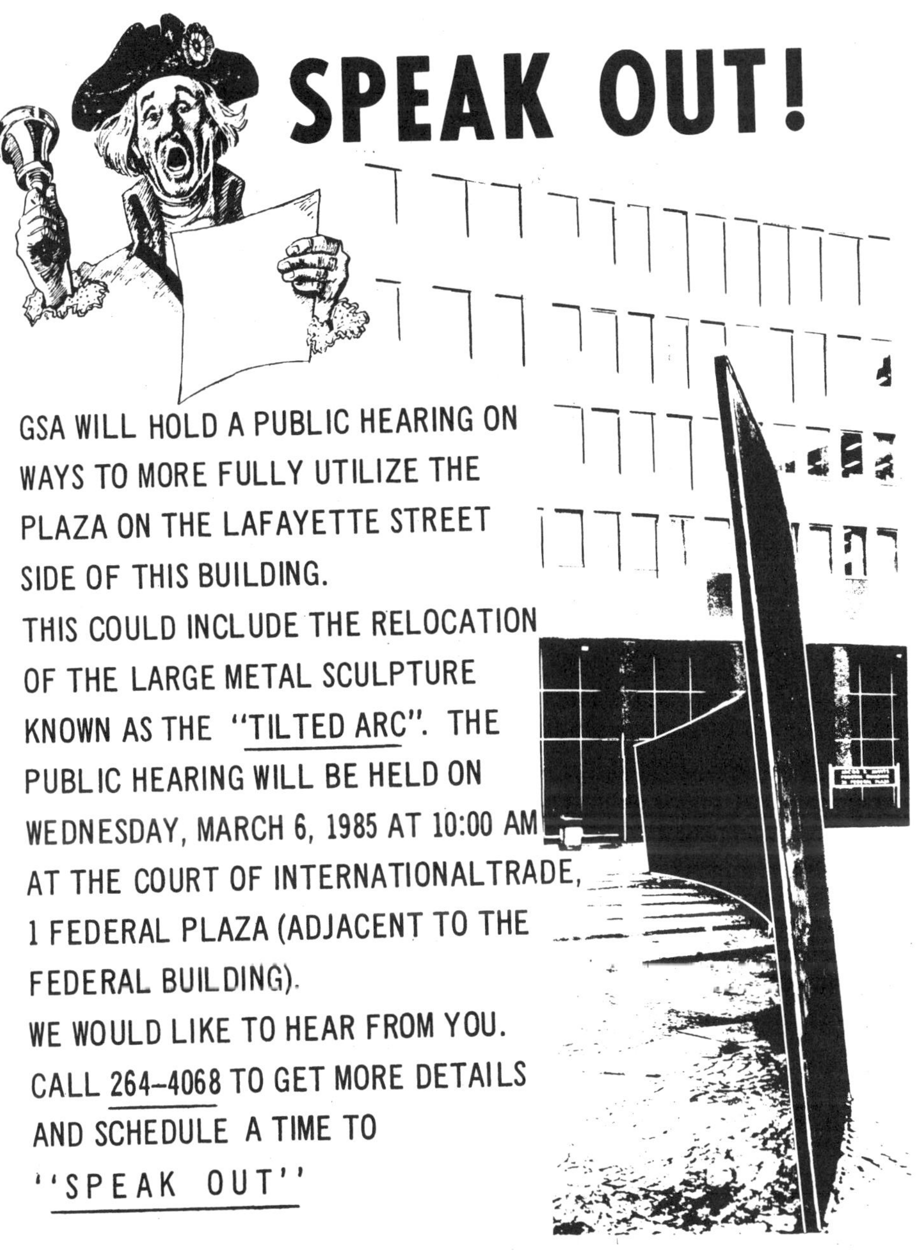

Figure 16. "Speak Out!" flier, 1985 hearing, Federal Plaza, New York City.

presided over the meeting and judged its outcome. Two were members of his staff who at the time did not hold permanent titles to their jobs: Gerald Turetsky, acting deputy regional administrator, and Paul Chistolini, acting assistant regional administrator for public buildings services. The other two panel members were Thomas Lewin, a senior partner at the New York law firm of Simpson, Thatcher, Bartlett, a prior acquaintance of Diamond's, and Michael Findlay, vice president of Christie's auction house (invited by Diamond's wife in a letter dated February 15) and the only panel member who later voted against relocating Serra's sculpture.

In a press release issued at time of the hearing, Diamond asserted, "The panel will not make an aesthetic judgment as to the worth or value of *Tilted Arc* nor will it recommend that any precedent be established that would affect any other piece of art." Instead, he linked the sculpture to the issue of excessive government spending:

> The United States government paid $175,000 for the Richard Serra sculpture. We strongly believe that the public has a right to tell us how they feel about the way in which their government spends their money. We in Government have the responsibility to provide that opportunity. The fact that we are holding this hearing is evidence of our good faith in this effort. We trust that today's proceedings will further encourage future dialogue between artists and their audience.[34]

Although Diamond's wording implied that Serra was paid $175,000 for *Tilted Arc,* this fee included the cost of creating and installing the piece. In fact Serra, like many artists, made no money on this commission.

For three days the spectacle—the hearing, complete with reporters and television crews—took place in the International Court building at Federal Plaza. Serra began by "giving some background information about what I do, why I do it, and how I build my sculpture, what site-specific sculpture means and why site-specificity and permanence are inseparable."[35] He described the GSA Art-in-Architecture program and the process he followed, his assurances of the permanency of the piece, and the implications of the hearing.

In all, 122 people spoke for keeping the sculpture, and 58 were in favor of removal.[36] Supporters came predominantly from the art world or related cultural professions. Artists, museum directors, gallery owners, curators, arts administrators, a few musicians and filmmakers, and art patrons addressed issues of the sculpture's site specificity and the hearing's violation of due process and issues of artistic freedom and the need for time to appreciate the sculpture. (These and other issues are discussed in detail in chapter 2.)

For the federal office workers and community residents who spoke against the sculpture (i.e., for removal), art-world elitism and the imposition of taste were the issues. They also objected to not having been consulted, the obliteration of the view and the obstruction of the plaza, the graffiti, and the cost; and many just hated the piece.

Before testimony was over, on the evening before the last day of the hearing (March 7), Diamond appeared on television asserting that the commission had taken place in Washington and that "there was no idea the sculpture was going to bisect the plaza and make it practically impossible for any public function to be held in the plaza as it happened for years in the past."[37] This was patently false and obviously prejudicial.

In spite of the "public" response (two to one) in favor of keeping the sculpture, on April 10 Diamond's panel recommended by a vote of four to one that it be removed from Federal Plaza. On May 1, in a formal letter to Dwight Ink, the acting head of GSA in Washington, Diamond stated that he could not play a numbers game in justifying his decision, could not address the question of artistic merit (that would make it a censorship issue), and could not find any guarantee of permanence in the GSA contract. He argued instead for removal on the grounds of the need for open space, the danger of the piece, and its invitation to vandalism:

> I was impressed by the statements of the federal agencies, and employees, collectively and individually, who passionately sought the return of the plaza to its original space and openness; to its prior capacity for public events; to its freedom of physical passage and visual perspective; and to its originally designed integrated serenity. It should be noted that the basic design concept of the plaza area contemplated and focused upon openness. . . . There can be no doubt that these original concepts have been severely compromised by the placing of the "Tilted Arc" in the middle of the plaza. There can be no controversy that the space has been bisected, physical passage obstructed, visual perspective distorted, and the atmosphere of the plaza turned into affrontry *[sic].*

Diamond, using a legal comparison, suggested that Ink "correct a mistake by restoring a *status quo*—in this case, the artwork first in place, e.g. the open plaza itself."[38]

After the Hearing

Although the decision as to whether to remove or retain the sculpture was now up to the Washington office, there were no precedents or models, and the *Tilted Arc* controversy continued to evolve in an ad hoc fashion. The GSA's general counsel, Allie B. Latimer, determined that the agency's administrator had the ultimate power to decide the outcome, but she cautioned Ink "not to give any special weight to the recommendation/vote of the panel" because it apparently was not set up within federal guidelines. Rather, Ink could "start all over again with a properly established advisory committee" including "at least some members of the private sector." Or he could "totally ignore the panel recommendation/vote, and make a decision based solely on the record which was developed via the public hearings and other material generated on the subject." Latimer advised that he first develop an "independent, official recommendation" with a detailed rationale.[39]

In the meantime, Manhattan's Community Board 1 (a group of local individuals who discuss and act on issues of common concern) recommended that the sculpture be removed. However, apparently Diamond strongly urged the ten-member subcommittee responsible for the decision to come to this conclusion. When the vote came before the full community board of forty-seven, only twenty-two were present. The subject of the sculpture had not appeared on the agenda and was not open to debate. Serra, who lives within the board's jurisdiction, was not informed. Thus, although Diamond gave much weight to the community board's recommendation, the final vote of twenty-one to one may not have been representative.[40]

While Diamond argued that to remove *Tilted Arc* would actually strengthen the Art-in-Architecture program because many GSA regional administrators were holding up funds for scheduled art projects until the controversy was resolved,[41] Thalacker presented Ink with nine reasons to keep the sculpture at Federal Plaza.[42] He pointed out that relocation would be problematic since no suitable site had been found and that it might not be possible to find one. (In fact, no new site was found.) He questioned the validity of Diamond's hearing and of Community Board 1's recommendation, noted the absence of public events at the plaza during the seventeen years of its existence prior to *Tilted Arc,* and reiterated the need for time to appreciate the sculpture's aesthetic qualities. In addition to the expense of relocation, removal of the sculpture would, he felt, precipitate a loss of faith in the Art-in-Architecture program and in the credibility of GSA.

Ink received pressure from both sides, including a letter signed by two senators and six representatives cautioning him that "regardless of one's views on abstract art, or this sculpture in particular, the preemptive move to destroy this work presents an alarming precedent for subjective criticism and disregard for due process."[43]

Shortly before he left office, Ink ruled in favor of finding a new site for *Tilted Arc.*[44] As an acting administrator, Ink had limited responsibility. Had he left the decision to the next administrator of GSA, Terence C. Golden, the result might have been different. As it was, Golden adopted a holding pattern involving the NEA and yet another panel. (These events are discussed in greater detail in chapter 3 in the section "The Public Policy Context.")

The NEA Site-Review Advisory Panel

Like the GSA, the NEA was operating in an area with no precedents. Because this agency had suggested the original selection panel, Richard Andrews, director of the Visual Arts program, felt strongly that the NEA should continue to be involved with the project.[45] In lengthy discussions and memos to officials at both agencies, Andrews explored various possibilities.

Initially there were plans to improve both the plaza and the public perception of *Tilted Arc.* Thalacker prepared a brochure on the sculpture, and it was available, for a time, in the lobby of the federal building. The NEA considered "a quick design contest to improve the plaza."[46] Adele Chatfield-Taylor, director of the NEA's Design Arts program, was charged with determining what could be done "to 'temporarily enhance' the site of *Tilted Arc.*" Feeling the necessity to do something, since "Mr. Diamond had in mind food kiosks," she recommended, as the least-expensive and most effective solution, asking landscape architect Peter Walker, a dean at the Harvard Graduate School of Design, to suggest a temporary improvement.[47] After submitting an initial proposal to study the problem, Walker and his partner, Martha Schwartz (who subsequently redesigned Federal Plaza), withdrew in concern over potential negative publicity.[48]

The NEA then decided to concentrate on setting up a site-review advisory panel to consider alternative locations for *Tilted Arc*.[49] Although the GSA was to assume administrative costs (not to exceed $40,000 for fiscal year 1986) and serve as the sole recipient for relocation proposals, the committee was appointed by the NEA to act until such time as an appropriate site was found, either the NEA or GSA terminated it, or the committee itself reached an impasse. When the NEA *Tilted Arc* Site Review Advisory Committee was officially chartered in June 1986, it was anticipated that it would function for a year, meeting four times at designated sites as required. As it turned out, one meeting was enough.

Diamond sent out some 150 queries to institutions (museums, universities, and arts organizations) across the country asking if they would be interested in acquiring the sculpture. After two universities—Clemson University and Long Island University—answered in the affirmative, the committee convened at Federal Plaza. On December 17, 1987, in the pouring rain, Serra stood in front of *Tilted Arc* and explained its site specificity to panel chair Theodore Kheel, noted mediator of labor disputes, and architects James Ingo Freed and Jaqueline Robertson, artist Robert Ryman, art historian Sam Hunter, Brenda Richardson (deputy director of the Baltimore Museum of Art), and Los Angeles city councilman Joel Wachs. Richard Andrews of the NEA represented the federal government. Each proposed site was represented by two individuals, one from the local community.

Serra began the proceedings by stating categorically, "I am not here to participate in site-finding activities. There is no alternative site for *Tilted Arc*. . . . to remove the work is to destroy the work." As a result, the representatives from Clemson University and the South Carolina Art Commission withdrew their proposal for the creation of "an entirely new site-specific work by redefining *Tilted Arc* in another location to be chosen by the artist."[50] They had not been informed that Serra would not, under any circumstances, approve a new site.

The delegates from Long Island University were less clear. Judith Collischen Van Wagner, curator of their public art collection, stated that she wished *Tilted Arc* would stay at Federal Plaza, although she would welcome Serra to make a piece for their C. W. Post campus. Since other university officials were vague about their commitment, Kheel concluded that their remarks were conditional and not an unequivocal proposal.

Panel deliberations raised several significant issues. Serra, after discussing the barren state of the plaza prior to *Tilted Arc,* stated that he was not averse to amenities being provided as long as they did not disrupt the sculpture. The question of site specificity was debated at some length. One panel member observed that without GSA input it was difficult to determine if there were "cogent urban reasons" to move the sculpture or if Diamond's decision was "willful, capricious, and individual." Significantly, Kheel observed that it was not clear whether the GSA had made a final decision to remove the piece.

The panel in its advisory role could only vote on the appropriateness of each proposed site; they could not decide whether Serra's sculpture should stay at Federal

Plaza. Not surprisingly, the vote was unanimous. Neither proposed site was deemed appropriate, Clemson because it had withdrawn and Long Island University because its offer was not sufficiently clear or firm. Kheel stated that Serra had the moral right to withdraw his name from the sculpture should it be moved. Given the artist's position, Kheel concluded that it was improbable that an appropriate site could be found and that for the committee to proceed would be "at the least academic and at most an exercise in futility." On January 5, 1988, NEA Chairman Hodsoll informed GSA Administrator Golden of the result.[51]

In its own way, this panel's recommendation was as predictable as the result of Diamond's hearing. Composed of art-world professionals and supporters, all knew Serra's work and could reasonably be expected to honor the artist's wishes. It was an art crowd talking about art. Although all involved took the panel seriously, it too had the feeling of a charade.

The Outcome

Over the next few years Serra pursued legal measures addressing contract, copyright infringement and trademark violation, and First Amendment issues to protect his sculpture. (Legal issues are discussed in detail in chapter 3 in the section "The Public

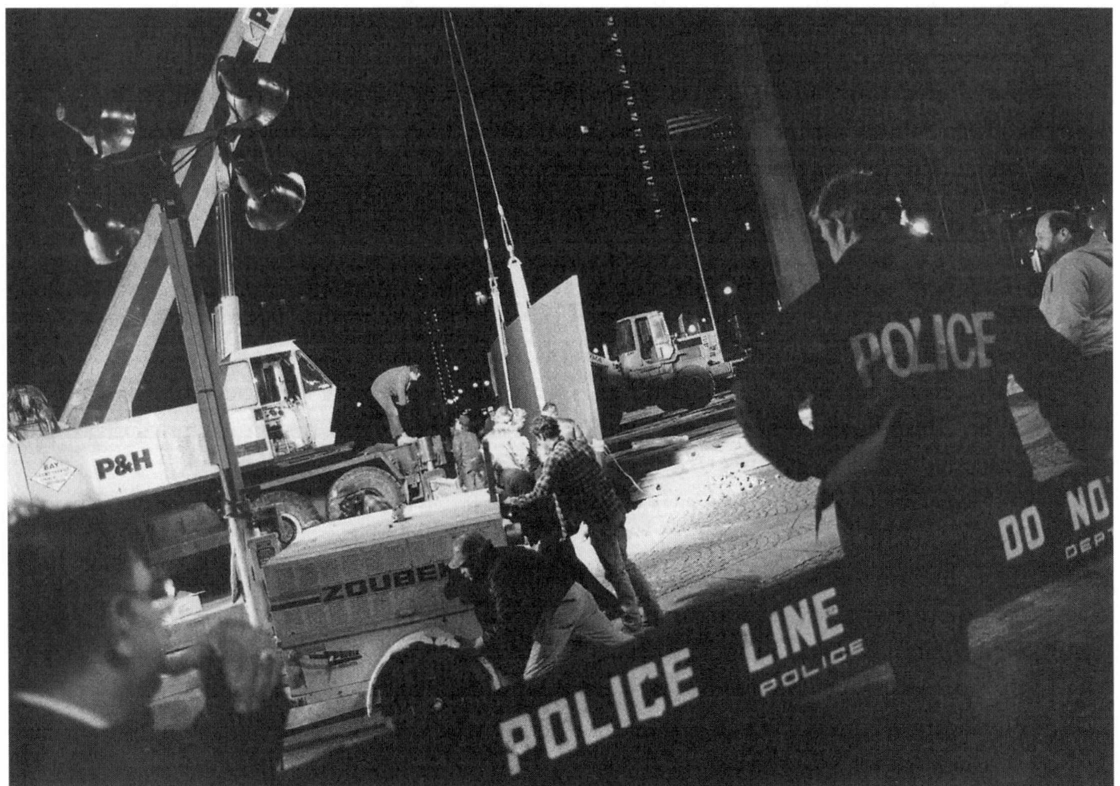

Figure 17. Removal of *Tilted Arc,* March 15, 1989, New York City. Photograph by Jennifer Cotter; courtesy of Richard Serra.

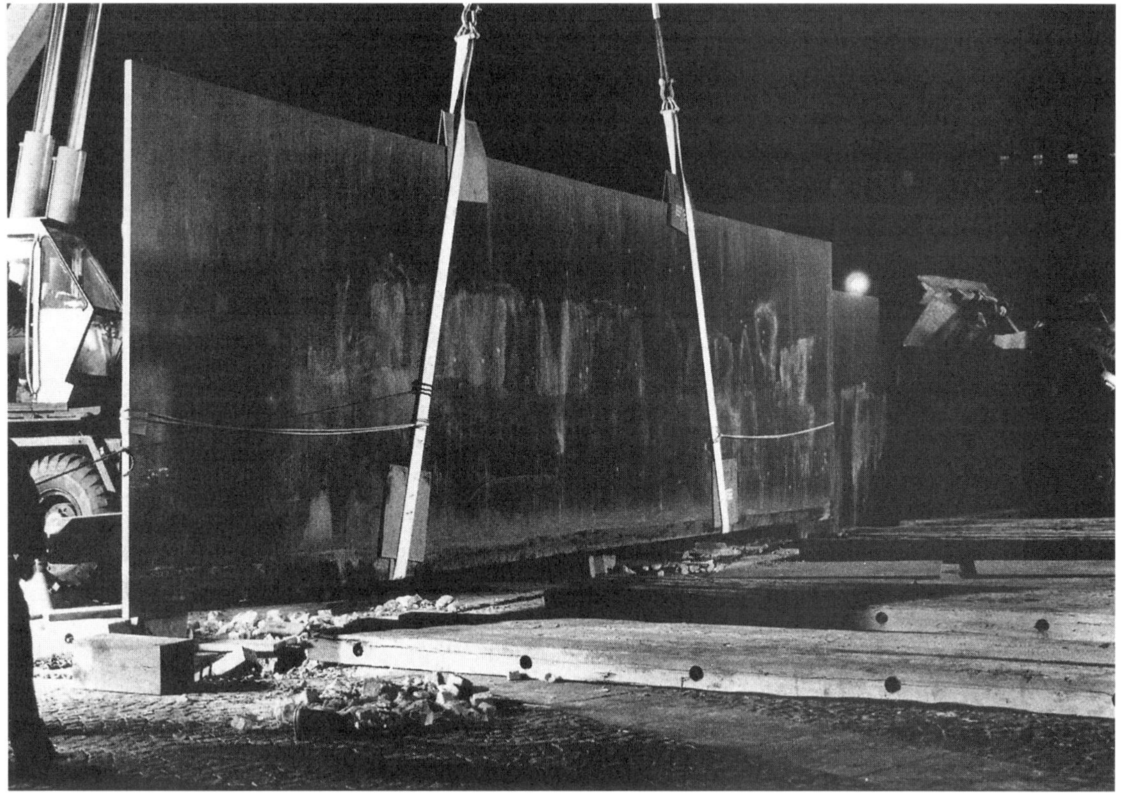

Figure 18. Removal of *Tilted Arc,* March 15, 1989, New York City. Photograph by Jennifer Cotter; courtesy of Richard Serra.

Policy Context.") After a number of unsuccessful appeals, a scant ten years after it had been commissioned and eight years after it was installed, *Tilted Arc* was removed from Federal Plaza. On the night of March 15, 1989, at a time when the GSA had another acting administrator (Richard Austin) in Washington, and the NEA was also without a permanent director, the sculpture was dismantled and "stored in three stacked sections in an outdoor government parking lot in Brooklyn, at Third Avenue and 29th Street." (See Figures 17, 18.) In September 1999 "the three 5-ton sections were moved by flatbed truck to a storage building in Middle River, Md., where they were unloaded and stacked by an oversized 80-ton forklift. The move cost $36,000." Recently, GSA spokeswoman Renée Miscione said that the agency "will not destroy or discard the pieces. However, we will honor Richard Serra's wishes, and we will not erect it anywhere else."[52]

2. Public Opinion

> You cannot take 2,000, 4,000 or 10,000 people at a particular time and place. . . . *Tilted Arc* belongs to 230 million people.
>
> **—Bradley Arthur, citizen and neighbor, at the Hearing**

Contrary to nearly all published commentary, there is no accurate measure of public response to *Tilted Arc.* Although there is a surviving archive of letters at the GSA and NEA, the actual numbers of people represented are relatively small and may not be representative. Nevertheless, even this sample reveals that although the controversy was always presented as an "us versus them" narrative, with "us" variously constructed as the art world, the government, or the public at Federal Plaza, there were *Tilted Arc* supporters and detractors in all the alleged camps. Common to all of them was a self-righteous rage that set the tone of the controversy.

The media only furthered what Diamond characterized as an "atmosphere of effrontery." Television presented art and artists as objects of ridicule. Accounts in the general press were divisive and simplistic, if not downright misleading. For those without an art education or interest in art, there was no alternative to counter the prevalent media marginalization and mockery.

Arguments for relocation of the sculpture emphasized the perceived loss of use of the plaza, the expenditure of public money (taxes) for this "thing," and the absence of public participation in the selection process. Other complaints included the proverbial "it isn't art" objections to "the wall" and especially objections to its rusty surface and the graffiti it attracted.

Arguments against relocation focused on the primacy of professional opinion over popular taste, the time needed for new or difficult art to be accepted, the nature of site-specific art (i.e., removal would be the same as destruction), preexisting problems with the plaza, the violation of freedom of speech, and, though only occasionally, the patently undemocratic process of removal. Surprisingly, this last issue, an essential feature of the controversy, was missing from most reportage and critical commentary.

Contemporary critics expressed a range of positive and negative opinions about the significance of the sculpture and the controversy, a situation very different from the nearly monolithic art-world support of *Tilted Arc* represented in the media and evidenced at the hearing and in letters to GSA.

Sources of Public Response

Public opinion in the *Tilted Arc* controversy was expressed in hearing testimony, letters, and comments on distributed fliers as well as in published critical writing, newspaper articles, and TV footage. But only those who were motivated responded in the form of oral testimony or written words, and they may not be representative of even the population at Federal Plaza.

There were some 10,000 employees at Federal Plaza in 1985. Although the hearing generated more than seven hundred pages of testimony, fewer than two hundred people testified. Of these, only some fifty were federal employees. It has been suggested that the public hearing may have been intimidating (certainly the media circus surrounding it was), but I suspect the imbalance has more to do with the nature of bureaucracy. Government workers learn early on that talk (at meetings) is meaningless; only leaving a paper trail (memos, letters, etc.) counts. The art professionals who turned up in numbers were those who were used to having their spoken words count. Many more federal employees signed various petitions: an initial one circulated in 1981 by an employee of the Army Corps of Engineers, Dick Wood, and those distributed by Diamond at the time of the hearing in 1985.

Defining the Public

Who was the public in the *Tilted Arc* controversy? In sculptor Donald Judd's view, "The public is not only the office workers . . . but people everywhere including me discussing this destruction and writing this statement from Switzerland."[1] Certainly, the public extended beyond the changing workforce at Federal Plaza to include a steady stream of visitors to the building, as well as other workers and residents in the immediate area around Foley Square. An even larger public became involved as the controversy was publicized, historicized, and became a subject for commentary on the Internet.

Many who spoke of "the public"—government administrators, judges, and other federal employees; artists, curators, and arts administrators; and art reporters and critics—meant different things. Most often, only two publics were identified: the larger general public (i.e., the people) and the smaller art world (i.e., the elite). Both were framed as inherently monolithic, in direct opposition to the other.

Sociologists Judith H. Balfe and Margaret J. Wyszomirski defined three general "parties" in public art, each with its own interests: the artists, the commissioning public agency, and the public.[2] More recently, historian Casey Blake suggested a three-way power struggle among "artists and art administrators . . . conservative judges, officials, and commentators . . . and [those who] insisted that the public be given more control over public affairs."[3] Blake observed that "the two elite discourses that dominated the *Tilted Arc* controversy rarely recognized the existence of a popular esthetic that was as hostile to the official iconography of Federal Plaza as it was to *Tilted Arc*."

But even the acknowledgment of three publics or discourses is insufficient to frame the range of expressed opinions. As Robert Storr pointed out, the opinions expressed by art professionals varied widely in substance as well as language, and Serra had the firm support of some government officials.[4] Any attempt to define a community, no matter how common their perceived interests seem, is bound to be problematic.[5] An analysis based on grouping voices by professional identity may obscure issues as well as differences.

There are numerous government agencies represented at Federal Plaza: the Departments of Agriculture, Commerce, Health and Human Resources, Housing and Urban Development, Justice, Labor, State, Transportation, and Treasury; the Air Force, the Army Corps of Engineers, the Merit Systems Protection Board, the National Labor Relations Board, the Port Authority of New York and New Jersey Federal Credit Union, the Railroad Retirement Board, the Social Security Administration, the Small Business Administration, and the New York bureau of the Voice of America. An adjacent smaller building houses the International Court of Trade, with its judges and legal staffs. Each agency at Federal Plaza has its own middle management and support staffs. Levels of education range from advanced professional degrees to high school equivalency diplomas. All employees are salaried, most are middle class, some barely. Generalities are risky.

Consider Wendy Harris, an archaeologist with a Ph.D. in anthropology, working for the Army Corps of Engineers.[6] Hardly a fan of the GSA (although she finds her coworkers interesting and likes them), indeed an activist in improving working conditions, she was predisposed to like large-scale public art because her father is a sculptor and she loves rust as a surface. Nevertheless, when she came to work at Federal Plaza in 1988, she experienced the sculpture as overbearing and oppressive. She was convinced that the sculpture blocked her path, especially on her way to lunch in nearby Chinatown. It made her feel cut off from the rest of the city. Not having been there before the sculpture was installed, she assumed that the plaza's barren appearance was something Serra intended. It had never occurred to her that seating might have been added and that the plaza might be used for concerts with *Tilted Arc* as a backdrop; she thought that would have made a big difference. She also thought *Tilted Arc* "mirrored the federal bureaucracy" and acted as "a magnet for transference."

For many during the 1980s, work and life in lower Manhattan became increasingly stressful. While the dynamic rise of Wall Street fortunes was taking place a few blocks away and the real estate boom was evident in the development of Battery Park City further east, the homeless became a visible part of daily life at Federal Plaza and elsewhere.[7] In the midst of political scandals revealing corruption at city hall and in the nation's capital, government employees, themselves the object of mounting public scorn, were caught in a squeeze.[8]

As Reagan, true to his campaign promises, trimmed the nondefense government workforce, mostly through random attrition, the remaining overburdened staff was consistently expected to do more with less. Government salaries, already well below those in the private sector when Reagan took office, fell even further behind during the 1980s, especially for upper-rank managers. At the time of Diamond's hearing, many new law and business school graduates were earning more in their first year out of school than were federal judges and heads of major government agencies. Not surprisingly, the turnover rate doubled, and not just for economic reasons. In 1986 one executive stated, "I think Ronald Reagan's lasting contribution to government in the next decade or so will be that he completely illegitimatized government service."[9]

Working conditions at Federal Plaza were (and continue to be) appalling. In 1985 employees complained of overcrowding, inadequate maintenance, and vermin. One man who voted against relocation of the sculpture reported that he was "appalled at the working conditions *inside* the building. . . . In 6 months there has been no effort to clean the floors in the office spaces, roaches are everywhere and just getting a light changed takes weeks. . . . we work with garbage on the floors and roaches living in our desk drawers." Another wrote that GSA's "incredible disregard for the workers' comfort and morale is like a slap in the face."[10]

The Anger

A certain level of frustration was presumably shared by workers at Federal Plaza before Serra's sculpture came on the scene. It acted as a catalyst, a focus for generally diffuse and mounting frustration expressed not only at the hearing but in letters to critics who defended the sculpture.[11]

The object of rage varied. Some people, including federal workers, blamed the government. An employee of the Army Corps of Engineers commented, "It is frequently referred to as being symbolic of all that is wrong with federal government." But the artist and art establishment attracted greater rage. Peter Hirsch, an attorney, stated, "The public is saying we don't like it and we are not stupid and we are not Philistines and we don't need some art historians and some curators to tell us we will like it. We don't like it." For some, this perceived disrespect from the art world was the last straw. To Shirley Paris, Serra's sculpture was

> [a] nose-thumbing gesture at the government and at those who serve the government, the civil servants and those of us who comprise much of the daytime population of Foley Square. It is bad enough for the government and its civil servants to be the perennial targets of the public and the press alike, but for us to be denigrated by artists as well, as exemplified by the affront embodied in *Tilted Arc,* is to say the least compounding the insult.[12]

The elitist/populist split was reinforced by many art-world comments. Even sculptors like George Segal, whose figural work embodies humanist themes, and

George Sugarman, whose public pieces provide seating and are abstract, colorful, and open, expressed opinions that revealed a basic distrust if not contempt for public opinion. At Diamond's hearing, Segal testified, "If we start backing down on public objections we are in danger of establishing the same standards for outdoor public sculpture that we have for television and we would be in a terrible state if our public sculptures . . . were on the same level as a TV sitcom program." Sugarman also equated public taste with television culture. As artists, he insisted, "We are not appealing to a TV taste. We are not appealing to . . . MacDonald's hamburgers, you know, quick taste."[13] Yet both artists, whose public art is radically different, have also been the object of bitter controversy as well as widespread admiration.[14]

Serra was even more dismissive of the public. In an interview given three years before his GSA commission, he stated categorically,

> I don't have any assumptions of humanistic values that art needs to serve. If you are conceiving a piece for a public place, a place and space that people walk through, one has to consider traffic flow, but not necessarily worry about the indigenous community and get caught up in the politics of the site. There are a lot of ways in which one could complicate the problem for oneself. I'm not going to concern myself with what "they" consider to be adequate, appropriate solutions.[15]

In 1980, when *T.W.U.* and *St. John's Rotary Arc* were installed in New York and *Tilted Arc* was in process, Serra stated, "Placing pieces in an urban context is not synonymous with an interest in a large audience even though the work will be seen by many people who wouldn't otherwise look at art. The work I make does not allow for experience outside the conventions of sculpture as sculpture. My audience is necessarily very limited."[16] Serra was clear. He considered the general public only as figures moving through the space, distinct from his true constituency, an art audience.

Although the controversy was defined by polarized images of an enraged public and arrogant art world, this was far from representative. As in most things, the art world was hardly a united community. Art critic Patricia Phillips, writing in *Artforum,* arguably the most influential art magazine at the time, sided with those who wanted Serra's sculpture removed. She criticized Serra for creating "a behavioral autocracy" at Federal Plaza and argued for the public's right to ignore public art or avoid engaging it.[17] Robert Storr, writing in *Art in America,* was sharply critical of his art-world colleagues "who have learned their politics from Benjamin, Lacan and Foucault," and he found "the palpable contempt they expressed for the opposition pointlessly antagonistic and self-indulgent."[18] Unfortunately, their comments appeared only in specialized journals and did not reach a larger audience. Neither did the less oppositional comments from the general public.

The Mediated Controversy

Attitudes toward art and visual culture are formed by personal experience, education, and media exposure. And taste, as Pierre Bourdieu has demonstrated, is largely a function of class. Early home environments establish attitudes as well as cultural preferences.[19] Subsequent art education may provide exposure to alternative visual forms, offer a context for understanding, and encourage an open mind. But if one's only exposure to art is making it in kindergarten or rare encounters with "visiting artists," then art remains a diversion (a hobby or entertainment) rather than an expression of serious content in visual form.

Many have argued for an art component at all stages of public education on the grounds of aesthetic justice.[20] In 1977, two years before *Tilted Arc* was commissioned, a national panel chaired by David Rockefeller published a report recommending that "the arts become central to the individual's learning experience, in or out of school and at every stage of life" in order to realize "the fundamental goals of American education."[21] Nevertheless, an important study by the Getty Center for Education in the Arts published in 1985 (the year of the hearing) found that 80 percent of all individuals in the United States graduate high school without any art education (studio, appreciation, or history). In elementary schools, less than 3 percent of weekly instruction time was devoted to the arts.[22] The study found widespread opinion that art was not an academic subject but a frill and that people needed little or no formal education to experience, create, or comprehend it.

According to a survey by the NEA published three years later, in 1988, 75 percent of the participants reported no education in making art, and 84 percent had had no instruction in art appreciation.[23] In a 1992 public policy study, Laura Chapman concluded that current art education is "haphazard, inconsistent, unbalanced, and not evaluated."[24] Not surprisingly, our culture manifests various conflicting attitudes toward art. In a 1993 survey conducted by the National Cultural Alliance, 81 percent of the respondents thought the arts were essential for well-rounded communities and individuals, but 68 percent said the arts played little to no role in their lives.[25]

Art is generally ignored by the media, except as the object of controversy, theft, or the expenditure of great sums of money. During the Reagan years the most influential medium, television, became ever more sound-bite simplistic.[26] A CBS news piece on *Tilted Arc,* aired on March 26, 1985, after Diamond's hearing, reached an audience of millions. Dan Rather introduced the three-minute-ten-second segment with a favorite television frame, asking a familiar question: "But is it art?" Reporter Jane Wallace's voice was heard over "images of rusting, junked cars along the Hudson River," referring to *Tilted Arc* as a "seventy-five-ton slab of steel." Only negative comments by passersby were heard. The reporter asked someone if the work was pretty and quoted the price of the sculpture, $175,000, without explaining that this was the total GSA cost, not Serra's profit. Wallace's remarks were facile and snide: "The *Tilted Arc* may soon become the 'Jilted Arc' because government workers want it out of their sight [site?]"; "The artist was driven to abstraction"; and her concluding comment, "The Federal Government has more than a month to decide if *Tilted Arc* is a monument to abstract art or just a monumental mistake." Serra's serious comments were juxtaposed with images of sleepy panel members at Diamond's hearing or laughing security guards. Dan Rather ended the segment by mocking Serra's explanation of his sculpture: "And that ends our space, place, and time."

The CBS evening news had actually enlisted Serra's assistance in preparing this piece. According to the artist,

> They told me that they were going to support the concept of site-specificity by showing other site-specific works, so I spent a week helping them organize TV crews in Holland, France, Germany, and Japan. It seemed like a responsible project, and I was looking forward to the broadcast. When the segment was finally aired, I was stunned. For the first thirty seconds, the camera panned across abandoned, wrecked cars; cut to burnt-out buildings and urban rubbish; and then cut to *Tilted Arc,* with a voice-over stating: "New Yorkers have had enough of this." I'd been had once again. I should have known that television delivers people, and that all public opinion is manipulated opinion. The pragmatics of television do not admit rejoinders or resistance. There is no equal time.[27]

According to Jeffrey Scheuer, "Television . . . is a relentlessly simplifying and atomizing medium. It simplifies by personalizing and dichotomizing; by truncating and foreshortening events and personalities; by ignoring organic relationships and suppressing uncertainty and ambiguity."[28] A detailed study of art and artists on network news by sociologist John Ryan and curator Deborah A. Sim confirmed a consistent pattern of representation.[29] Of the art features aired on the three major networks from January 1976 to August 1985, "only 14 (28 percent) dealt with art or artists that could even remotely be considered as representative of the main currents, past or present, of the art world." Those who learned about art only from television literally saw a different art world, one consisting of "baglady art, art made with the exhaust of jet engines, sports art, space shuttle art, freeway art and a sculpture made by crashing a plane into the ground." Always aired in the last ten minutes of the program after the serious news was over, art was the subject of "cute, poignant, or humorous stories."

Television reporters bonded with their audience in marginalizing the art world. Although not quite as unifying as a common enemy, a common laughingstock offers a welcome release, enforcing a false elitist/populist dichotomy by turning it upside down. Television news, like Diamond's hearing, trivialized art, obviating both the need for and possibility of dialogue.

Coverage of the *Tilted Arc* controversy in much of the press was consistent with television reportage. The *Daily News* treated art as an object for scorn or ridicule, frequently juxtaposing cartoons with articles. The *New York Times,* although seemingly more evenhanded, nevertheless simplified issues, obscured facts, and avoided mention of the more questionable aspects of the controversy, such as Diamond's hearing. The *Washington Post* news reports were glib and inaccurate, and the editorials, although more thoughtful, also avoided difficult themes. The most cursory, inflammatory, and politicized account I read appeared in the *Washington Times.*[30] The writer identified Serra as a loser, comparable to Walter Mondale in his bid against Reagan, while dismissing supportive comments by artists with the statement "The artists, like Mom, know best." And as for the vice president's wife, "Mrs. Mondale, naturally, gets to wait out eternity on a quiet street of little children and big dogs in Cleveland Park, where urgent old men do not relieve themselves against rusting steel walls flung across the neighborhood's spacious lawns."

An absence of respect and an inability to listen, to suspend prejudice, or to consider that art is inherently a serious endeavor, on the part of people whose only exposure to art came from the media, was (alas) understandable. It was inexcusable for the press and art-world professionals not to try to counter those prejudices or to consider that individuals may be uninformed but not unintelligent. The inability to listen to differing views affected both sides of the controversy.

Arguments for Removal (against Keeping the Sculpture)

Ballots distributed at Federal Plaza offered employees the option of voting for or against removal. In this polarizing frame, a positive vote expressed a negative opinion.

Considering the arguments for removal required looking at Serra's sculpture in terms of a real-world context, in the context of "the practice of everyday life."[31] The perception that the space was no longer usable was arguable. Misperceptions—mistaking the sculpture for something else, such as a wall or a ship, or taking offense at its rusty surfaces—could have been addressed through a public-art education program. Complaints about graffiti and danger reflected the experience and quality of urban life in general. The money spent for art and the absence of public participation in the selection process were public-policy issues. Hardly unique to *Tilted Arc* or Federal Plaza, they implied larger, more pervasive problems in the public art enterprise.

It Ruined the Plaza

Federal Plaza existed for ten years without Serra's sculpture. In that time people got used to things as they were. Change is always disturbing; that's why public art policy, as a rule, stipulates that art be installed before the building opens. Complaints that *Tilted Arc* ruined the plaza, rendered it unusable, and made it unsafe are discussed in more detail in chapter 3 in the section "The Public Space Context." Arguments that Federal Plaza was not a livable space before *Tilted Arc* and that the sculpture did not prohibit its use are included in the section "Arguments against Removal" below.

Reasoned written and oral comments that objected to *Tilted Arc*'s placement without denigrating the sculpture or public art in general were not reported. Federal employee John F. Tavolaro felt that a fountain sculpture would work better in a city with already limited open space. Robert Crawford of the U.S. Department of Labor credited the sculpture with "aesthetic merit" but disliked the "brutal and arrogant" way it dominated the plaza and "conflicted with people's use of that space." And Keith Lawrence liked Serra's *St. John's Rotary Arc,* preferring a visual rather than visceral experience.[32]

It Isn't Art

> From the time it was built it was hard to see
> just what it was supposed to be.
> A windbreaker was the general guess
> or a tilted wonder more or less.
> We soon found out it was none of the above
> but a great work of art we would grow to love.
> Unfortunately it just didn't work out that way
> but has dampened our spirits every day.
>
> **—Hank Perveslin, U.S. Department of Education employee**

Accounts on television and in the general press rarely referred to *Tilted Arc* as sculpture; for the most part it was called a "wall" or a "piece of rusty steel." Although reporters didn't directly challenge its status as art, many at Federal Plaza, who undoubtedly had never heard of Richard Serra, did.[33] As Dario Gamboni has shown, mistaking a work of art for something else, especially something disposable, has become a standard public response to modern art. It is a contemporary version of a narrative, popular from antiquity through the late nineteenth century, about art that is so realistic it is mistaken for the real thing.[34] These anecdotes acknowledge an immediate reaction that the rational mind then corrects—something like "That looks so real I can't believe it's painted" for illusionistic works, or "What *is* that?" for abstract modern art. The first is the highest compliment; the second the most comprehensive dismissal. The object in question is not art but something else with no claim to special treatment. If not worthless, it definitively becomes worth less. As verbal vandalism it is a way of disparaging something that, one way or another, challenges our ability to identify what we see.

The Wall Context

At the hearing, Shale Brownstein pointed out, "We are a wall culture when it comes to art. That's where it seems to belong. Not out in a room with tables, chairs, and other things we use. I think we can be uneasy with other objects that actually co-exist with us in the room, in space. Their special presence intrudes and the fact a sculpture is there is enough to feel it's imposing on our life space." Without a museum or gallery frame, an object is related to other everyday objects, not to other art. Serra's sculpture looked and functioned something like a wall, and observers, reacting to the feeling of being controlled, compared it to real and symbolic walls of dictatorship. Art critic Kim Levin had already invoked the Berlin Wall in a 1981 gallery review of a similar Serra sculpture. Shirley Paris observed that immigrants applying for citizenship within the building "cannot help but be painfully reminded by *Tilted Arc* of the iron curtains from which they escape." Ray Slizys of the Environmental Protection Agency observed that the Javits building "may be the first U.S. government office building that they've ever seen. In light of this, a structure which looks like a wall designed to keep people out seems amazingly inappropriate."[35] All these associations implied that *Tilted Arc* was definitely un-American.[36]

One FBI employee suggested, "Rename it 'Great Wall of China Meets Wailing Wall' and dedicate it to Richard Nixon for every malcontent in the world to attach notices to its surface." Others saw a retaining wall, a firing squad wall, or a windbreak necessitated by bad planning.[37]

By relating Serra's sculpture to other known walls in the public realm, people reframed it. That process is what museums do all the time. They first decontextualize art (from its place of origin and function) in order to recontextualize it (as art from a particular culture, period, style, etc.). Only the visual contexts are different. In either case the art is tamed and implicitly or explicitly redefined.

Compared to a Ship

Many FBI employees suggested relocating the sculpture in the East River, the Hudson River, the bottom of the Atlantic Ocean; an employee of the National Labor Relations Board suggested it be "put . . . with Noah's Ark." More directly, one individual observed, "To me it looks like the remnants of a sunken battleship," and another saw "the forlorn remains of part of a vessel." One employee observed, "If I wanted to see a rusted side of a ship, I'd go to the shipyard." Others suggested that the sculpture be relocated to New York City's seaport since it would make an "excellent sea wall," to Fire Island "to be used to prevent erosion of the shoreline," or even to the Netherlands "as a retaining wall for their dike system." These observations were prompted, I suspect, either from a direct or subliminal perception of the work's similarity to the side of a ship, acknowledged by Serra only years after the piece was made.[38]

A "looks like" approach to seeing works of art, although disparaged by art practitioners, is to be expected, especially in a public space. This type of seeing enables navigation in the real world (e.g., "It's a chair; I can sit in it"; or "It's a car; I better get out of the way"). It is not so different from what occurs in a museum or gallery, where the process of identification results in the ability to contextualize a work as belonging to a particular artist or style (e.g., "It looks like an early Serra," or "It's an abstract sculpture"), prompting thoughts about that kind of art (e.g., the artist's intentions, the work of his contemporaries, the critical issues of the time).

The Rust Problem

> Now the whole thing about rust shows a kind of prejudice against the oxidation of steel.
>
> **—Gerry Rosen, attorney, at the Hearing**

Although self-rusting Cor-Ten steel became as common to postwar sculpture as marble and bronze were in earlier times, in a contemporary urban setting rust is associated with deterioration and decay.[39] Gregory W. Carman of the U.S. Court of International Trade observed in a letter to Diamond, "In its rusted condition, it unfortunately appears to be part of the construction for the new subway." One Public Health Services worker wrote, "New Yorkers have enough rust and decay to look at," and an employee of the Environmental Protection Agency commented, "The spirit of his work is exemplified by rust. If there is anything we don't need here it is something that symbolizes the destruction and decay that is prevalent in the city." Even for some who liked *Tilted Arc,* rust was seen as negative. A worker at the Bureau of the Census who admired the design of the sculpture and its functionality as a windbreak, wondered if there were "any kind of treatment that could refinish it and rust proof it."[40]

Graffiti and Worse

Not surprisingly, *Tilted Arc,* like other "walls" in urban environments, attracted graffiti, but here the sculpture rather than the graffiti writer was held responsible. Judge Carman stated that it "invites vandals to place graffiti upon it," and Dr. Bernard Kilbourn (regional director for the Health and Human Services Agency) noted that "*Tilted Arc* unfortunately has been a magnet for ethnic graffiti. Racial and religious epitaphs abound on it." And worse than graffiti, the sculpture attracted human and animal excrement. Federal employee Bert Haggerty complained, "It's not an uncommon sight to see people urinating on the wall and this is what the wall has done."[41]

Although it was irrational to blame the sculpture, in a sense it was understandable: Without the sculpture there would have been no graffiti in the middle of Federal Plaza. And although a sewer smell permeated the area around the low perimeter wall of the plaza for years after the sculpture was removed, offending actions presumably were less visible or more easily ignored. It has been suggested that works not immediately recognized as art are particularly subject to vandalism, perhaps because they, more than others, seem to emphasize the hierarchical distinction between those who get it and those who don't.[42] But considering the current pervasiveness of graffiti, I am not sure that art can be singled out as a special case.

An anonymous act of physical aggression, vandalism has increasingly become an annoying fact of urban life.[43] More seriously, so has the threat of random violence. The comments alleging the sculpture was dangerous indicated that people felt safer before the sculpture was installed when they could see in all directions. (Issues of public safety are discussed in detail in chapter 3 in the section "The Public Space Context.")

No Money for Art

Two widely repeated complaints went beyond reactions to *Tilted Arc* per se. They addressed issues of public policy, arguing that public money should not be spent for art and that if it were, the public should have a say in the choice. Central to every public art controversy and every discussion of the NEA, the debate over the appropriateness of national art patronage dates back to the origins of the country. Questions about the selection process raise issues of citizen participation and professional expertise.

Art is perceived by many as elitist entertainment, not as serious as, say, literature or classical music but equally peripheral. The *work* of art is not acknowledged. Artists are told to get day jobs or real jobs, and money for public art is resented, especially if the price exceeds the annual salary of many of those who see it.

Although Serra made no money on the commission, many assumed that the price of *Tilted Arc* was the artist's profit rather than the total allocation for creating, building, and installing the sculpture. And they were enraged that one way or another, they would have to pay for any relocation costs. One Army Corps of Engineers worker favored moving the piece, "as long we don't get a 5 percent pay cut to fund its relocation."[44] Realizing that all government activities involving the sculpture were costing taxpayers money, some people felt that Diamond "should have 'let sleeping dogs lie.' It would have been cheaper." A few felt that Serra should pay for relocation of the sculpture.

The larger issue, of course, was how to justify spending public money on art when funds were scarce and living conditions were worsening. One employee complained, "Art is for private charities—taxes are to be spent for *needs* of the people—not enrichment of Serra. . . . *NO MORE TAX MONEY FOR FOOLISHNESS!* " Another stated, "This should *NEVER HAPPEN AGAIN*. Why is the government buying junk at exorbitant prices when our real salaries are shrinking?" Comments that identified the sculpture as "a tribute to government waste and stupidity," "another rip-off of the U.S. taxpayer," and a "waste of taxpayer dollars in view of unemployment" reflected a larger dissatisfaction with decreased earning power and governmental use of taxes. After all, the hearing took place about a month before federal income taxes were due.

We Weren't Asked

Tilted Arc was commissioned in the way representative democracy usually works: by designated individuals without direct input from the general public. Nearly a month before the hearing, Patricia A. Nelson, a federal employee, wrote to Diamond, "It would have been far wiser to seek public comment prior to the installation of the piece instead of at this late date."[45] For the most part, however, people seemed to value any venue to express their rage at not being considered, an anger that implicated far more than the public art selection process at GSA.

Joseph Lombardi, clerk of the court at the International Court of Trade, recognized that "for as long as that wall remains, it stands as a symbol to the public that its agents, government employees even though acting with the well intent and sense of artistic noblesse oblige, can impose their opinions on the public and worse, the symbol demonstrates that the public is powerless to re-assert its rights."[46] As with graffiti, many blamed the sculpture for their sense of victimization and impotence.

Paul Goldstein, district leader of Community Board 1, protested, "We feel that the people who live and work in this community and wish to utilize this plaza deserve to be heard and to have their needs and opinions respected."[47] But how can this public be identified? And who would best represent them? How can they best participate in the selection process? And what is the place and value of art expertise in the selection process?

The problem of acknowledging art expertise rests with attitudes toward both art and expertise.[48] Distrust of "expert opinion" is expressed inside the academy, in mass media, and on the street. It is reflected in a commonly held assumption that John or Jane Q. Public could, if given the chance, do a better job than the professionals in charge[49] or that, when it comes to modern art, there's nothing to it ("My six-year-old can do that"). If art is considered only a matter of taste, knowing what one likes is paramount, more important than understanding what one sees. And if expertise is discounted, and all opinions are equal, then anyone is qualified to select public art. That is not, however, the way of representative democracy in any other area.

Arguments against Removal (for Keeping the Sculpture)

Although art-world support for Serra's sculpture at the hearing appeared unanimous, it was usually expressed indirectly. Those who opposed the work's removal emphasized the time needed for new or difficult art to be accepted, the principle of freedom of speech, the illegality of removal procedures, and violation of the artist's government contract.

The Test of Time

At the time of the hearing, *Tilted Arc* had been up for four years. Joan Mondale suggested, "Sculpture which may be provocative to our eyes can be seen more clearly by those who come after us," and sculptor Gene Highstein stated, "A work of art is never seen clearly at the time of its creation and the judgement of the public upon seeing the work of art for the first time is notoriously wrong."[50]

Since change is inevitable in life, Mimi Johnson, codirector of Performance Art Services, argued, "Public opinions on the appropriateness, scale, and public usage are as likely to change as anything else. . . . it is very likely that once again habit and familiarity will work their magic allowing all of us in ten years time to feel that *Tilted Arc* is a beautiful, old friend." William Rubin, director of the department of painting and sculpture at the Museum of Modern Art, also posited ten years as a reasonable test of time.[51]

Taking a long view was not the American way in the 1980s. The long-term effects of junk bonds and leveraged buyouts, the savings and loan crisis, and environmental damage, to name just a few, were routinely ignored by politicians, especially by those who gained handsomely in the prevalent laissez-faire atmosphere. In a climate of threatened funding for art when the standard political modus operandi was an immediate and unreasoned response to perceived public opinion, even a hint of protracted discontent or controversy over art could lead to a loss of already limited dollars.

Freedom of Speech

National identity in the United States is in many ways defined in terms of the First Amendment; any threat to its principles are, by definition, un-American. Senator Jacob K. Javits, for whom the federal office building was named, argued that removal of the sculpture would compromise "the kind of integrity which makes art in our society the symbol of what freedom means in the world." Speaking for the National Emergency Civil Liberties Committee, Betty St. Clair stated, "Artistic expression no less than religious freedom or political expression is entitled to full and complete constitutional protection."[52]

Conversely, removal of the sculpture (which was equated with its destruction) was associated with dictatorships. Egregious comparisons to Hitler notwithstanding, the issue of censorship can be argued and is discussed in chapter 4 in the section "*Tilted Arc* and the Culture Wars."

The Contract Guarantees Permanence

Serra and other artists who had worked for the GSA's Art-in-Architecture program believed that their commissions, once approved, were permanent, and Julia Brown, the GSA administrator in charge of the Federal Plaza project, stated unequivocally that permanence was always assumed. As Brenda Richardson, assistant director of the Baltimore Museum of Art, noted, "Acclamation by popular taste was not a condition of the contract."[53] The clause in the contract allowing the government to move art under special circumstances had been considered a precaution to protect the works from threats of physical harm but the wording was not specific enough. The legal ramifications of this vagueness are discussed in chapter 3 in the section "The Public Policy Context." In the end, the controversy was determined by the artist's contract; it all boiled down to a legal issue.

The Process Is a Sham

There were serious objections to the removal proceedings in general as well as to the obvious bias of the hearing panel. Victor Ganz, chair of the Fine Arts Committee of Battery Park City, queried "Is a work of art, legally commissioned by a government and designed by contract for a specific public space subject to removal at the sole discretion of the agency which commissioned it?" And Senator Howard M. Metzenbaum objected,

> I am concerned about the propriety of the recent action by the General Services Administrator for New York in convening a public hearing to solicit views on the sculpture *Tilted Arc*. The convening of a hearing by an Administrator, who, according to news accounts, has already made up his mind about the art, appears to be a breach of proper procedures and violative of the explicit agreement with the artist as to the display of the sculpture. . . . I believe that it constitutes an improper and unfortunate precedent to reopen the process after the installation. I am concerned that this is a precedent which would severely hamper the vitality and perhaps the continuation of the Art-in-Architecture program.

Serra tried to separate the issue of whether the hearing could reverse the commission "after the fact" from the "quite different question of whether a local community should have input into the process prior to selection and installation."[54]

George Kubler, Sterling Professor of History of Art at Yale University, questioned Diamond's right "to convene public hearings meant to reverse a national decision through an ad hoc process," and Abigail Solomon-Godeau, photography curator and critic, accused Diamond directly:

> Last night, Mr. Diamond, you appeared on a cable news program and announced—midway through this hearing—that the GSA had obviously made a mistake in commissioning *Tilted Arc,* that something was wrong with the commissioning process, and that the plaza should be restored to its original empty state and made available to other purposes. . . . Last night you proved what others said, this is not an open hearing, it is a show trial . . . a parody of the notion of a public forum. You, Mr. Diamond, have in your statements revealed the utter bankruptcy and the total fraudulence of these proceedings.

And Gus Harrow, Serra's attorney, observed that the hearing "was unauthorized if not illegal; . . . it was convened in order to reach a foregone conclusion, not an informed one; and the manner in which it was constituted is an effort to mask its illegitimacy." And furthermore, Harrow remarked, "the entire panel presiding at this hearing is improperly constituted, since the official who should have disqualified himself, chose and designated the panel, which will evaluate the hearing. These acts disregard the responsibilities of public office and violate the terms of its trust."[55]

After the hearing Terry Adams Murray, a resident of Manhattan's Upper West Side, wondered whether the gathered opinion on *Tilted Arc* was representative of anything. He wrote to acting GSA administrator Dwight Ink in Washington:

> The whole effort to have the art-work removed has been built up by a small group of red-necks who think this is a chance to make a stand against modern art. The sculpture was planned and approved in a most methodical and democratic way . . . and it is simply fascistic to have a small group of reactionaries carry so much weight. If there were to be a serious effort to find out what the public wants, it would be different. Instead of heavy lobbying through friends of the opponents of the art-work, there should be a survey tailored to get a genuine reading on the pros and cons, carried out by a reputable research group, such as The Roper Organization.[56]

But as long as the spectacle of the hearing seemed to satisfy the media, there was no motivation to do things differently. The hearing, consisting of the testimony of fewer than 180 individuals, came to frame and stand for the controversy.

The violation of any semblance of impartial procedure was rarely mentioned in media reports and had no impact on the outcome. Considering the political coverups of the 1980s, not the least of which involved a covert foreign policy that aided governments the United States did not officially support in Central America and Iran, Diamond's charade appears insignificant. (At least he made an attempt to look as if he were following a reasonable protocol.) However, the practice of deception and the promotion of spectacle are serious issues where and whenever they are condoned, indicative of a corrupt and corrosive cultural climate.

Critical Opinion

Since critical opinion was written in response to the hearing, it was largely framed by the same question: Should *Tilted Arc* be removed? Published in newspapers and periodicals, another form of public opinion, it reflected a diversity of art-world approaches. Some argued for removal based on public response or because *Tilted Arc* was not good public art; others thought the sculpture should stay based on contract or process issues, or, oddly, for didactic reasons.

Even before Diamond's hearing, two critics passionately attacked Serra's sculpture. Grace Glueck suggested that the sculpture "may conceivably be the ugliest outdoor work of art in the city," and Peter Schjeldahl raged, "It should be removed. It should never have been commissioned. With this installation—so mistaken, so wrong, so bad—the esthetic and moral failure of recent public art should at last be clear to everybody."[57] Although contextualized by opinions about appropriate public art, he and Glueck responded as many of the using public did: Just get rid of it.

But since public art is rarely reviewed, there was little critical commentary until the hearing. Then Paul Goldberger, architecture critic of the *New York Times,* and Patricia Phillips, writing in *Artforum,* argued for removal based on the perceived overwhelmingly negative public opinion. Goldberger wrote, "When a work of public art fails to communicate to those who see it daily as completely as this one seems to have done, the sad question that must be asked is what benefit its continued presence has." Phillips argued less reluctantly. Seeing *Tilted Arc* as "a demagogue who insistently attacks independent activity," she concluded that "aside from all the things that public art can and should do, the public should have the option to ignore it or avoid participation."[58] This argument would allow a sampling of public opinion expressed after the fact to determine the fate of public art.

Not all critics who did not like the sculpture (and in some cases, the artist) argued for removal. Gary Indiana wrote in the *Village Voice,* "It would indeed be a dangerous precedent for the GSA, which failed to consult the public in the first place, to blithely expunge the detested object without Richard Serra's agreement." Indiana, directing his venom at the artist, his high-minded supporters, and government alike, ended his article railing, "In case Richard Serra never heard this from anybody else, I'd like him to hear it from me: lie down with dogs, get up with fleas."[59]

In a milder tone, Michael Sorkin, architecture critic for the *Village Voice,* disparaged *Tilted Arc* as "[m]inimal sculpture mocking minimal architecture," but he felt that "Richard Serra and his measly one half of one percent take are taking the heat for the vastly greater failures of the 99½ [the architecture and the plaza]." Sorkin's observation that *Tilted Arc* is taking the rap for both the plaza and the building refers to the curious ability of public art to prompt a kind of unconscious transference, focusing all manner of local discontents onto itself. Considering contract issues and the potential impact of removal for the GSA art program, he observed, "I may not much like *Tilted Arc,* but the man did have a deal. What did the GSA think it was buying in the first place? Serra hadn't exactly been carving scrimshaw before he got the commission. . . . I wouldn't really shed tears over the Serra—the troubling question is who gets trashed next."[60]

Although others, notably Robert Storr, expressed concern over the improprieties of the removal process, only Michael Brenson, writing in the *New York Times,* made that a primary basis for judgment: "Before the hearing," he wrote,

> it may have been possible to feel caught between the need to be responsive to those who live with the sculpture, dislike it and resent the loss of their once-open plaza, and the need for the Government to honor its word, resist popular pressure and preserve the integrity of its enlightened Art-in-Architecture program. Because of the testimony, however, and because of the questions raised by the way the hearing was conducted, it is now emphatically clear that removing the sculpture from the site for which it was commissioned and conceived would be a serious mistake.[61]

The outrageous process, however, did not necessarily mean that the sculpture should not have been removed, only that it should not have been removed in this way.

Taking a different tack, Arthur Danto, writing in *The Nation,* observed, "*Tilted Arc* made vivid the truth that something may succeed as a work of art but fail as a work of 'public' art." Conversely, he posited that "it is possible that a work of art might be good public art though bad or indifferent as art, which would then make esthetic criteria irrelevant to the matter." He argued instead for a kind of public art that "embodies societal values, such as Grant's Tomb or Maya Lin's Vietnam Veterans Memorial."[62] Similarly, Calvin Tomkins, writing in *The New Yorker,* emphasized the social function of public art, as evidenced in the new "community-minded approach" taken by artists like Siah Armajani, Scott Burton, and Elyn Zimmerman.[63]

There is, however, room for more than one kind of public art, and social functions may arguably be better served by good art. Scott Burton or George Sugarman, say, provide a richer seating solution than standard benches from a catalog. And the experience of the Vietnam Veterans Memorial is more profound, more affecting, than that of its touring half-size replica or of the numerous imitations it engendered. There is simply no evidence to suggest that art that provides urban amenities is better appreciated by its immediate audience; Sugarman's *Baltimore Federal* (1977) was the object of a bitter controversy that did not lead to removal.[64]

Although Robert Hughes, art critic for *Time* magazine, dismissed Serra's art as "blue-collar minimalism, a pugnacious combination of muteness with extreme manipulations of space," he thought that *Tilted Arc* should stay, "if not as a source of general pleasure, than as a didactic monument to the follies that can arise at the juncture of undemanding patronage and truculent aestheticism." Robert Storr, in an otherwise thoughtfully nuanced article in *Art in America,* also concluded that the sculpture should stay as a lesson. Observing that Serra's sculpture "is a truly impressive work" if "approached on its own terms," he felt it should remain at Federal Plaza not for aesthetic reasons but "because it exists as a constant reminder that it is not just the public that has something to learn, but also all those who presume to speak for, and make, art in the public interest."[65]

The lesson argument appears to ignore public experience more blatantly than Serra did. He at least thought he was providing provocative art. Leaving artists and arts administrators with a lesson of things gone wrong, an "art as punishment" argument, would make a certain limited sense if the public consisted only of those directly responsible for the commission. In any event, as the legion of ignored public art (including war memorials) attests, visible reminders of our mistakes rarely lead to change or even reflection.

As this summary of public response indicates, the public is far from monolithic. Opinions that strayed from the main story line of art versus the public were rarely reported. General categories, such as art world, federal workers, or government officials, rarely stood for unanimity of opinion or communal response. Individuals proceeded from perceived self-interest, previous experience with art, available information, and certain (often unstated) expectations that determined their primary frame of reference.

Perhaps some of our expectations for public art are a direct response to what increasingly seems to be a misnomer, if not an oxymoron. The NEA early on defined its funding program as "art in public spaces," recognizing that it was the art's location, not its essence, that was public. In the same vein, it might be more useful to consider the audience for this art rather than its public. As T. J. Clark noted, "The public is different from the audience; the latter can be examined empirically and should be. . . . The public is a presence or a phantasy within the work and within the process of production."[66] And also, to be sure, in theories of democracy.

3. Reframing the Controversy

The *Tilted Arc* controversy raised many issues in related but distinct arenas: art, public art, public space, and public policy. Each context suggests a different primary audience with different expectations. In every frame, the controversy was caught in a paradigm shift of monumental proportions.

To the art world, however fractured, an art frame is always present, so much so that it becomes invisible. It is our given. To the art-informed audience, an art frame is at least implied. To the art-interested public, the frame is desirable but may not be immediately apparent. Whatever art may be—allusive, metaphorical, experiential—it is not literal. Without an art frame, one sees a rusty wall and not a Richard Serra sculpture. In the context of the 1980s art world, Serra, a product of the rebellious 1960s, had come to represent establishment modern and was consistently honored as such in major museum exhibitions and installations. At the same time, modernism was in decline, and various postmodern styles with implicit and explicit political content enjoyed greater critical acclaim at modernism's expense.

Public art practice has its own art parameters, with evolving criteria different from those of museum art. In the public art world of the 1980s, a single sculpture in an urban space was as disparaged as modernism was in the art world. Public art had evolved in a number of different directions, and the definition of site-specific art, an important aspect of arguments for keeping the sculpture at Federal Plaza, had been both challenged and redefined. Increasingly for those commissioning public art in the 1980s, the audience experiencing it in an everyday (as opposed to art) context became a primary focus. This had come to include community participation in the process, an issue not at play at the time of the Serra commission.

Public space, like public art, is perceived as a function of everyday life. People inhabit it whenever they leave their homes or workplaces, and its meaning may be variously interpreted according to the dominant critical theories of the day. Public space, on the most direct level, encompasses all existing visual and experiential parameters (architecture et al.). Public art is often expected to do what city planning and urban renewal have failed to do: to provide a civic image, to include someplace pleasant to sit, to upgrade the property values, and so on. Federal Plaza, with its own history related to a specific period of public land use and zoning, and the Serra commission coincided with a worsening of urban conditions and a heightened sense of danger in public spaces.

Public policy, the primary determinant of public art, is largely invisible. It is formed and analyzed in different institutions and disciplines, separate from the art world and the more general public. For public policy makers, public art, above all, must be politically expedient. During the Reagan era public support for art was consistently undermined. Although *Tilted Arc*'s fate was ultimately determined by the Serra-GSA contract, the controversy revealed significant deficiencies in GSA policies but prompted changes of an entirely different order. It underlined the need for a public-education component in the public art process and, most significantly, for a deaccessioning policy, but it led instead to the elimination of the NEA in the commissioning process, a further devaluation of art-world expertise.

Each section of this chapter suggests a different frame for discussion. Each frame has its own critical and problematic issues. None tells the complete story; they all pertain.

The Art (Historical) Context

Serra's sculpture entered the art world at a time of transition. For most of the twentieth century, modern art, expressed in various styles ranging from cubism to abstract expressionism, was championed as avant-garde, aesthetically and politically suited to an ever changing era.[1] Variously defined in terms of its self-referential concerns, its intention to shock, and its obsession with originality, it was often considered synonymous with abstraction.[2] In the postwar milieu of New York, abstract expressionism as practiced by artists such as Mark Rothko and Barnett Newman became a form of self-definition imbued with the mission of providing spiritual content for an era bereft of viable beliefs.[3] Underlying the premise of modern art was the fervent conviction that abstraction, freed from the ideological burden of content, would prove to be a viable visual language, capable of communicating with a broad audience. This was not, however, the case.

The position of modernism, and with it abstraction, was increasingly challenged with the advent of pop art in the early 1960s with its reintroduction of recognizable images and its focus on the commercial world of popular culture. This, as has been convincingly argued by Andreas Huyssen, marked "the great divide" between modernism and postmodernism.[4] Although it is debatable whether postmodernism began in 1961 or 1968, there is no doubt that it was, however defined, in full swing by 1980. Characterized by an ironic stance, much postmodern art was informed by an awareness and often an embrace of the mediated, commodity-based art world. By 1980, in response to the civil rights and feminist movements of earlier decades, much art focused on expressions of personal identity defined through gender, race, and ethnicity. Although the definition and even the existence of postmodernism has been seriously debated, there seemed to be no doubt that modernism, and with it abstraction, was and should be a thing of the past.[5]

In 1978 the Whitney Museum mounted an influential exhibition called *New Image Painting,* signaling that some kind of recognizable subject matter had reappeared, and the New Museum hosted *Bad Painting* challenging the emphasis on abstraction that had characterized modernist art and criticism. In 1979, the year Serra got his GSA commission, Joseph Beuys, the influential European artist who directly engaged the public in provocative performances and compelling tactile work, was the subject of a retrospective at the Guggenheim Museum. And Judy Chicago created what has since become a feminist icon, *The Dinner Party* (1974–79), a collaborative installation consisting of ceramic plates with vaginal imagery honoring important women from the past.

Two years later Hal Foster edited *The Anti-Aesthetic: Essays on Postmodern Culture,* a collection of writings from different perspectives, all but one sharing the belief "that the project of modernity is now deeply problematic." Coincidentally, New York's East Village became the focus of media attention as the latest incarnation of the avant-garde. Young artists like Keith Haring and Kenny Scharf used glaring psychedelic colors and cartoonlike shapes to launch an attack on what was now perceived as an elitist and insular Soho.[6]

In 1984 Brian Wallis edited an important anthology, *Art after Modernism: Rethinking Representation,* and Lucy Lippard published *Get the Message? A Decade of Art for Social Change.*[7] Wallis included essays that defined the "dismantling of modernism" as well as the "theorizing of postmodernism," ending with a section on "gender/difference/power." This collection provided a frame not only for the critique of modernism but for the kind of criticism that dominated the next decade. Lippard concentrated on overtly political art whose message was clear.

In 1985, the year of the *Tilted Arc* hearing, Suzi Gablik published *Has Modernism Failed?* and the New Museum featured an exhibition titled *Difference: On Representation and Sexuality.* Gablik, proceding from the premise that the modernist mission of constantly redefining art in new formal terms was exhausted, urged a look to the past to redefine the limits of art. Posing pluralism as modernism's opposite, she, like many others, looked to the potential of multiple approaches expressed from different vantage points to revitalize art. The New Museum's exhibition challenged modernism (and art in general) by revealing the ways in which it was hardly the universal expression it claimed to be. *Difference* focused "on the ways in which representation, purporting to be neutral, is informed by differences in gender."[8]

The following year, Rosalind Krauss's *The Originality of the Avant-Garde and Other Modernist Myths*[9] appeared, challenging this central defining tenet of modernism, and the Los Angeles County Museum mounted an exhibition called *The Spiritual in Art: Abstract Painting, 1890–1985,* insisting that abstraction has content. This premise directly challenged the prevaling interpretation of modernist art as being about nothing but itself. Throughout the 1980s and into the 1990s, abstraction was reframed, modernism was debunked, and identity issues came to dominate the discourse of the art world.

Within this constantly changing art milieu, Richard Serra continued to be celebrated in well-established venues. In 1979 and 1981, the years of the commission and installation of *Tilted Arc,* he was included in the Whitney Biennial. Serra's retrospective at the Museum of Modern Art in New York occurred a year after Diamond's hearing, and throughout the 1980s he had one-person exhibitions in prestigious museums and galleries in the United States (New York; Los Angeles; St. Louis; Dallas; Washington, D.C.), Europe (France, Germany, Italy, Netherlands, Sweden, Denmark, Greece, Switzerland), and Japan.

In the 1980s art world of shifting paradigms, any stylistic categorization became problematic, if not beside the point. Serra, sometimes classified as a minimalist and sometimes a postminimalist,[10] was in some essential ways a modernist.

Contextualizing Serra's Sculpture

Fashionable or not, Serra, in both his art and his writings, defined his work exclusively in formal terms, and critics followed his lead. In museum installations and public works, he redefined existing space in ways that are specific and consistent. In his 1967–68 *Verb List,* Serra identified his sculptural ambitions according to a variety of processes (starting with "to roll, to crease, to fold" and ending with "to continue"), enacted upon by a series of forces (beginning with "of tension, of gravity, of entropy").[11]

Over the course of nearly three decades, Serra developed and refined a powerful vocabulary of forms that often prompt instantaneous and profound visceral unease. Not surprisingly, this experience, in which a familiar space suddenly feels threatening, often evokes anger. Serra's sunken geometric volumes raise questions about the stability of the ground we stand on. With their limited openings, his vertical structures, a bleak echo of urban architecture, appear to both invite and bar entry. The disjuncture between their exterior forms and interior spaces implies a pervasive disparity between visual appearance and physical reality. The large-scale curves and arcs reconfigure spatial experience in their own terms, challenging the human vertical position defined by gravity and introducing an element of velocity, forcing the spectator around or through their volumes without visual clues to what awaits on the other side or at the other end. Perpetual tension and implicit instability characterize most of Serra's works, especially those in urban spaces.

In the tradition of modernism codified by the influential critic Clement Greenberg, art was defined as an activity of self-criticism, with each discipline establishing its own "unique area of competence" according to "the nature of its medium." The quest of modernist painting and sculpture became one of purification through self-definition, an ambition that has since come to be analyzed as having distinct ideological overtones.[12] Any reference to the outside world through realism, illusionism, or symbolism was considered bogus, an evasion of the mission of modernist art to define itself in its own terms. Serra has always insisted that his works be understood this way: "There are certain misreadings of abstract works that seem to preclude any comprehensive understanding. Imagistic and metaphorical associations lead by definition to the dismissal of abstraction by making it needlessly referential. It's a way of domesticizing it, of trying to integrate it into a vocabulary that has been canonized by tradition."[13] His belief in the integrity of abstraction and its innate ability to communicate are modernist at core.

Serra and Phenomenology

A more contemporary context for discussing Serra's work is provided by the French philosopher Maurice Merleau-Ponty, who insisted that the true nature of all phenomena (including art) may only be apprehended subjectively through experience. When his *Phenomenology of Perception,* published in 1945, became available in the United States some twenty years later, it was widely used by artists and critics as a means of explaining the content of abstract art. When art historian Rosalind Krauss introduced Serra's work to a French audience in 1983, she spoke of its relationship to Mearleau-Ponty's writings.[14] Armin Zweite also used this approach, and Serra himself advocates a phenomenological reading:

> The only way to understand this work is to experience the place physically, and you can't have an experience of space outside of the place that you're in. Any linguistic mapping or reconstruction by analogy, or any verbalization or interpretation or explanation . . . is a linguistic debasement, in a sense because it isn't even true in a parallel way.[15]

A phenomenological reading focuses on the physical experience of the art; it does not interpret the precise nature or significance of that experience in any other context.

Serra and Minimalism

Serra's work is often discussed in the context of minimalism, a movement that emerged in the mid-1960s and was largely defined by its practitioners, who were more involved with three-dimensional form than with painting. The sculptor Robert Morris spoke of "structures" that occupied a scale somewhere between monument and ornament and were related more to manufactured objects than to past art. Minimal sculptures were often composed of identical, manufactured modules whose configuration was determined by their exhibition space. Serra shared a minimalist interest in industrial materials and processes, a rejection of any symbolic content, and an insistence on the primary importance of site. But he differed in his ongoing production of unique sculptures that evoked an intense emotional and visceral response totally absent from minimalist work. Kenneth Baker saw Serra's contribution to minimalism as bringing its "human" content into focus.[16]

Serra and Abstract Expressionism

Serra may be best understood as a latter-day modernist in the tradition of abstract expressionism.[17] In 1995 Serra singled out Barnett Newman and Jackson Pollock as major influences in his development.[18] He was strongly aware of Newman's work during his formative years as an artist. Newman was on Serra's mind when he took a trip in 1969 with *Artforum* editor Phil Leider to see Michael Heizer's sculpture *Double Negative.*[19] Serra considered his own sculpture *Strike: To Roberta and Rudy* of 1969–71 (Figure 19) a homage to "the efficiency and directness with which Newman had used

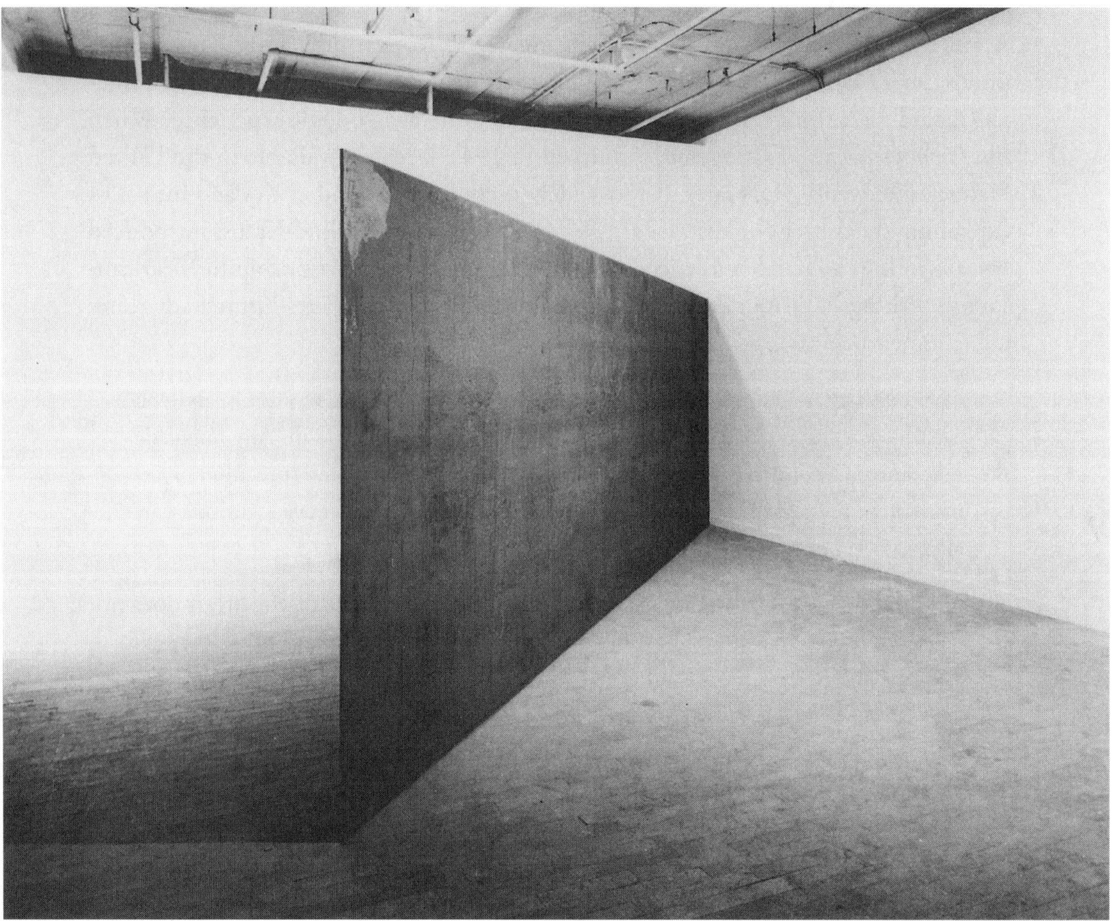

Figure 19. Richard Serra, *Strike: To Roberta and Rudy,* 1969–71, Varese, Italy, collection of Giuseppe Panza di Buomo. Courtesy of Richard Serra.

the sequence of surface-line-surface as a means of refusing to obey the commandment of the Cubist spatial concept any longer."[20]

But in spite of his insistence on nonmetaphorical readings of abstract art, Serra suggested a humanistic interpretation of Newman's paintings: "It could be that the vertical in relation to the horizontal is fundamental to how we perceive and understand time, place, and space; that he touched upon something that has to do with how we move and how we think when we move; it could be that the zip which sets up the coordinates of the field, top, bottom, right, left, corresponds to the vertical axis of our body."[21]

In recent years exclusively formalist readings of modernist art have been challenged. In 1978, the year before Serra's sculpture was commissioned, E. A. Carmean Jr. curated *American Art at Mid-Century: The Subjects of the Artist* at the National Gallery in Washington. He suggested that abstract expressionist paintings "can be said to have a dual identity: an almost objective existence, as the subject of the work was separate from them, and appeared much as it might to the viewer of their works, and a subjective one, as the subject arose out of, and was capable of expressing, personal concerns."[22] This gap between what the artist means and what the viewer sees remains a critical issue with much abstract art and was central to the controversy surrounding *Tilted Arc.*

A New Interpretation

> The personal is not expunged by using a neat technique; anonymity is not a consequence of a highly finished painting. The artist's conceptual order is just as personal as autographic tracks.
>
> **—Lawrence Alloway**

Sculpture, more than painting, has traditionally been read as an extension of the human body, even after it departed from figurative subjects.[23] Existing in the same space as the body, sculpture implies a way of being in the world. And Serra's work, either seemingly on the verge of collapse or apparently sinking unevenly into the ground, conveys a threatened existence. Kenneth Baker saw its verticality as "analogous both to one's upright posture and to the vulnerable immanence of the powers that sustain it" and the "threat of collapse as an aggressive reminder of mortality."[24]

In a 1976 interview Serra said, "[one] way of dealing with space is to project an analogue for a psychological condition which can be manifested symbolically or existentially, given the definition of your world as stable or unstable; the work could be defined by concepts of entropy or gravity, or on the other hand stasis or disequilibrium."[25] Serra's need to define a given space sculpturally in terms of implicit instability and explicit tension, if not immanent danger, may be understood in terms of his personal history of repressed Jewish identity.

Nearly fifty years after the fact, in a 1992 essay, Serra recounted this harrowing exchange with his Russian-Jewish mother: "When I was five years old [in 1944] I would ask my mother: What are we, who are we, where are we from? One day she answered me: If I tell you, you must promise never to tell anyone, never. We are Jewish. Jewish people are being burnt alive for being Jewish. I was raised in fear, in deceit, in embarrassment, in denial. I was told not to admit who I was, not to admit what I was."[26] In the same essay he observed, "It is difficult to defend yourself against retributions for an unknown. There is no preparation. To keep good faith with yourself, to understand yourself, requires truthfulness, sincerity, a moral effort. Is that possible if part of your identity cannot be revealed?" In 1995 he elaborated, "I was raised in denial. I went to Catholic, Presbyterian, and Episcopal churches. I didn't like any of them. It was reading Primo Levi [the Italian chemist who wrote so powerfully of his Holocaust experiences] that finally put me over the hill."[27] Serra began reading Levi while considering the 1993 commission for a sculpture for the U.S. Holocaust Memorial Museum in Washington, D.C. (Figure 22).[28]

Serra's revelation of his Jewish identity appeared in a small catalog for an exhibition in Pulheim, Germany, commemorating local synagogues destroyed during World War II. He named his sculpture *The Drowned and the Saved* (Figure 20), after a chap-

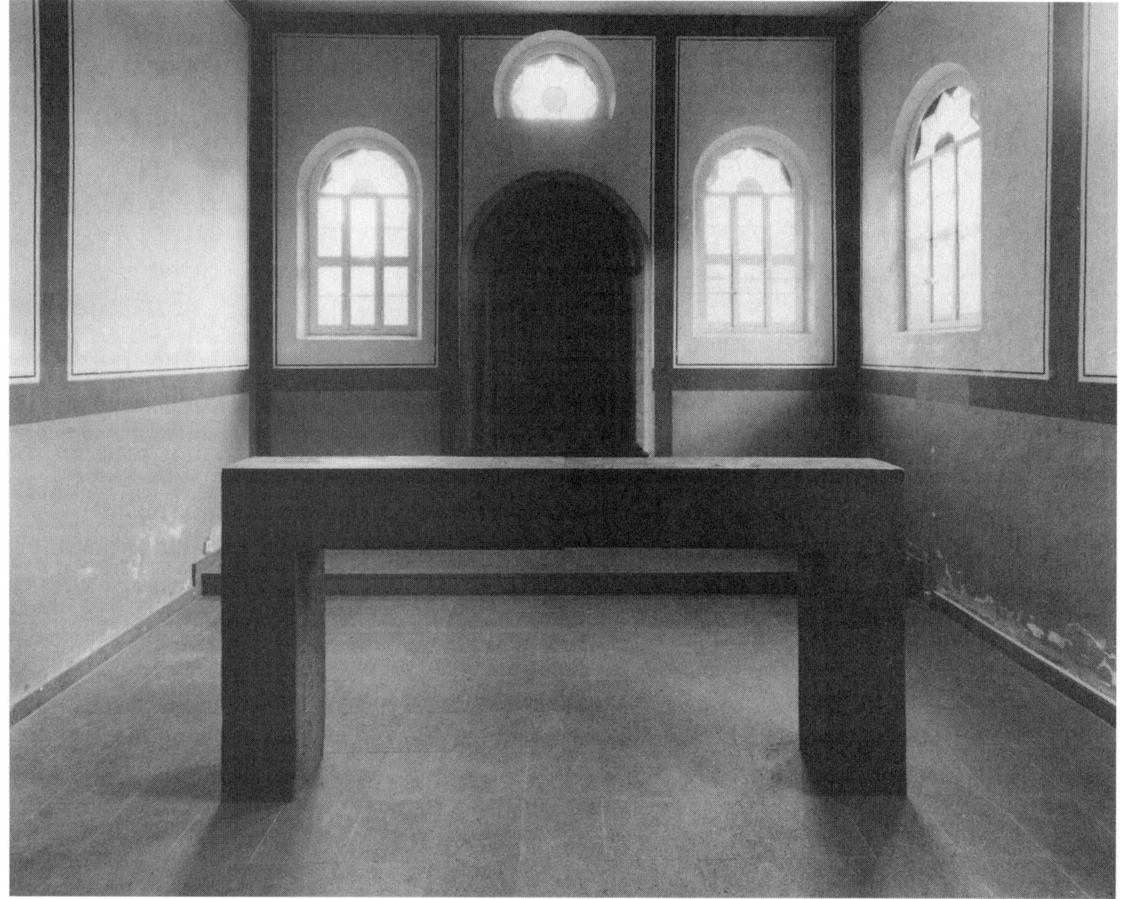

Figure 20. Richard Serra, *The Drowned and the Saved,* 1992, installed at Synagogue Stommeln, Pulheim, Germany. Courtesy of Richard Serra.

ter in Primo Levi's *Survival in Auschwitz* (originally published as *Se questo e un uomo* in 1958). A nearly identical piece, titled *Primo Levi,* exhibited in the 1995 Whitney Biennial, refers even more directly to the "survivor" author, who committed suicide in 1987 (Figure 21).

Both sculptures, differing only minutely in their dimensions, consist of two L-shaped pieces of forged steel, joined to create a form resembling a wide, squared off, upside-down U. Their size is ambiguous, too high and narrow to suggest a bench, too low to suggest an arch. They suggest a barrier of sorts, visible and tangible but apparently surmountable, held in tense equilibrium. The historical experience of Jewish identity, fraught with issues of both persecution and apparent assimilation, might be similarly described.

Issues of identity and its denial have been a major focus of the postmodern era. Jewish identity, encompassing more than religion or nationality, is difficult to define and has received less attention than have characterizations based on gender or race. This is distinctly relevant because art history in general and the modern and postmodern art worlds of New York in particular have been largely defined and populated by Jews. Ironically, even though Jews are often members of elite cultural and economic groups, historically, especially in the twentieth century, they are also paradigmatic victims.

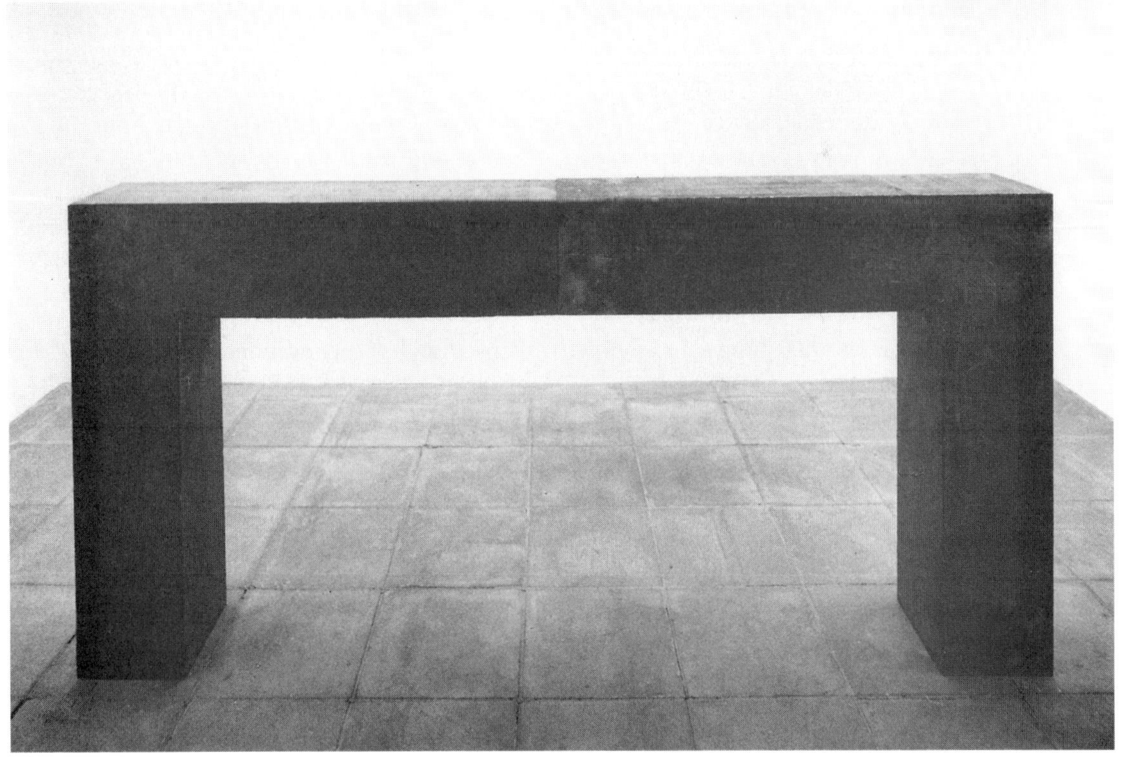

Figure 21. Richard Serra, *Primo Levi,* 1995, private collection, Atherton, California. Courtesy of Richard Serra.

As social psychologist Simon N. Herman observed, "There can be no proper understanding of contemporary Jewish identity without consideration of the profound and continuing impact on it of the memory of the Holocaust. It is a constant background factor—moving from time to time into the foreground—affecting the way Jews see themselves and the way they perceive their relationship to the non-Jewish world." Sociologists David Theo Goldberg and Michael Krausz compare the defining experience of the Holocaust for Jews with the experience of slavery for American blacks.[29]

Writer Helen Epstein has described her experience growing up in silence as a child of survivors, "possessed by a history" she had never lived: "For years it lay in an iron box buried so deep inside me that I was never sure just what it was. . . . I conceived *lead walls* around the dangerous parts. . . . The box became a vault, collecting in darkness, always collecting, pictures, words, my parents' glances, becoming *loaded with weight*."[30]

The experience and aftermath of the Holocaust affected all Jews, not just German Jews, not just concentration-camp survivors and their children. As art historian Ziva Amishai-Maisels concluded in her 1994 book on the Holocaust and art, "[B]oth as a specific event and as an archetype of human behavior, the Holocaust is still with us, an active part of our collective memory as an event, and a growing part of our collective subconscious as an archetype."[31]

Although Serra's mother, Gladys Feinberg, was born in Los Angeles, her mother was from Odessa, and Russia had a national tradition of persecution. By impressing the need for silence on her son, Serra's mother undoubtedly believed she was protecting him. Widespread silence was a common enough response to the Holocaust. But even without overt acknowledgment, its repercussions were passed on. As Yehudit Shendar observed, "By way of transfusion and by identification, the parents transferred their own sense of pain and loss to their children and bestowed upon them the legacy of becoming a living *yahrzeit* (memorial candle)."[32]

By equating the acknowledgement of his true identity with a life-threatening position, Serra's mother imposed a stigma that carried with it a condition of perpetual risk. Herman observed, "Membership in a socially stigmatized minority group generally has far-reaching psychological implications. . . . *Uncertainty of belonging implies instability of the social ground* [emphasis added]." Or as sociologist Alan Montefiore stated, "Not to know who one is in this sense of personal identification is to lack a certain kind of ballast or stability." An individual may try to distance himself from his identity, but he cannot ultimately escape it. Jean Paul Sartre, in his much debated essay, described the Jew who denies or tries to escape from his Jewish identity as achieving not the sought-after anonymity among Christians, but instead a *"perpetual tension."*[33]

One reaction to denying one's identity is to find a substitute one.[34] For Serra, an alternative identity may have been provided by making art and gaining recognition in the art world. He went to prestigious schools, has been represented by well-established dealers, and has exhibited in major museums in this country and internationally. By all accounts, he might be said to be assimilated. But assimilation may be a form of denial or repression, and repressed content tends to find an alternative mode of expression.

Stephen C. Feinstein, cocurator of *Witness and Legacy,* an exhibition of contemporary art about the Holocaust, observed that especially for second-generation Jews who did not have a direct experience of this event, often "art provided an appropriate entry for quests of memory absence, presence and identity."[35] Additionally, in abstraction Serra found a language that made it possible to discuss art only in its own terms, without reference to the outside world.

Thus Serra could explain the use of black in his drawings in terms of its density, which he considers "comparable to forging," and its lack of allusion to nature, since it refers to graphic or print processes.[36] More conventionally, however, black is interpreted as the color of death. Serra also has frequently worked in lead, a metal Primo Levi associated with death: [L]ead is actually the metal of death; because it brings on death, because its weight is a desire to fall, and to fall is a property of corpses, because its very color is dulled-dead. . . . lead is a material different from all other materials, a metal which you feel is tired, perhaps tired of transforming itself and that does not want to transform itself anymore; the ashes of who knows how many other elements full of life, which thousands upon thousands of years ago were burned in their own fire."[37]

The title of the sculpture Serra created for the Holocaust Museum in Washington in 1993, *Gravity* (Figure 22), refers to a force that he associates with death: "We are all restrained and condemned by the weight of gravity. . . . Everything we choose in life for its lightness soon reveals its unbearable weight. We face the fear of unbearable weight; the weight of tolerance, the weight of resolution, the weight of responsibility, the weight of destruction, the weight of suicide, the weight of history."[38]

Serra's Jewish identity, already fraught with issues of denial, is further complicated by his well-established professional and personal ties to Germany. In 1979, the year *Tilted Arc* was commissioned and the year his father died, he made a film with Clara Weyergraf, a German art historian who at the time worked at Galerie m in Bochum, Serra's gallery in Germany. *Steelmill/Stahlwerk* explored working conditions in a German steel mill.[39] In 1981, the year *Tilted Arc* was installed in Federal Plaza, Serra and Weyergraf were married.

Ten years later, in January 1991, in Duisburg, when he accepted the Wilhelm Lehmbruck Preis for excellence in sculpture, Serra noted that

> the development of my work and life is inseparable from my relation to this country. Not only is Clara from Germany, but I really started my sculptural activity here. My first lead props were built here, my first one-man show was in Cologne, *Circuit* [Figure 23] was built for Documenta, my first large-scale vertical structure, *Terminal* [Figure 9], was built for the railroad station in Bochum, my very first forged piece stands in front of the National Galerie in Berlin and was conceived and worked on at the Henrichschuette in Hattingen. It is a German museum, the Lenbachhaus in

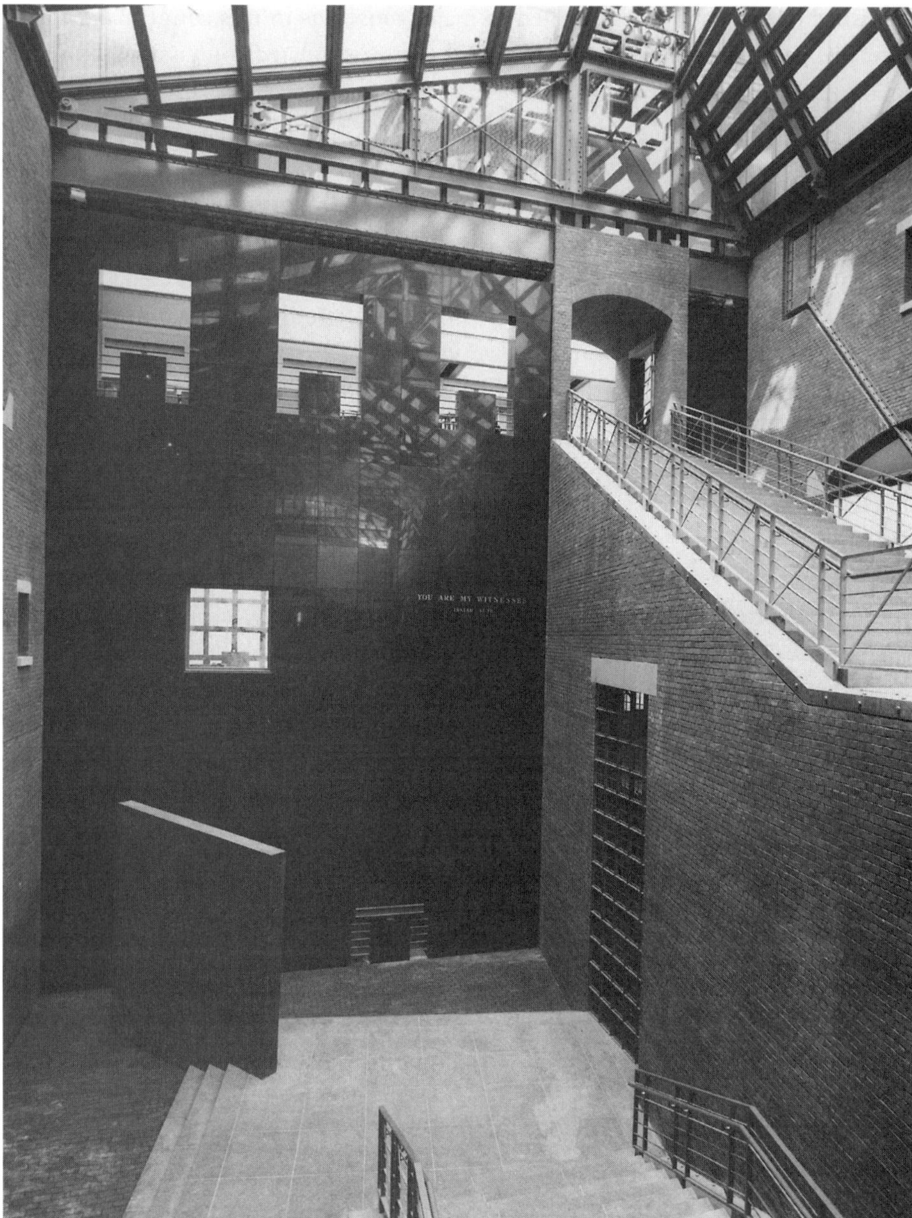

Figure 22. Richard Serra, *Gravity,* 1993, U.S. Holocaust Memorial Museum, Washington, D.C. Courtesy of Richard Serra.

> Munich, which will install seven permanent site-specific sculptures, originally conceived for an exhibition in seven rooms of the museum.

Comparing the treatment of artists in the United States, and specifically his own experience with *Titled Arc,* to conditions in Germany, he concluded, "I have been victimized by one and greatly supported by the other."[40]

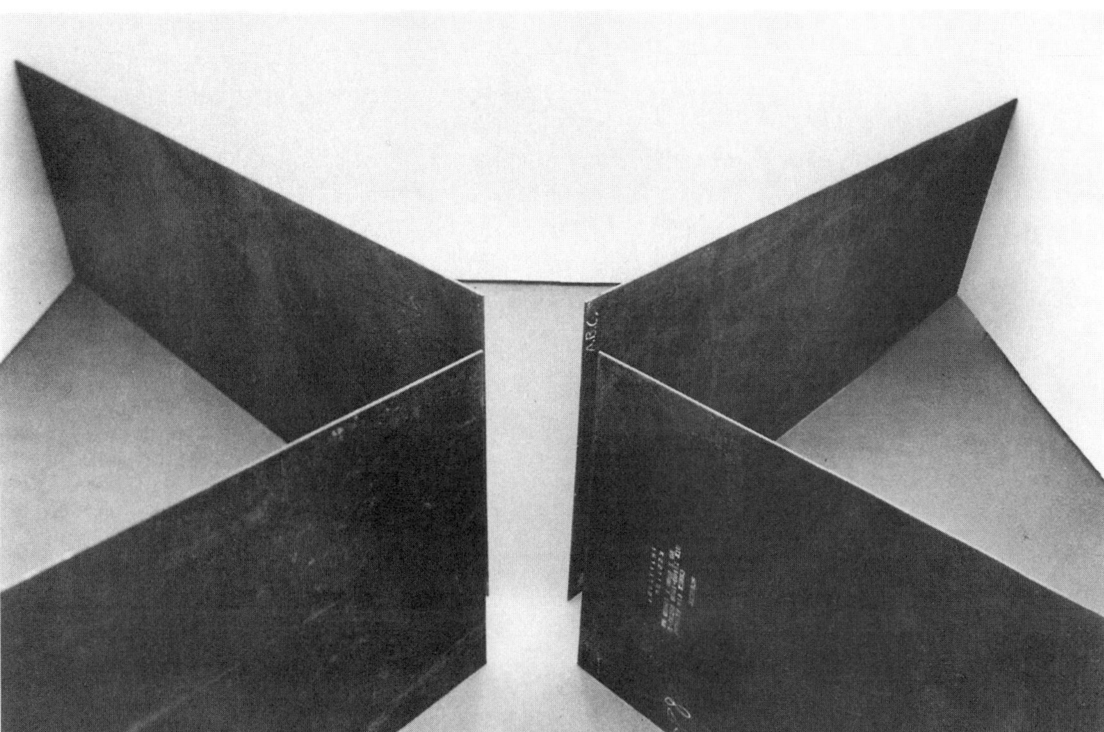

Figure 23. Richard Serra, *Circuit,* 1972, Galerie m, Bochum, Germany. Courtesy of Richard Serra.

In the context of the Holocaust, this statement is fraught with painful and impossible contradictions for a Jew. Even more problematic in terms of his Jewish identity is the permanent installation of *Berlin Junction* (originally displayed at an exhibition at Martin-Gropius-Bau) at Tiergartenstrasse No. 4, once an infamous part of Nazi history, now next to the Berlin Philharmonic (Figures 24, 25). Although there were plans to erect a memorial to mark Tiergartenstrasse No. 4 as the place where war crimes of euthanasia were planned, Serra did not object to the re-siting of his 1987 piece there.[41] Insisting, however, that his piece would not serve a memorial purpose, he suggested that a bronze plaque recounting the history of the site be installed in the ground a few feet from the sculpture. Since a music building was already at the site, he did not consider the addition of art a problem.[42]

Although issues of Serra's Jewish identity (determined in Judaism by matrilineal descent) and his relationship to Germany appear fraught with ambivalence, his memories of his Catholic father, Tony Serra, and his connection to his father's country of birth, Spain, are positive. His paternal grandfather was a woodcarver, and his father, a factory worker, was very supportive of his son's art interests. The Serra name in Barcelona is linked with a large artisan family, and this may have helped him obtain a subsequent commission (*La Palmera,* 1982–84, Figures 43, 44).[43]

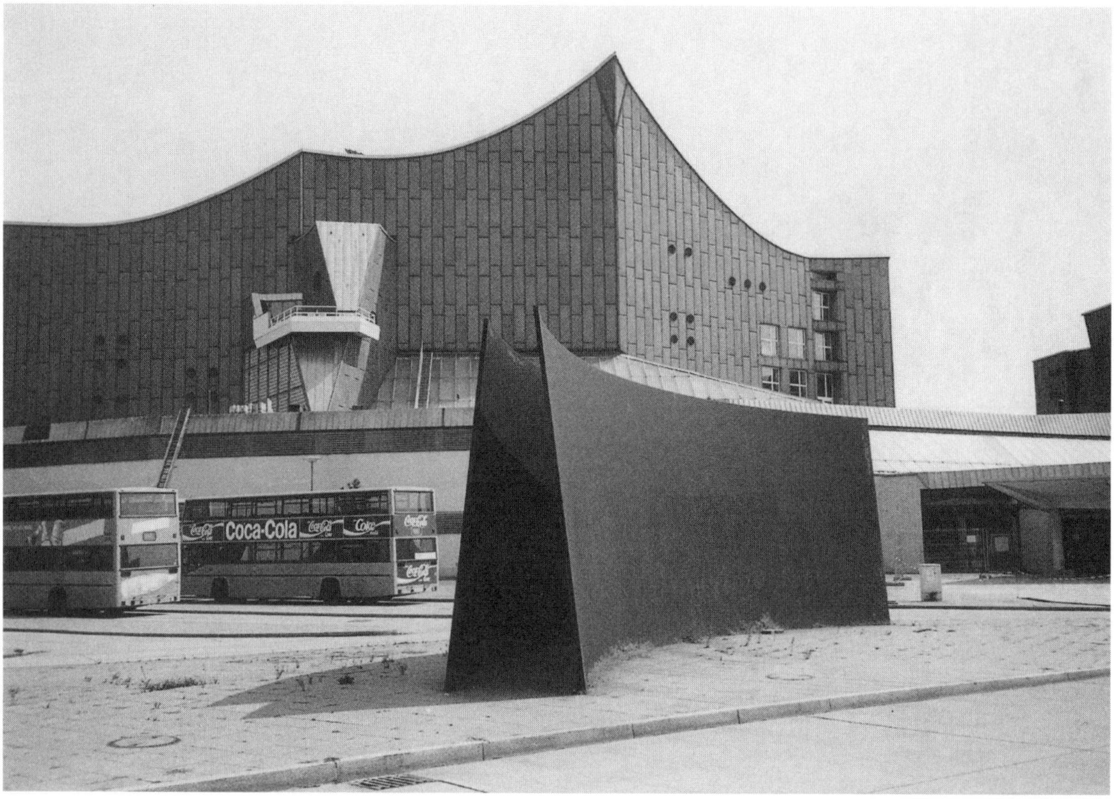

Figure 24. Richard Serra, *Berlin Junction,* 1987, Berlin Philharmonic, Berlin, Germany. Photograph by Burt Roberts.

Serra has also recalled an important early childhood experience: When he was four, his father took him to a ship launching near the Golden Gate Bridge in San Francisco:

> It was a moment of tremendous anxiety as the oiler en route rattled, swayed, tipped, and bounced into the sea, half submerged, to then raise and lift itself and find its balance. Not only had the tanker collected itself, but the witnessing crowd collected as the ship went through a transformation from an enormous obdurate weight to a buoyant structure, free, afloat, and adrift. My awe and wonder of that moment remained. All the raw material that I needed is contained in the reserve of this memory which has become a recurring dream.[44]

Thus Serra attributed much of his subsequent inspiration as an artist to this event that occurred at age four (a year before his mother warned him of the danger of acknowledging his Jewish identity). These associations present a very positive frame for defining Serra's paternal roots, a frame linked to art and prominence, not to victimization and death.

However, it is the latter that seems embodied in much of his work. It was primarily Serra's mother, herself a painter, who directly encouraged his art interests. In

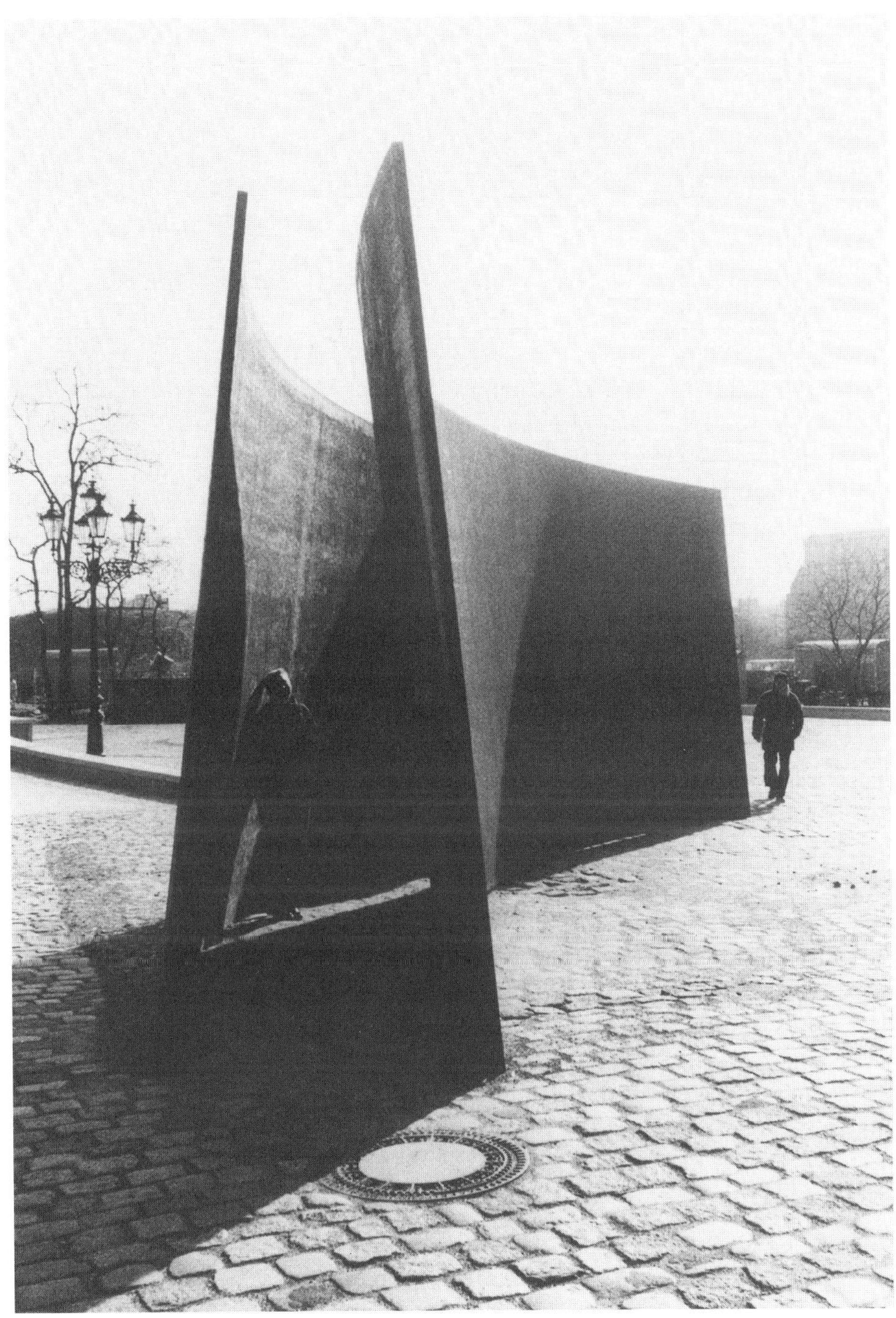

Figure 25. Richard Serra, *Berlin Junction*, 1987, Berlin Philharmonic, Berlin, Germany. Photograph by Alexander von Berswordt-Wallrabe; courtesy of Richard Serra.

1977, the year she committed suicide, Serra created three new forms, all relating to death—two specifically in their title. A forged-steel sculpture titled *Tot* ("dead" in German) is the first single-slab sculpture in Serra's oeuvre (Figure 26). Its form suggests an oversized gravestone, partially sunk into the ground. His first vertical piece, of four leaning plates of Cor-Ten steel, *Terminal* (Figures 9, 27), is sited in Bochum, Germany, next to the train station, but its title has another obvious meaning as well. His first sunken volumetric sculpture, *Berlin Block for Charlie Chaplin,* a seventy-ton forged cube, is next to the Nationalgalerie in Berlin (Figure 28). The reference to burial is palpable.

Applied specifically to *Tilted Arc,* this biographical context helps explain both the assertiveness of the piece and, perhaps, something of its significance to him. The 1979 commission of a permanent piece by the U.S. government, located next to the building where new citizens take their oath of allegiance, was an affirmation of Serra's identity as an officially recognized artist of this country. His father, who died the year *Tilted Arc* was commissioned, was born on the boat from Majorca and never became a U.S. citizen. The sculpture's eventual removal only reaffirmed the "unstable social ground" to which so much of Serra's work alludes.

Serra may (unconsciously) have distilled the complex postwar experience of Jewish identity into his work in such a way that its essence (not its particularity) is conveyed to viewers who, whether they want to or not, must share it. The experience of personal threat in a victim-defined age is not, of course, restricted to Jews. As Amishai-Maisels has observed, the Holocaust was all "too fitting an archetype for all that is dangerous in modern society."[45] Ongoing discrimination, random killings, and fears of terrorism were at that time a part of daily life in New York and elsewhere. And a sense of helplessness or victimization pertains as well to the distrust and perceived threat of all governmental authority that Serra, with his 1960s heritage, espouses.[46]

In his work Serra tried to incorporate both the pervasive threat to individual freedom (personal identity) and the powerful struggle of the individual to withstand it. The heroic and solitary struggle, however, is isolated, concentrated, and magnified in the art experience. But for many, as we have seen, Serra's sculpture was interpreted only in terms of a visibly imposed threat, a reflection of imposed limitations, not as an invitation to struggle against them.

Certainly *Tilted Arc* was not an easy sculpture to read (Figures 29–31). Perhaps, like Serra's conflicted Jewish identity at the time, the sculpture was not completely resolved.[47] In any event, its implicit threat and perpetual tension, typical of much of Serra's work, cannot be explained through formal terms alone. The complex issue of Serra's Jewish identity provides what has thus far been a missing component in considering both the force of his art and its power to provoke such an impassioned public response.

Figure 26. Richard Serra, *Tot,* 1977, Staatsgalerie Stuttgart, Germany. Courtesy of Richard Serra.

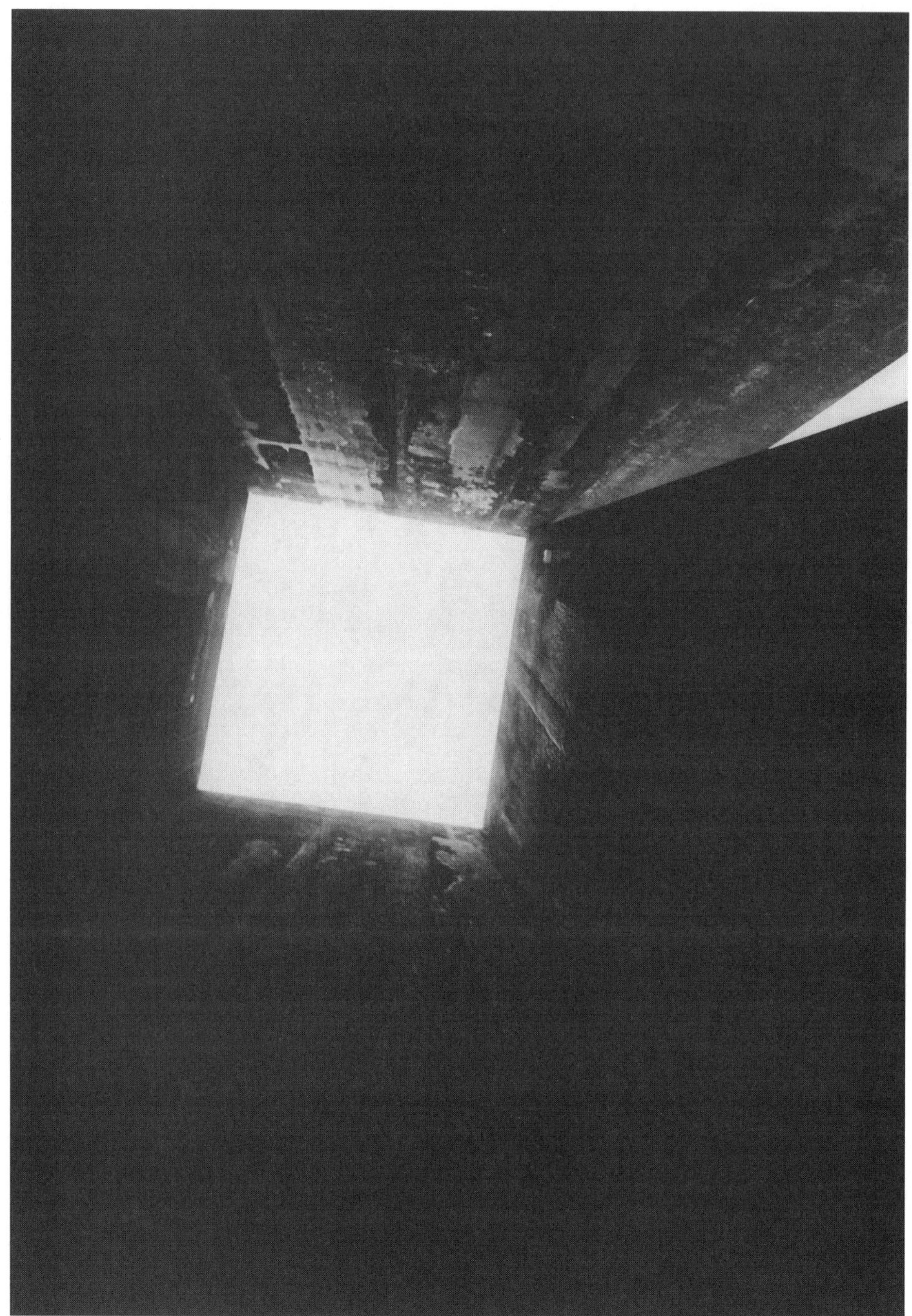

Figure 27. Richard Serra, *Terminal,* 1977, interior, Bochum, Germany. Photograph by Burt Roberts.

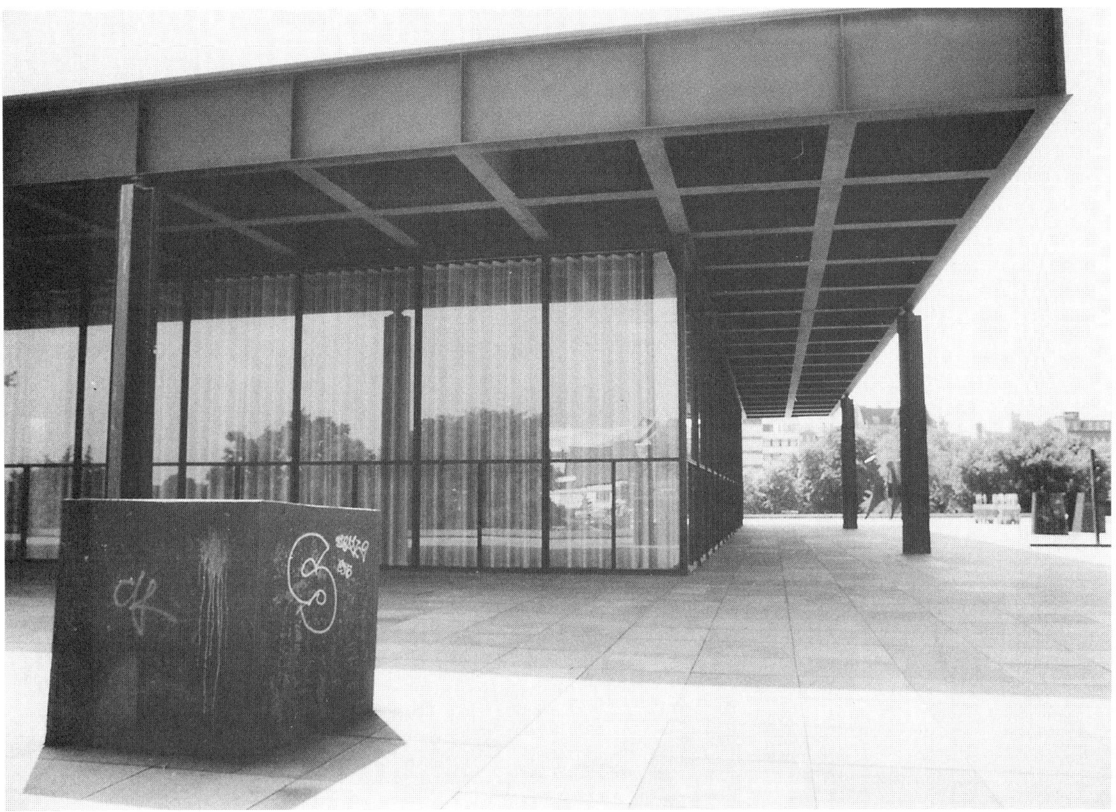

Figure 28. Richard Serra, *Berlin Block for Charlie Chaplin,* 1977, Nationalgalerie, Berlin, Germany. Photograph by Burt Roberts.

The Public Art Context

> *Tilted Arc* made vivid the truth that something may succeed as a work of art but fail as a work of "public" art.
>
> **—Arthur Danto**

The art world and the public art world are not the same, although artists who make public art are often affiliated with a gallery and exhibit in museums. (It is difficult to make a living on public art alone.) The art world is supported by an interconnected system that links private collectors, galleries, museums, and a slew of art writers and publications. Public art exists in a different economic sphere, sponsored by patrons who do not take out ads in art magazines and newspapers. Exhibitions in museums and galleries get reviewed; public art, for the most part, does not unless it becomes the focus of controversy.[48] And it is much more vulnerable. Left unguarded on the street, it has a different audience, a different history, and a different context.

Although (or perhaps because) New York, with its many museums and galleries, has a strong art identity, it is not a public art town like, say, Chicago or Seattle. The reception of public art in New York has been no more enthusiastic than elsewhere,

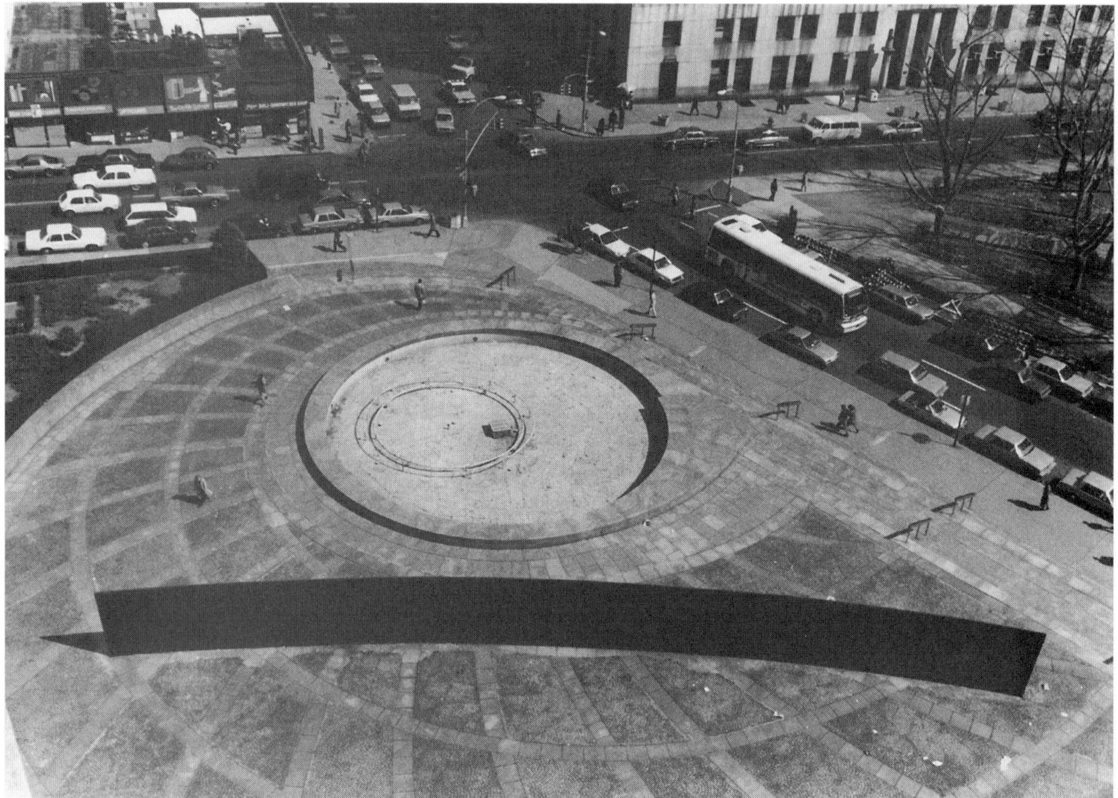

Figure 29. Richard Serra, *Tilted Arc,* 1981, New York City. Photograph by Michael Abramson; courtesy of Richard Serra.

another indication that public art is outside the critical art-world loop. In 1964, at a time when the art of Alexander Calder and Henry Moore was a staple of modern art in museums worldwide, it was difficult to get city Art Commission approval for the permanent siting of privately financed sculptures by them destined for Lincoln Center.[49]

Although the first municipal percent-for-art law was passed by Philadelphia in 1953, New York did not enact one until 1982, the year after *Tilted Arc* was installed. (Percent-for-art laws mandated that a small percentage of construction costs of public buildings be used for art, usually 0.5 to 1 percent.) As a result, the national public art revival that began in the late 1960s seemed for a time to bypass New York. Gordon Bunshaft of Skidmore, Owings, and Merrill included sculpture by Noguchi in his projects at Chase Manhattan Bank Plaza (1961–64) and Marine Midland Bank Plaza (1968) in lower Manhattan (Figures 32, 33). Real estate developer Mel Kaufman sponsored a few successful projects, such as the one at 127 John Street (1969), where an undistinguished office building by Emery Roth and Sons was enlivened by a huge neon display clock designed by Corchia-de Harak Associates and a street-level cluster of colorful public seating, red pipe, and canvas canopies surrounding a pool.

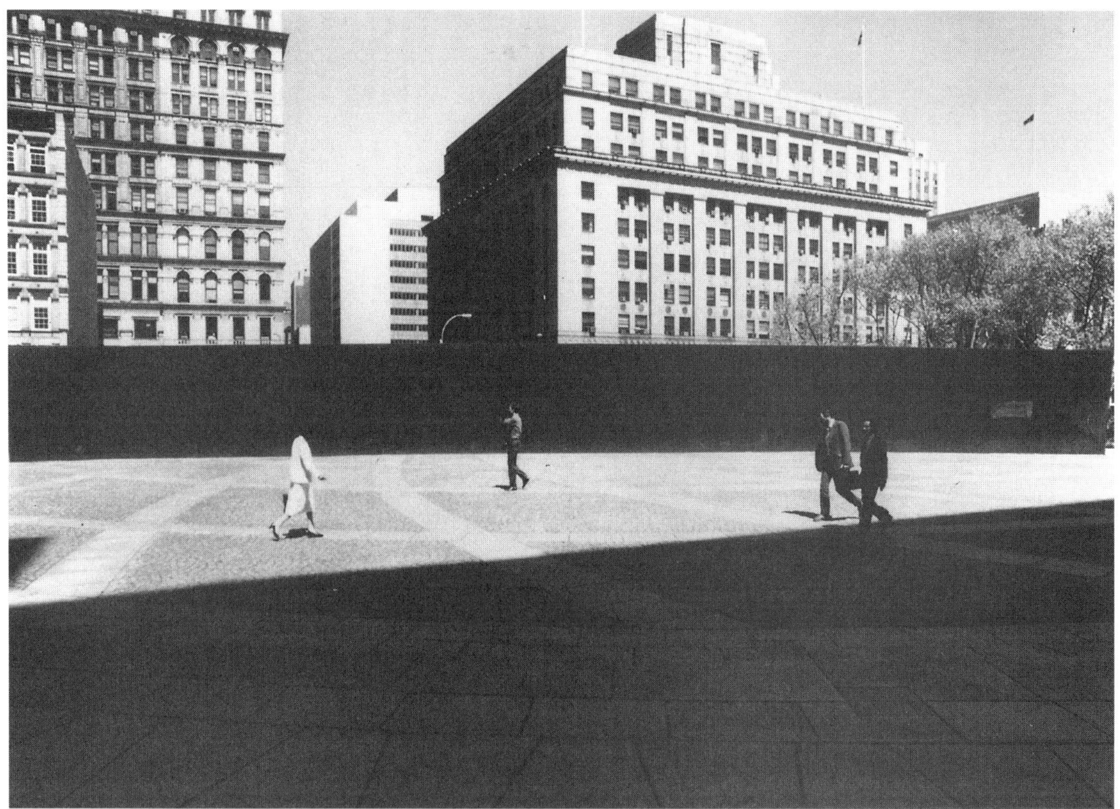

Figure 30. Richard Serra, *Tilted Arc,* 1981, New York City. Photograph by Robert McElroy; courtesy of Richard Serra.

Although similarly motivated, as an enhancement to the building that would make it a more desirable rental property, these (financially) unnecessary additions were considered public amenities: good urban design perhaps, but not public art.

The start of the contemporary public art revival of the late 1960s was signaled by the placement of large-scale sculptures by already famous artists in a variety of urban spaces. Precedent-setting sculptures like the Chicago Picasso (1967) and the Grand Rapids Calder (*La Grande Vitesse,* 1969), which eventually functioned as civic logos, led to the proliferation of works by other artists in spaces not specifically designed for them but deemed appropriate for that use by their architects.[50] Usually installed well after the building was complete, these sometimes seemingly interchangeable sculptures were referred to disparagingly as "plop" art.

Site-Specific Public Art

To make public art more meaningful, artists began to consider the nature, function, and meaning of its site. The concept of site specificity was at the core of Serra's aesthetic position and was integral to his legal arguments. He maintained that since he had conceived *Tilted Arc* for Federal Plaza and only for that site, the site was part of its

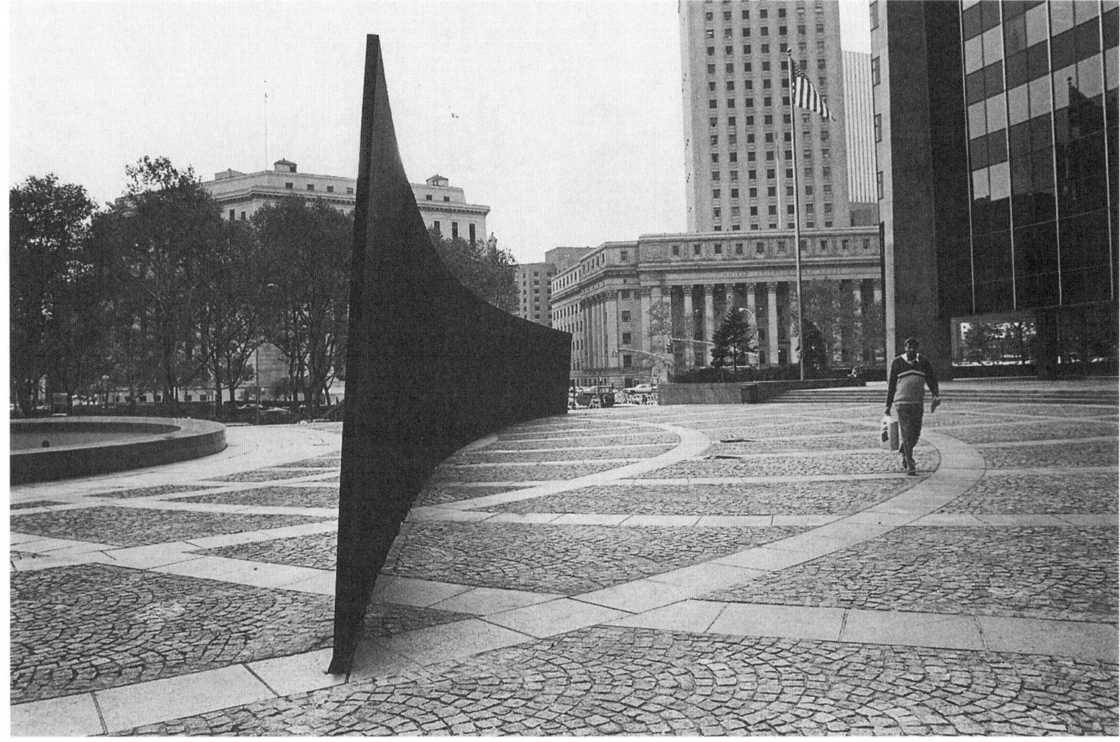

Figure 31. Richard Serra, *Tilted Arc,* 1981, New York City. Photograph by David Aschkenas; courtesy of Richard Serra.

content and therefore to move the work was to destroy it. "Site specificity," commonly used today to describe both museum installations and public art, has become something of a catchall phrase.[51] It is, however, hardly a new concept.

Site-specific art is an updated version of architectural art that derived its form and content from the building it enhanced. The caryatids supporting a Greek temple or the ornamented facades and columns in a Gothic cathedral are integral to their sites, as are Michelangelo's frescoes in the Sistine Chapel. To the extent that they depend on their architectural frame, they could be considered subservient to it, that is, merely decoration. Indeed, the development of contemporary public sculpture was partially prompted by the need for an ornament after the fact for modern architecture.[52]

Site specificity in contemporary art was a response to different circumstances. During the 1960s, coincident with the development of minimal art, artists and critics began to question art's status as precious object or commodity. Gallery art was insufficiently distinct, it was felt, from other luxury items—highly priced and prized elitist symbols of wealth. Questioning both the heroic status of the artist and the iconic nature of the modern art object, minimal sculptors like Carl Andre, Donald Judd, and Robert Morris began in the mid-1960s to focus on the environment in which art was seen, to involve viewers in a more active relationship with art by engaging gallery space.[53] Arguably, as Anna Chave has suggested, contemporary practices in dance per-

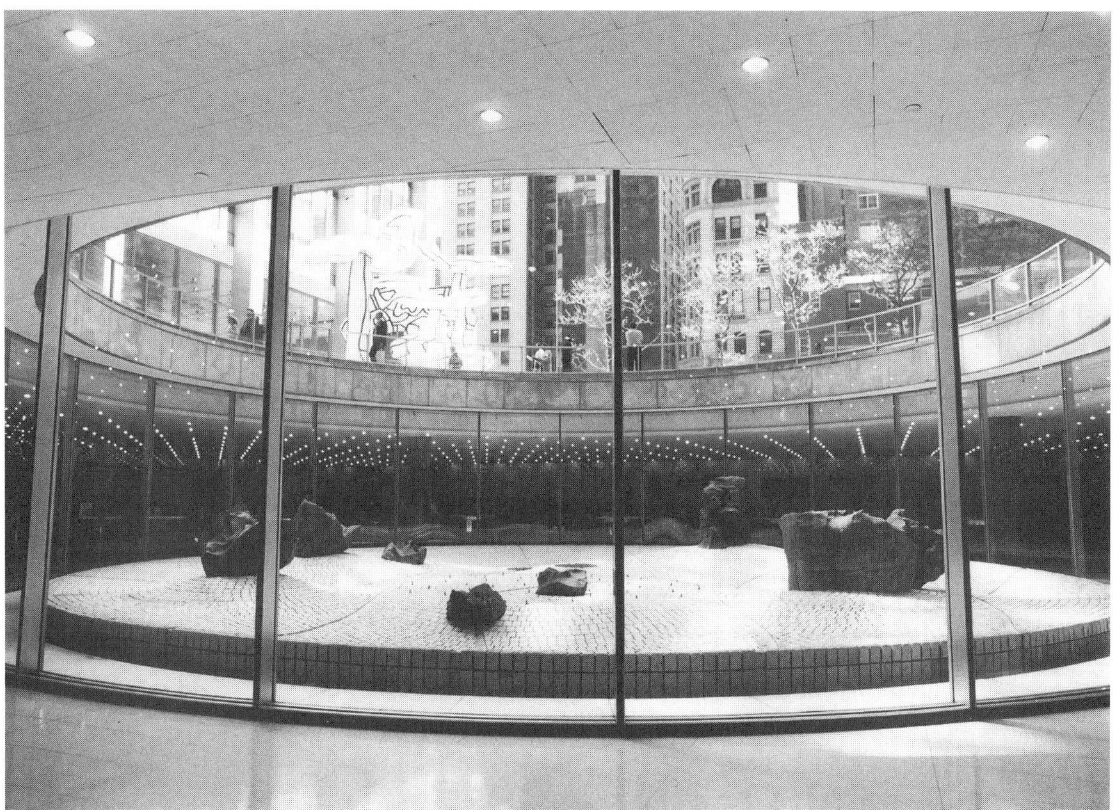

Figure 32. Isamu Noguchi, Garden for Chase Manhattan Bank Plaza, 1961–64, New York City. Photograph by Burt Roberts.

formance by women artists such as Simone Forti and Yvonne Rainer were both influential and more successful in this enterprise.[54]

A number of exhibitions in 1967 reflected the expanded definition of sculpture and the new concern with site and by implication site specificity. *American Sculpture of the Sixties,* curated by Maurice Tuchman at the Los Angeles County Museum, contained 25 (out of 166) works created specifically for their exhibition spaces. *Scale as Content,* curated by Eleanor Green at the Corcoran Gallery of Art in Washington, D.C., included interior works by Tony Smith and Ronald Bladen whose form and dimensions were determined by the gallery configuration. In December 1968 Robert Morris organized an exhibition called *Nine at Castelli* at a warehouse on the Upper West Side of Manhattan usually used for gallery storage.[55] Serra's contribution, *Splashing* (1968), involved tossing molten lead into the juncture where the floor meets the wall. Created in the gallery, the piece took its shape and form specifically from its structural parameters.

Interest in nonart outdoor sites developed at the same time. *Sculpture in Environment,* an exhibition of 1967 sponsored by the New York City Department of Cultural Affairs under the aegis of Doris Freedman, placed the works of twenty-four

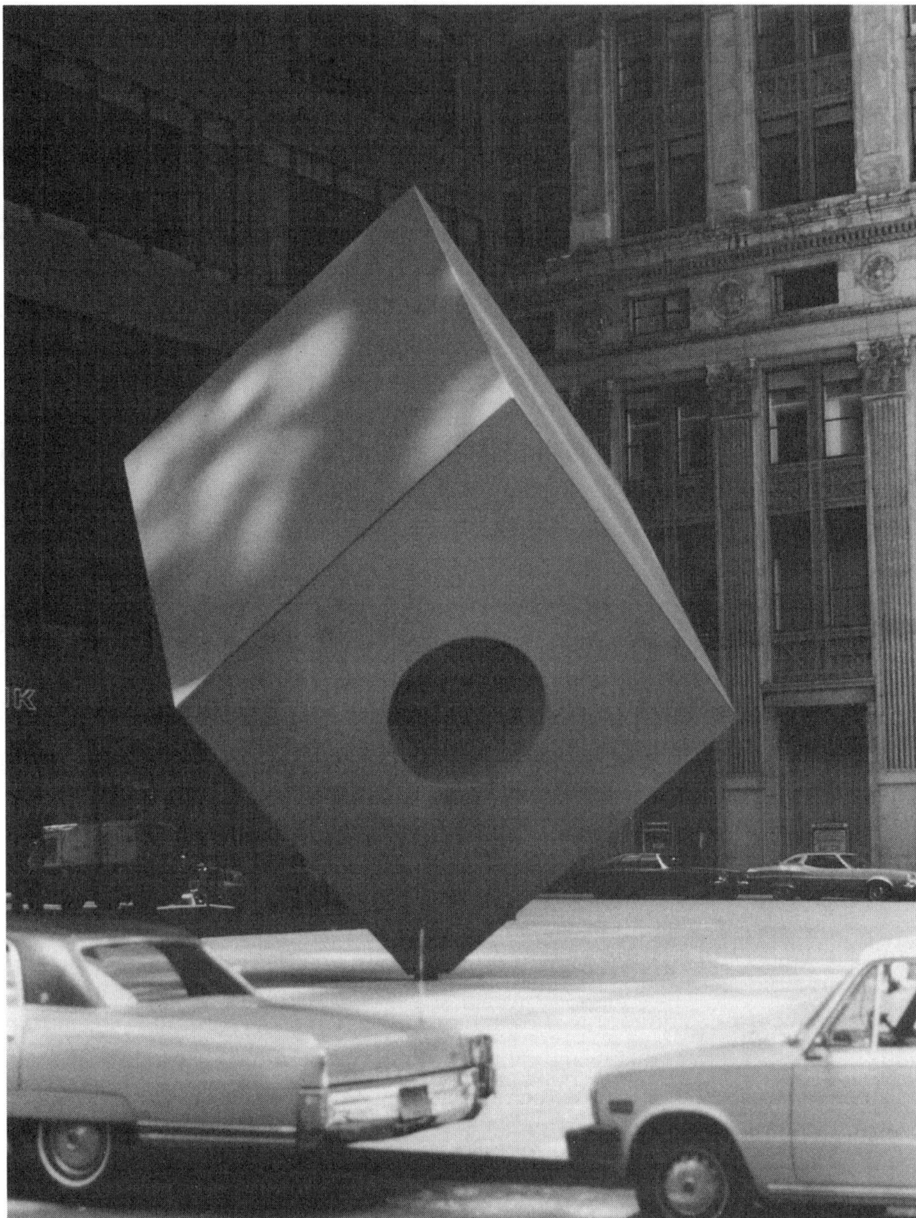

Figure 33. Isamu Noguchi, *Red Cube,* 1968, Marine Midland Bank Plaza, New York City. Photograph by Harriet F. Senie.

artists in a variety of outdoor city spaces. All the artists were involved with the choice of sites, and more than half created works specifically for those sites.[56]

By the end of the decade, environmental artists like Walter de Maria, Michael Heizer, and Robert Smithson, who shared with minimal artists the desire to circumvent the precious-object nature of gallery art, began to create works in remote landscape sites, sponsored by galleries, notably Virginia Dwan, and important private patrons.[57] Robert Smithson's *Spiral Jetty* (1970) is both part of and inseparable from its site, the Great Salt Lake in Utah. Earthworks were explicitly site specific in terms of form and implicitly in terms of content. Although many of the artists insisted their work was about art and not nature, the fact that it was sited in the landscape and not the gallery had philosophical as well as formal implications.

Serra's concept of site specificity was directly influenced by both environmental and minimal art. In 1969 he went to see Michael Heizer's *Double Negative* (1969–70), near Overton, Nevada. In 1970 he visited Robert Smithson and Nancy Holt during the construction of *Spiral Jetty* and helped with its layout. After Smithson's death in 1973, he worked with his widow, artist Nancy Holt, and his art dealer, Tony Shafrazi, to complete *Amarillo Ramp* (1973) in Texas.[58] Like the minimalists, Serra was "interested in a behavioral space in which the viewer interacts with the sculpture in its context."[59] After studying Federal Plaza and determining that it "was essentially used only as a place of transit, through which people passed from street to building," he conceived a sculpture "for the moving observer" (Figure 34):

> *Tilted Arc* was constructed so as to engage the public in a dialogue that would enhance, both perceptually and conceptually, its relation to the entire plaza. The sculpture involved the viewer rationally and emotionally. . . . The work, through its

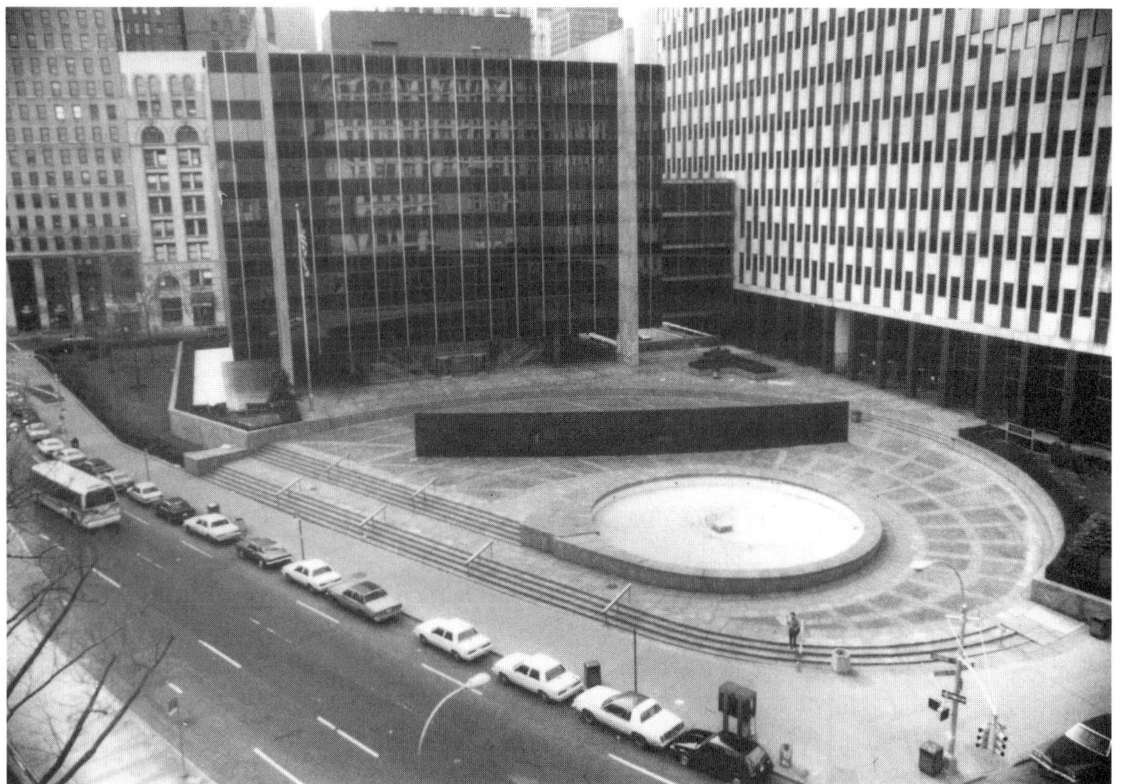

Figure 34. Richard Serra, *Tilted Arc,* 1981, New York City. Photograph by Burt Roberts; courtesy of Richard Serra.

> location, height, length, horizontality and lean, grounds the viewer into the physical condition of the place. The viewer becomes aware of himself and of his movement through the plaza. As he moves, the sculpture changes. Contraction and expansion of the sculpture result from the viewer's movement. Step by step the perception not only of the sculpture but of the environment changes.[60]

As the controversy evolved, so did Serra's explanation of his site specificity. When he addressed the NEA-appointed Kheel panel of 1987, he spoke more of environmental factors than of behavioral space:

> Site-specific works deal with the environmental components of given places. The scale, size and location of site-specific works are determined by the topography of the site, whether it be urban, landscape or architectural enclosure. The works become part of the site, and restructure both conceptually and perceptually the organization of the site. . . . The specificity of site-oriented works means that they are conceived for, dependent upon and inseparable from their location. Scale, size and placement of sculptural elements result from an analysis of the particular environmental components of a given context.

At Federal Plaza, Serra intended to "(1) structure the plaza and create directions, accentuating existing pedestrian traffic patterns; (2) link the two sides of the federal enclave in that the sculpture should act as a bridge, connecting and visually gathering the different federal architectures; (3) create a sculptural space within the plaza which could be experienced by those crossing the plaza on their way into and out of buildings."[61]

At the Kheel hearing, Serra also acknowledged the significance of the site's "social and political characteristics":

> Site-specific works invariably manifest a value judgment about the larger social and political context of which they are a part. Based on the interdependence of work and site, site-specific works reveal the content of their site critically. A new behavioral and perceptual orientation to a site demands a new critical adjustment to one's experience of the place. Site-specific works primarily engender a dialogue with their context.

In 1991, after the sculpture had been removed from Federal Plaza, Serra was more specific:

> Works which are built within the contextual frame of governmental, corporate, educational, and religious institutions run the risk of being read as tokens of those institutions. One way of avoiding ideological co-optation is to choose a leftover site that cannot be the object of ideological misinterpretation. However, there is no neutral site. Every context has its frame and its ideological overtones. It is a matter of degree. But there are sites where it is obvious that an art work is being subordinated to/accommodated to/adapted to/useful to. . . . In such cases it is necessary to work in opposition to the constraints of the context, so that the work cannot be read as an

> affirmation of questionable ideologies and political power. I am not interested in art as affirmation or complicity.[62]

Throughout the controversy, Serra's argument for the site specificity of *Tilted Arc* was undermined by temporary installations of *St. John's Rotary Arc* at the exit of the Holland Tunnel in Manhattan and *Clara-Clara* in Paris. *Clara-Clara* was originally intended for a site next to the Beaubourg that proved structurally impossible. It was then situated in the Jardin de Tuileries at the entrance to the park, was subsequently placed in a residential neighborhood near the Square de Choisy but later removed for political reasons, and at the time of this writing was awaiting a site to be approved by Serra. Although Serra argued that the New York sculpture was built as temporary and the Paris commission was not conceived as site specific, at a public lecture in 1993 he stated, "If you move one work to another site, it's not the work you would have built for that site, nor the best solution, but there are reasons for it, mainly economic. You build the work you want to initially; every decision after that is a lesser decision."[63]

Beyond Serra's own shifting position, the concept of site specificity has been challenged within the art world. Rosalyn Deutsche has argued that defining site-specific art as permanent invalidates its underlying principle of being responsive to "history, politics, everyday life" and not part of "an eternal sphere superior to the rest of the social world." Tom Crow defined the strength of site-specific works as lying in temporality, as opposed to the permanence advocated by Serra and others. James Meyer posited a functional as opposed to a literal definition of site specificity, characterized by a "mobile notion of site and a nomadic subjectivity [of the artist]" with roots in Happenings, among other art practices. Miwon Kwon analyses three different paradigms: "phenomenological, social/institutional, and discursive." The first was Serra's approach; the second expressed an institutional critique of the site's cultural framework (Mierle Ukeles or Hans Haacke); and the third was "ungrounded, fluid, virtual." Thus the artist was reconceptualized from being "a maker of aesthetic objects" to a "facilitator, educator, coordinator, and bureaucrat." In each paradigm, however, the artist remained central, the giver or progenitor of meaning and experience. Linking these contemporaneous practices, Kwon saw site-specific art used as a corrective to the uniformity of spaces produced by an increasingly global economy. By providing unique civic or local identity, such art arguably acts as a validation of these practices. And Dario Gamboni provides an interesting historically based argument demonstrating that moving a site-specific work does not destroy it.[64]

Other critiques of Serra's site specificity centered on pragmatic rather than philosophical issues. Albert Elsen challenged the implicit moral claim to site specificity in public places if no landmark designation guarantees that a site's buildings will be permanent.[65] Structures that once defined a site may be razed or radically altered; new buildings in a different style may be added to the visual parameters. The urbanscape is subject to seasonal change as well as long-term transformation. A sculpture sited next to a sapling may be totally hidden by the mature tree. And on and on . . . At what point does a sculpture cease to be site specific? Does it then have to be removed?

Another critical issue is that however site specificity is defined, its intended purpose of making contemporary public art more meaningful and/or political may not be clearly communicated. For art critic Douglas Crimp, *Tilted Arc,* "situated at the very center of the mechanisms of state power," conveyed "the truth of our social condition" as a "society constructed upon the principle of egotism, the needs of each individual coming into conflict with those of all other individuals." The function of the state was thus revealed as the "defense of private property—the defense . . . of the conflict between individuals," and Serra's achievement became "the redefinition of the site of the work of art as the site of political struggle."[66] Far from universally accepted by art critics, this interpretation certainly appeared to be beyond the conscious grasp of many or most in the sculpture's immediate audience.[67]

Site specificity, Serra's chief argument for keeping *Tilted Arc* at Federal Plaza, has thus been challenged philosophically and pragmatically, according to shifting art paradigms in art and criticism. Certainly today it seems inherently flawed. Even at the time, it was only one accepted and acceptable premise for making public art.

Alternative Public Art Solutions

Almost from the moment *Tilted Arc* appeared, members of the art world as well as the general public suggested alternative public art solutions for Federal Plaza. In November 1985, some seven months after Diamond's hearing, the Storefront for Art and Architecture (a small gallery in lower Manhattan with a reputation for innovative exhibitions) hosted *After Tilted Arc: The Aesthetic Quest and Public Life.* The challenge was "to bridge the gap between the aesthetic elite and the public." Curators Tom Finkelpearl, Glenn Weiss, and Kyong Park framed the options: "(1) Explain, narrate, or invent the public mythology that *Tilted Arc* can provide for the average *and* sophisticated viewer. (2) Redesign the plaza or *Tilted Arc* to provide a synthesis of the needs of the public and the *Arc.* (3) Propose a new public artwork for the plaza."[68] Although the exhibition was based on the assumption that something was wrong with Serra's sculpture and that it should (and could) be modified, the press release, like many official statements issued by the GSA, denied its true intention:

> This exhibition is not intended to be critical of *Tilted Arc* or Richard Serra. Rather, it is an attempt to redirect the argument surrounding the piece. While the highly emotional debate has centered on whether the Arc is legally and morally assured of a future in the Federal Plaza, few have sought to clarify the issues behind the controversy: What is public art? What work can be accepted and understood by the "average viewer"? What is the artist's responsibility when proposing a work for a public place?[69]

Finkelpearl (then director of the nearby experimental exhibition space, The Clocktower) had been director of public relations at the Hudson River Museum in Yonkers, New York, during a Serra exhibition in 1981. After struggling to explain

Serra's work to a very resistant public, Finkelpearl "began to think seriously about artistic communication and the relationship between a work of art and its audience." Weiss saw *Tilted Arc* as part of an avant-garde mythology that favored a "formal, phenomenological art" and criticized it for "accentuating . . . pain to bring awareness" rather than attempting to "heal the wounds inflicted upon people by modern urbanism." He hoped that the exhibition would help make *Tilted Arc* a turning point toward new work that "merges the aesthetic quest and public life."

The resulting artistic solutions varied: Six involved various forms of burial. Toshio Sasaki suggested sinking the sculpture into the ground without changing its material. Kristin Jones and Andrew Ginzel proposed a brass strip as a memorial to the sculpture, and Sandford Kwinter and Françoise Schein suggested outlining the absent sculpture with a beam of light. After asking a number of people how they felt about rust, Sandy Gellis suggested burying *Tilted Arc* so that only its top edge was exposed.[70]

Allan Wexler addressed the blocked-view problem by suggesting the addition of high chairs (the kind used by lifeguards or referees at tennis matches) facing each other over the top of the sculpture.[71] Nancy Spero "feminized" the sculpture with imagery depicting the subjugation of women. David Hammons threw twenty-five pairs of sneakers over *T.W.U.,* Serra's piece on Franklin Street, as a Harlem gesture toward a downtown macho piece.

Sound artists Bill and Mary Buchen taped public reactions to the sculpture, finding, to their surprise, much more approval and far less hostility than was expressed at Diamond's hearing. Greenmarket, a collective selling fresh produce, proposed installing their vendors in Federal Plaza. And Mierle Ukeles suggested transforming the unused fountain into a space for public art and Federal Plaza into an amphitheater for public discussion of public art.

Like the artists in the exhibition, but in the form of comments on Diamond's questionnaires, members of the general public also suggested public art alternatives for Federal Plaza. Some wanted to unblock the view and open access across the space; others wanted to provide content or decorative amenities by adding things to the sculpture.

Ben Goldfrum, a federal employee who made metal sculpture, suggested "having openings at strategic points for walking through it, adding a sculpture to it to make it more interesting, making it part of a memorial, turning it from a cold and bland mass of metal into something enjoyable and useful." B. G. Pollock of the Army Corps of Engineers thought that *Tilted Arc,* like the Washington Monument and the Vietnam Veterans Memorial, "offends by massive understatement." She favored painting it and hanging art shows from it or exhibiting traveling sculpture exhibitions in front of it and at the same time emptying the lobby of "art junk." Another federal employee proposed cutting holes in it and hanging flowers and wind chimes from it.

An employee of the Health and Hospitals Corporation suggested painting it a bright color, and one from the Internal Revenue Service wanted to cover it in mirror-like chrome. Someone from the Human Resources Administration proposed that a scenic mural be painted on it or that it simply be replaced with trees. Similarly, a private citizen, Emil P. Norman, wrote to Dwight Ink suggesting that *Tilted Arc* could "be modified into a thing of beauty"[72] by painting panoramic scenes on both sides, and a federal worker preferred a mural with either symbols of the agencies at 26 Federal Plaza, historical scenes, or famous faces. Someone else suggested that the sculpture be decorated with famous patriotic quotes.

Alternative public art solutions for Federal Plaza were in no short supply. Although lacking the sophistication and irony of the artistic responses, the public statements suggest that Ukeles's proposal for an ongoing forum at the site was feasible. At least, the basis for a dialogue was there.

The Evolution of Public Art

The *Tilted Arc* controversy was interpreted by many as a warning that public art in the form of single-object sculptures, site specific or not, was no longer viable. In 1979, when the GSA commissioned Serra to create a work for Federal Plaza, a number of artists were practicing alternative approaches to public art. Some tried to transplant the vocabulary of landscape art into the largely urban realm of public art, incorporating elements like rocks and water.[73] Some sculptors, like Isamu Noguchi, admired natural stone for its own sake; others, such as Carl Andre and Michael Heizer, used it in a more conceptual way. The fountain, a traditional form of public sculpture, was variously revitalized by artists such as Claes Oldenburg and Coosje van Bruggen, and Nancy Holt.

The definition of public art was gradually expanded to include the entire site. Working largely with natural elements, Elyn Zimmerman created "spaces apart" that provided a place for people to sit quietly and enjoy their environments, and Alan Sonfist created landscapes using (and thereby commemorating) flora of centuries past. His *Time Landscape* (1965–78) was installed in Manhattan, just north of Soho at the corner of LaGuardia Place and Houston Street. In response to a growing concern with environmental issues, artists as diverse as Herbert Bayer, Patricia Johanson, Robert Morris, and Athena Tacha created public art that addressed or actually functioned as land reclamation.

During the 1980s another group of artists began making public art that also functioned as street furniture.[74] George Sugarman and later Scott Burton and Richard Artschwager made sculpture that provided seating; Donna Dennis, Lauren Ewing, and R. M. Fischer designed gates; Stephen Antonakos and Rockne Krebs made light sculpture; and Vito Acconci, Dennis Adams, Barbara Kruger, and Bruce Nauman, among others, used bus shelters for their public art messages. Still others, such as Andrea Blum, Jackie Ferrara, Robert Irwin, and Ned Smyth, created built environments that relied less on landscape elements and more on man-made sculptural components.

In New York City examples of this pragmatic approach to public art could be seen in Scott Burton's 1985 elegant outdoor seating for the Equitable Life Assurance

Building in midtown, and by the end of the decade at Battery Park City (southeast of Federal Plaza) in the individual sculptures by Ned Smyth and Richard Artschwager, the gate by R. M. Fischer, and the larger collaboratively designed spaces by Burton and Siah Armajani working with architect Cesar Pelli and Mary Miss collaborating with architect Stanton Ekstut and landscape architect Susan Child.

By 1990 critic Patricia Phillips observed that public art existed in a near critical vacuum burdened with the misplaced expectation that it would somehow save or restore public life. Increasingly of late, public artists have focused on the public, attempting to engage individuals in community issues. A variety of approaches to this socially based public art have been documented in anthologies by Suzanne Lacey, J. W. T. Mitchell, and Arlene Raven.[75]

Critic Eleanor Heartney saw *Tilted Arc* as the turning point in developments leading toward the dematerialization of public art. Curator Mary Jane Jacob experimented with different approaches in a number of exhibitions intended to make public art both more meaningful and more accessible to its local public. For *Places with a Past,* organized for the 1991 Spoleto Festival in Charleston, South Carolina, Jacob selected not the city's traditional tourist sites but those that revealed its "forgotten history" to be interpreted by a number of well-established public artists.[76] But the practice of importing artists to address local history is problematic even if their work appears to encompass social concerns. As Heartney observed, the artists "employed a visual and conceptual language that did not travel well outside the art ghetto, and the issues they chose to address often had more to do with the artists' own personal explorations than with concerns that might be easily recognized by Charleston's ordinary citizens."

In 1993 Jacob curated *Culture in Action* for Sculpture Chicago, involving artists directly with a variety of community groups rather than with a site. The resulting eight projects included a local parade, a workers' design for a new candy bar, and a community vegetable garden. Here the critical question became whether there was any art left in the public art equation. Heartney wondered, "What makes such projects art and not social work or community activism?" *New York Times* art critic Michael Kimmelman observed, "It is not always easy to distinguish [it] from social work." Despite critical reservations, Jacob's experimental exhibitions, including the conversations she conducted in Atlanta to coincide with the 1996 Olympic Games, were important in the way they pushed the limits of public art in provocative ways, all of them inherently challenging to Serra's practice.[77]

The Public Art Process

Much of the *Tilted Arc* controversy centered on who did and who did not participate in the selection process. The architects complained (erroneously) that they had not been consulted, as did many employees at Federal Plaza. What role should the public play and who should represent them?

Under the first federal programs to support public art during the New Deal, there was a tacit assumption that people would naturally like and appreciate art placed in their midst and that good art would overcome all resistance, even the desire for no art.[78] The same suppositions initially guided the public art programs of the NEA and GSA. Artists were primarily concerned with making their art and not with public interaction, and commissioning agencies installed art with little or no input from or accompanying information for its immediate audience.

At the time *Tilted Arc* was commissioned, the public was indirectly represented by three art-world professionals (two of whom lived in New York), a representative of the architect's firm, and the GSA staff in Washington, D.C., and New York who approved the project at every step of the way. During the Reagan 1980s, with its populist refrain, the art-world practice of consulting peer panels, widely used in other disciplines to award grants or contracts, was increasingly challenged for not including members of the general public. (The peer-panel process is discussed further in this chapter in the section "The Public Policy Context" below).

The distinction between professional expertise and public opinion may be more complicated in art than in other fields because people are accustomed to making aesthetic decisions regarding their own personal and environmental decoration (hence the "I know what I like" argument). Whether art professionals' expertise is valued for their ability to envision a range of possible artistic solutions or dismissed as reflecting an entrenched power structure continues to be a critical issue.

The question also remains as to who would best represent the public in the selection process. Ideally, each federal building would have a committee, headed by the local GSA director and consisting of a representative from each agency, to consider not just art but also working conditions and workers' needs inside and outside the building. Neighborhood residents representing local groups such as community boards or block associations might also participate in discussions about art.

Architecture provides a useful model in considering how these representatives of the using public might be included in the public art selection process. A responsible architect first establishes the client's specific pragmatic needs and more general wishes. The resulting design then, hopefully, incorporates and transcends both. Before construction, the client, usually represented by the chief executive of the institution, must approve the final solution.

In a public art process structured along these lines, art professionals consider the possibilities of the site as well as input from the using public to determine which artists might work best within the given parameters. The problem is that it is often difficult, either because of timing or lack of interest, to engage the community before a work is in place. With Serra's commission, conditions were exacerbated because the buildings had already been standing for more than a decade, and then no efforts were made to prepare the public for what was to come.

Art Education and the Public Art Process

At the hearing, Douglas Crimp noted that "although *Tilted Arc* was commissioned by a program devoted to placing art in public spaces, that program seems now utterly uninterested in building a public understanding of the art it has commissioned."[79] One of the most serious omissions of the public art revival of the late 1960s was the lack of an education component. Public art was, and often still is, launched into the public domain with little or no information—far less than is routinely provided in a museum to an audience that presumably is better informed and predisposed to be more receptive.

As an interim step after Diamond's hearing, Don Thalacker, working with the NEA, prepared a brochure on Richard Serra and *Tilted Arc*.[80] It informed the reader that the artist made no money on the commission and related Serra's choice of Cor-Ten steel (described as a "self-oxidizing [i.e., rusting] steel") to his experience working in steel mills. It suggested that people would have found the sculpture more acceptable if it "had been made of either stainless steel or polished granite," the materials of Eero Saarinen's *Gateway Arch* (1966) in St. Louis, Missouri, and Maya Lin's Vietnam Veterans Memorial (1981) in Washington, D.C., two works by architects that were initially very controversial. While acknowledging that the sculpture elicited diverse opinions, the brochure presented this as positive: "Through his exploration and searching, Serra indeed challenges our imagination, both as individuals and collectively, in a forceful, evocative manner. The *Tilted Arc* is a work that insists upon, and invariably receives, a spirited response from each of its viewers."

It is impossible to know now whether this brochure would have made a difference if it had been distributed at the time the sculpture was installed. At the very least, it would have obviated some widespread misconceptions (such as confusing the cost of the sculpture with Serra's fee) and clarified basic interpretive issues (regarding the use of rust in contemporary art).

Without an art frame (provided by a museum or gallery), public art is seen in a real-world context, and the "looks like" or metaphorical process of identification that constitutes seeing often leads to disparaging epithets. Thus *Tilted Arc* became "the Berlin Wall of Foley Square"; a proposed sculpture for Charlotte, N.C., by Joel Shapiro was dubbed "the headless Gumby"; and two very different sculptures utilizing natural stone in Seattle, one by Isamu Noguchi and the other by Michael Heizer, were related to the then popular "pet rock" craze.[81] If a work of art is not tamed or framed by placing it within a familiar context, a sense of unease or anger persists, a feeling that may escalate to vandalism.

Ideally, a public art education program begins with representatives of the public educating the selection committee about their community, and participating in the design concept in ways that are appropriate to the specific project.[82] But the sponsoring organization has a responsibility to continue to inform the public. The artist may "explain" and discuss his or her work with building inhabitants, community groups, politicians, and the press. The finished work may be amplified by information about the artist, a statement of artistic intent, critical comments, and pertinent technical information (often an effective hook). Public discussions, news stories, local radio and television coverage, advertising, and permanent documentation in any form (visible and close to the piece) may be reinforced by outreach programs to local schools, libraries, and corporations.[83]

The place of art education in the public art process is evolving. Its dual function is to ensure that the commissioned art is informed by community input and to provide access to a general audience, mitigating the distinctions that separate the public into those who know and those who do not.

The Public Space Context

> I would like there to exist places that are stable, unmoving, intangible, untouched and almost untouchable, unchanging, deep-rooted: places that might be points of reference, of departure, of origin.
>
> **—Georges Perec, *Species of Spaces***

Manhattan's defining public spaces are its streets and parks, not its plazas. There are few open spaces or places to sit in the midst of the acknowledged financial and cultural capital of the world. So New Yorkers make do with what there is, use anything they can, and cherish what little they have in direct proportion to its scarcity. It was the public-space frame of the controversy, pitting *Tilted Arc* against open space, that was ultimately the most damaging.

Every public space has an evolving history of multiple uses—political, social, visual, and so on. At the time of the *Tilted Arc* commission, there were conflicting concepts of the appropriate use of Federal Plaza. Employees walked across it on their way to and from work and lunch; sometimes they sat on the edge of the empty pool encircling an inoperative fountain. The architects considered Federal Plaza complete, defined by their buildings, their pavement design, and the pool. And Serra saw it as a space to be redefined by his art.[84]

Both the architecture of Federal Plaza and its open space were dreadful examples of paradigms outmoded at the time of Serra's commission. Many complaints about *Tilted Arc* focused on basic public amenities that appeared to have been specifically precluded by the sculpture but that had never been there in the first place. Created in response to a problematic urban space, the sculpture only emphasized its barrenness.

Different kinds of public art determine different spatial responses, and although *Tilted Arc* reinforced the function of the plaza as a walk-through, it also, by "attracting" human excrement, called attention to worsening problems of homelessness in the urban environment of the 1980s. Furthermore, by blocking an open view of its immediate surroundings, it appeared to threaten both personal safety and freedom of movement.

Public space is part of the larger concept of the public sphere, the philosophical arena where democracy is defined and negotiated. Considering various definitions of the public sphere and the experience of public space, *Tilted Arc* might be said to reflect (if not contribute to) all of them. It engendered public debate and protest. By drawing attention to Federal Plaza, it revealed the absence of urban amenities. And in the hostile reactions it prompted, the sculpture evoked, albeit obliquely, the history of the area, a history defined by past power struggles and present government offices, many housing the judicial system.

The Evolution of Federal Plaza

Federal Plaza is located opposite Foley Square (actually shaped "somewhat like a hatchet head")[85] at the intersection of Duane, Lafayette, and Centre Streets north of City Hall (Figure 35). Manhattan's grid comes undone here. A hodgepodge of federal, state, and city municipal courts and government office buildings reflect a piecemeal development.[86]

Initially under water, the area was drained and paved by 1911 and subsequently became a notorious slum.[87] Known as Five Points, the neighborhood was described as "a nest of saloons and old tenements" and the park (Foley Square) as "filled with men resting between drinking and brawling bouts."[88] In 1926 it was named for Thomas "Big Tom" F. Foley (1852–1925), a saloon keeper and alderman, sheriff, Tammany Hall district leader, and political godfather to New York State Governor Alfred E. Smith.

A decade later the site of Big Tom's last saloon had become respectable with the addition of buildings such as the U.S. Courthouse at 40 Centre Street, designed by Cass Gilbert and Cass Gilbert Jr. In 1967 the Jacob K. Javits Federal Office Building and Court of International Trade were added to the mix of beaux arts and art deco architecture that constituted the civic center of the city.[89] The area still abounds with courts and government agencies. City Hall is a few blocks away, as is the much disputed African Burial Ground.[90]

The 1967 GSA building, constructed during the post–World War II building boom in lower Manhattan, was typical of the banal modernist style of the time.[91] A western addition on Broadway was added in 1976 by the same architectural firms that had designed the 1967 building: Alfred Easton Poor, Kahn and Jacobs, and Eggers and Higgins. The buildings at Federal Plaza were criticized for destroying the coherence of Foley Square in much the same way that *Tilted Arc* was accused of ruining the unity of the plaza. Paul Goldberger, then architecture critic of the *New York Times,* observed,

> Whatever the U.S. Courthouse and the N.Y. County Courthouse do to bring coherence to Foley Square, this building undoes completely. . . . Designed with the subtlety of an airport concourse—each (building), in its own way, strikes a deep blow at the compositional order of Foley Square as a whole. . . . Not only does the courthouse wing clash with the office tower and both of them clash with the old courts across the square, but the rear section of the tower (added a few years later) clashes entirely with the front section. There are two skins used, both of them ugly, and they fight each other as much as they fight everything around them.[92]

The inclusion of open space at Federal Plaza reflected the New York City zoning ordinance passed in 1961. In the eighteenth century, public space in the United States had an institutional purpose directly associated with its architecture. It was "the place where inhabitants gathered to pay homage to the authorities within."[93] In the nineteenth

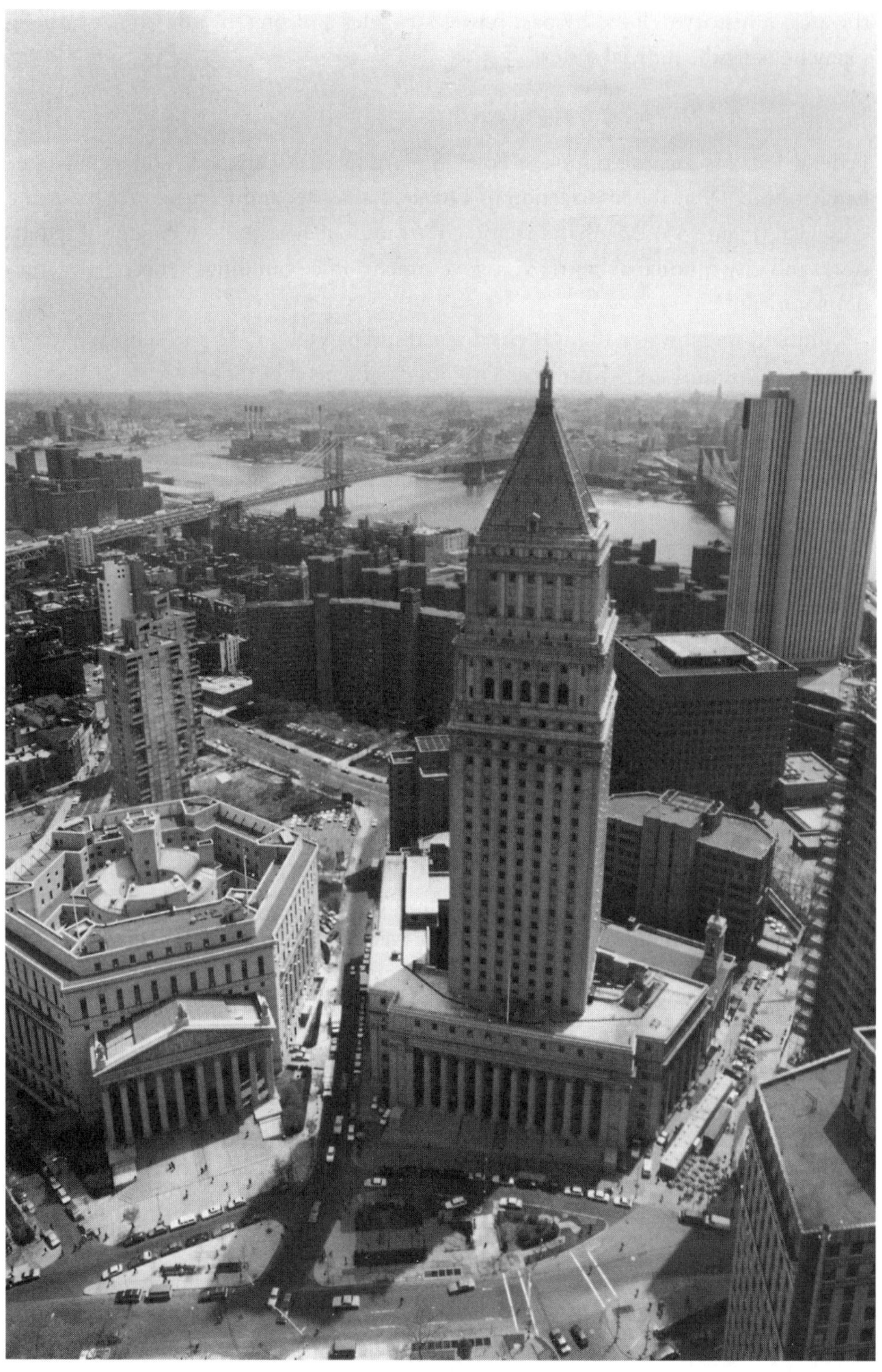

Figure 35. Foley Square, New York City. Photograph by Peter A. Sneed; courtesy of the General Services Administration.

century, squares were more often seen as parks and were developed independently from their surrounding environments. Gradually, other places such as train stations and in the next century shopping malls became the loci of public gathering, if not interaction.[94] Traditions of public space as both site of institutional power and idyllic landscape were incorporated into the urban planning of the late twentieth century.

Prompted by a concern with the absence of open space in the city and inspired by well-known European plazas and by the recently built Lever House and Seagram building on Park Avenue, New York City passed the so-called plaza law that granted bonuses (permission to build higher than area limits) for the inclusion of open space at ground level.[95] The new urban "plazas" (actually forecourts) of the 1960s often became the sites of public art. Sixth Avenue and Park Avenue were dotted with nondescript abstract sculptures that could easily be read as corporate logos. Even before Federal Plaza was built, these spaces were under attack.[96] Unlike their famous European precedents, they were actually private property, lacking either elegant design or public amenities.

Federal Plaza was arguably one of the worst examples of an already outmoded zoning code. It was so dismal that it was singled out by several architecture critics, as well as by members of the larger public, as being at the root of the objections to *Tilted Arc.* Robert Hughes in *Time* magazine described Federal Plaza as "one of the ugliest public spaces in America. Everything, from its coarse buildings—which look the way institutional disinfectant smells—to its dry, littered fountain, begs for prolonged shiatsu with a wrecker's ball." Goldberger was similarly scathing: "The fact is that, in a city of bad plazas in front of bad skyscrapers, this is one of the worst. Federal Plaza is a dreary stretch of concrete, punctuated by a poorly placed and poorly designed fountain; it was no urban oasis by a long shot." Michael Sorkin of the *Village Voice* summed it up as "horrible plaza, horrible buildings, horrible bureaucratic interiors, the worst." And in the "Notes and Comments" section of *The New Yorker* magazine, it was characterized as "an environment so ugly and inhumane that it would disgrace the Ministry of Truth in an East Bloc capital."[97]

A number of federal employees also felt that the plaza itself, not the sculpture, was the problem. C. F. Sweeney of the Department of Housing and Urban Development suggested improving the plaza rather than removing the sculpture: "Keep the arc, if you will, but incorporate it into a plaza that's meant for people. How about an outdoor cafe or lunchtime concerts, and flowers, trees, vendors, shows. Give the plaza some humanity." Renee M. Russell of the Army Corps of Engineers observed, "Were the 'arc' to be moved, few if any benefits would derive. The plaza surface is inhospitable and the local microclimate intolerable for people [to] use EXCEPT to walk across. The 'arc' does not interfere with this function."[98]

Serra's sculpture, sited in an architectural and spatial complex that was pragmatically and aesthetically flawed, to say the least, also existed during a time when living conditions for many New Yorkers dramatically worsened in the midst of rising prosperity.

Public Space in the 1980s

The increasing difficulty of assembling sites large enough to accommodate the plazas and the real estate industry's desire to keep the bonus of building an additional 20 percent of rental space led to a new focus on interior public spaces, commerical areas that reflected the national growth of shopping malls. Citicorp Center, Galleria, and Olympic Tower in midtown were all built in the late 1970s. In many parts of the country, these commercial ventures, under corporate control, already represented the dominant form of space open to the public.[99]

New York City's zoning amendments of 1982 shifted the definition of urban amenities away from the open forecourts fostered by the 1961 ordinance. Economic incentives were offered instead for improved subway stations, widened sidewalks, and off-site urban spaces within 1,000 feet of the building.[100]

While planners were experimenting with different ways to make the open spaces of Manhattan more apparently hospitable, the city was beset with the problems of a level of homelessness that had not been known since the Great Depression. As a result, for the sheltered, the experience of public space was one of nearly constant harassment of one sort or another; for the homeless, of course, it was much worse. New York, like the rest of the country, changed radically during the 1980s, as columnists Jack Newfield and Wayne Barrett pointed out:

> [T]he boom of the 1980s bypassed whole chunks of the city. Between 1977 and 1985, the proportion of New Yorkers officially classified as living below the federal poverty line increased from 17 to 25 percent. The homeless population grew to 60,000; the high school dropout rate rose 54 percent; AIDS became a plague; crack became an epidemic. . . . Manhattan was fast becoming the Ethiopia of the housing market, with a famine of rental apartments for the middle class and the working class starving for shelter. A city of scarce resources, dependent on its government to be honest and frugal, New York increasingly began to resemble a Dickensian city of extreme paradox, of poverty and overdevelopment, with diversity being swept away by the force of wealth.[101]

During the time of *Tilted Arc*'s existence, living conditions worsened and paradigms of public space design were changing in ways that benefited real estate developers.

The Spatial Impact of Public Art

A recent urban-design text considers public space "the stage upon which the drama of communal life unfolds" encompassing "a dynamic balance between public and private activities" that is culturally determined. Defining the primary function of public space as the creation of a hospitable environment that encourages personal exchange, the authors criticized *Tilted Arc* for paying insufficient "attention to the human dimensions and users of public space."[102] Public art may address just these aspects, directly or indirectly, as William H. Whyte suggests in a study of open spaces in New York City:

> Sculpture can have strong social effects. Before and after studies of Chase Manhattan Plaza showed that the installation of Dubuffet's "Four Trees" [Figure 36] has had a beneficent impact on pedestrian activity. People are drawn to the sculpture, and drawn through it; they stand under it, beside it; they touch it; they talk about it. At the Federal Plaza in Chicago, Alexander Calder's huge stabile has had similar effects.[103]

Different kinds of public art prompt different physical as well as social responses, and it is worth considering these obvious distinctions for a moment. When art enters public space, it leaves the institutional art frame behind. Government-commissioned art becomes part of the workday for its immediate public, something they pass every time they enter or leave the building.

A single-object public sculpture can provide a focus for a space, a civic emblem (Calder's *La Grande Vitesse* in Grand Rapids or the Chicago Picasso), or a landmark place to meet (Oldenburg's *Clothespin* [1976] in Philadelphia), or it may simply become part of the invisible urban environment, hardly noticed unless it is moved or removed.

Not too far from Federal Plaza, the Chase Manhattan Bank Plaza designed in 1961 by Gordon Bunshaft, the first new urban plaza in lower Manhattan built under the

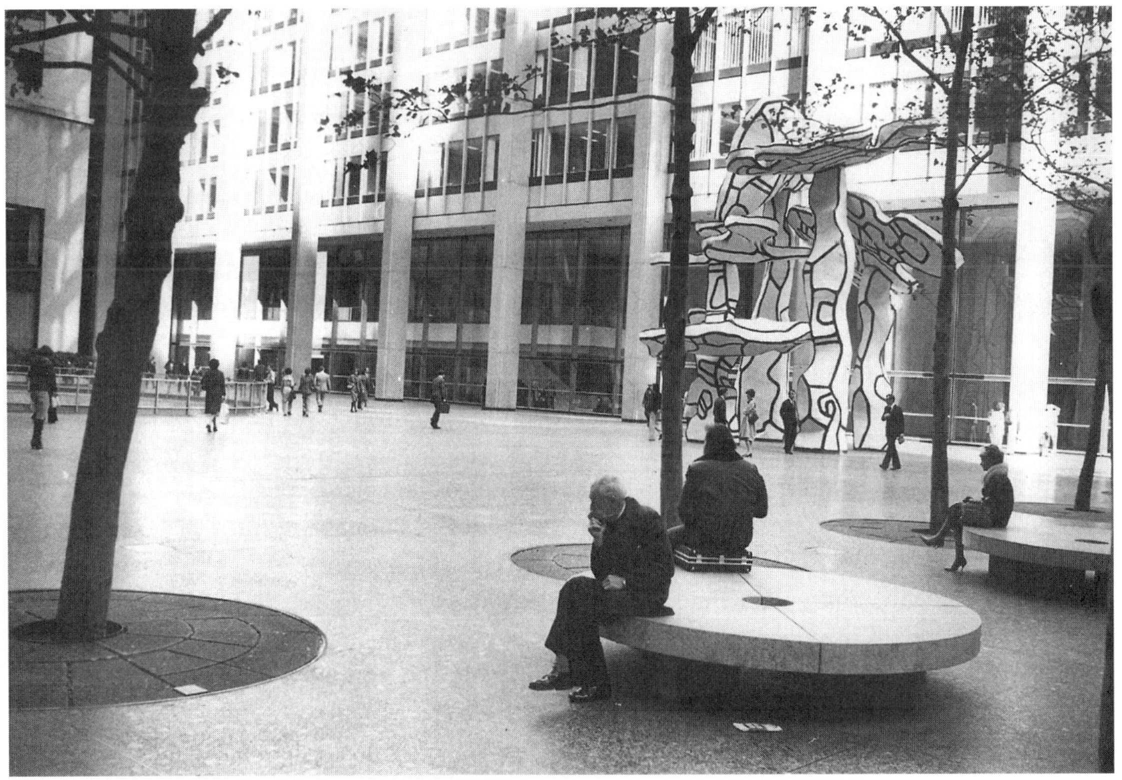

Figure 36. Jean Dubuffet, *Group of Four Trees,* 1969; installed 1972, Chase Manhattan Bank Plaza, New York City. Photograph by Frank Leonardo.

plaza law, was punctuated by Jean Dubuffet's *Group of Four Trees* (1969, installed 1972). The work adds a whimsical counterpoint to the architecture in an otherwise amorphous meandering space (Figure 36). Immediately to the west, at Marine Midland Bank Plaza, also designed by Bunshaft, Noguchi's *Red Cube* (1968, Figure 33) provides the focus.[104] A geometric form that complements the building, it interjects a striking note of color. Both *Four Trees* and *Red Cube* were decorative additions, Bunshaft said, for the corporate client, "just like he buys good furniture."[105] For the pedestrian, both invite visual and tactile engagement, and offer the possibility of walking around them, ignoring them, or using them as a photo op.

By the 1980s, the paradigm of the single object had been replaced with a type of public art that provided a more tangible spatial use: something to sit on, climb, or walk through—something that looked more like street furniture (loosely defined) than art. It answered a specific need or provided for a common activity in the space and aimed at becoming part of the urban environment in the same way that lighting fixtures or trash receptacles do. The art at nearby Battery Park City followed this model, as did Martha Schwartz's eventual design for Federal Plaza (discussed below).

The spatial experience of *Tilted Arc* was like neither of the above. Serra considered space to be a material: "I attempt to use sculptural form to make space distinct. . . . I admit, the work is disruptive. However, I want to direct the consciousness of the viewer to the reality of the conditions: private, public, political, formal, ideological, economic, psychological, commercial, sociological . . . or any of those combined. Part and parcel of making space distinct is to ground the spectator in the reality of the context."[106] *Tilted Arc* could not be viewed at a single glance and did not invite touch (although it attracted graffiti). And obviously, it filled no pragmatic needs (although some employees remarked that it functioned like a welcome windbreak). As Serra had observed in 1979, Federal Plaza was used primarily as a pedestrian crosswalk. Because he first measured the paths that people traversed entering and leaving the building, *Tilted Arc* underlined and reinforced this use of the space.[107] Indeed, its tilt, with its implied threat, strengthened the desire to keep moving.

But following John J. Costonis's useful frame, *Tilted Arc* functioned as an alien rather than an icon, something that threatened environmental stability by upsetting the status quo, thereby challenging a sense of self.[108] Serra's sculpture did this in a number of provocative ways: It made conditions of homelessness visible; it underlined the prevalent sense of a hostile, dangerous urban environment; and it challenged the illusion of personal freedom by seeming to curtail movement.

By "attracting" graffiti and human excrement, *Tilted Arc* made visible worsening conditions of the urban environment that were usually ignored. It brought the effects of current real estate redevelopment policies directly into the middle of an official federal space. These undesirable traces acknowledged the presence of a public that did not vote, that may have been homeless, and that was certainly unwelcome in the city's "public" spaces.

At the same time, by obscuring the sense of unobstructed vision at Federal Plaza, *Tilted Arc* threatened the fragile illusion of personal safety. It evoked the profound visceral unease that New Yorkers experience when they cannot immediately see where they are going. The fear expressed by many that someone or something might be lurking on the other side of the sculpture revealed the pervasive experience of the city's public spaces.

One employee at Federal Plaza observed, "Confrontational art, i.e., art designed to confront the beholder with annoyance and impedance and whose intent is solely to anger and annoy, doesn't belong in a city where every corner turned presents a nasty confrontation." Paul Goldstein, speaking for Community Board 1, observed that "in the minds of many the piece constitutes both a safety and fire hazard." One employee wrote, "The Arc promotes crimes such as muggings, rapes, etc. because it blocks the view of the plaza." John Gattuso feared that "the arc as a wall masks the plaza from both the interior of the building where there are security forces available and the exterior police on the street, so this is a perfect situation in today's growing crime down here for something to occur."[109]

Various unsigned comments stated: "Issue of safety, not art"; "I thought it was a barrier to stop terrorists"; "It would be a good backdrop for a firing squad." Federal worker Phil La Basi perceived the sculpture in a military context: "What I see there is really something that looks like a tank trap to prevent an armed attack from Chinatown in case of a Soviet invasion. In my mind it probably wouldn't even do that well because probably one good Russian tank would take it out." A worker at the Environmental Protection Agency also identified the sculpture as a defense structure: "My own thought is that the arc was really placed there to provide a barrier to protect the street level Custom Court building from bomb fragments and gunfire." Pete Wagner imagined the sculpture's "readiness for a military madman's executionary activities and the additional concealment for nefarious activities of muggers, assassins, or anarchists."[110]

Vickie O'Dougherty, a physical security specialist for the Federal Protection and Safety Division of GSA, in a much quoted excerpt of hearing testimony, also saw the sculpture in terms of potential danger:

> The arc is what I consider to be a security hazard or a disadvantage. My main contention is that it presents a blast wall effect. . . . The front curvature of the design is comparable to devices which are used by bomb experts to vent explosive forces. . . . This one . . . could vent an explosion both upward and in an angle toward both buildings. . . . It would, of course, take a larger bomb than that which has been previously used to destroy enough for their purposes, but it is possible and lately we are expecting the worst in the federal sector.

Her remarks, made well before the bombings at the World Trade Center and the Oklahoma City Federal Building and the recent shooting at the Empire State building, sounded paranoid in the extreme. As historian Casey Blake has suggested, such commentary can best be understood in the context of the pervasive Cold War rhetoric of the time.[111]

Although personal safety issues are raised so often in public art controversies that they might well be considered a reflection of their urban settings, much of Serra's work, in particular, embodies a sense of threatening precariousness that contributes to such a reading. His sculptures appear to be monumental balancing acts; their actual support is hidden belowground. A museum or gallery setting (an art frame) provides a guarded space where physical safety is assumed. Federal Plaza starkly intensified the experience of the sculpture as implicit risk.

By blocking a continuous view, *Tilted Arc* also appeared to block people's paths, although in fact it did not.[112] Even before the sculpture was placed, people could not move directly across the plaza without climbing in and out of the empty pool. Nevertheless, the visual barrier challenged the illusion of individual freedom to walk as one pleases. The paths we walk establish our individual experience of the urban environment. Whether we randomly vary our way in search of surprises or choose the comforting sameness of routine, the options are always open. Although this hardly constitutes freedom in a broad sense, as an aspect of daily life available free of charge to most, it is often experienced as such. It is the way we take possession of public space.[113]

The complexity of the spatial experience provided by *Tilted Arc* was never discussed as such, nor was it ever directly addressed. If Diamond's primary aim had been to "improve" the space at Federal Plaza by making it more "user friendly," he would have tried to add seating and greenery or to use the sculpture as a backdrop for concerts and performances. At Diamond's hearing, composers Philip Glass and Alvin Lucier expressed an interest in the latter. Serra offered to assist with improving the space at the 1987 NEA hearing; presumably he would also have been amenable to improvements two years earlier.

Federal Plaza after Tilted Arc

During the summer of 1989, after the removal of *Tilted Arc,* the fountain was briefly reactivated and Federal Plaza was furnished with a few benches and planters ordered from a standard federal order catalog (Figures 37, 38). A summer concert series was introduced to celebrate GSA's fortieth anniversary, and on July 6, 1989, there was a "rededication of Federal Plaza." William Diamond, who hosted the event, announced, "It will be a real pleasure to celebrate this anniversary with the opening of this concert series and with the return of Federal Plaza to the local workers and people of this community."[114]

Diamond designated the "renovated" plaza a new art form: "We are installing 15 benches and planters with trees so that the public can enjoy the plaza again. . . . It's a revolution in our thinking—that open space is an art form in itself and should be treated with the same respect that other art forms are." By declaring a new public art policy and ordering benches and planters, Diamond de facto became both selection panel and artist.[115]

In providing a place to sit, eat lunch, converse, or read, Federal Plaza followed the model of the new public art and addressed some of the basic physical and social needs of its primary using public. Over the next year the number of benches and planters was increased, until much of the plaza was covered with a hodgepodge of standard-order

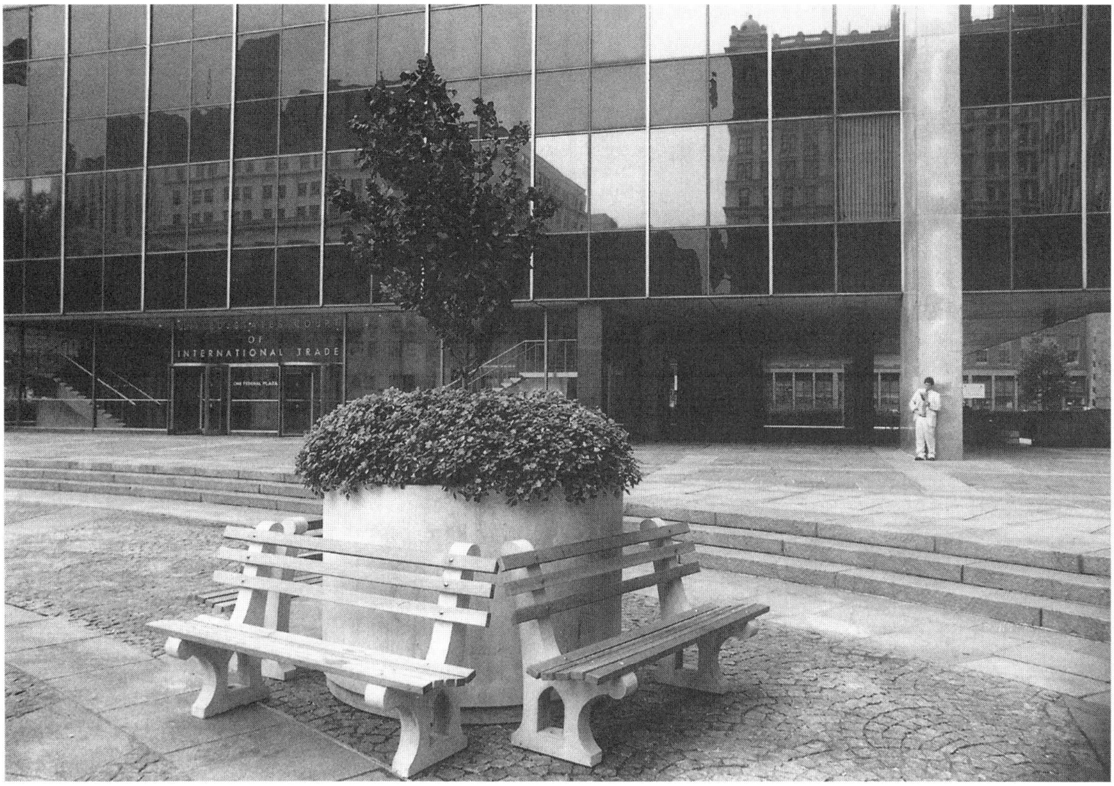

Figure 37. Federal Plaza planter, 1989, New York City. Photograph by Burt Roberts.

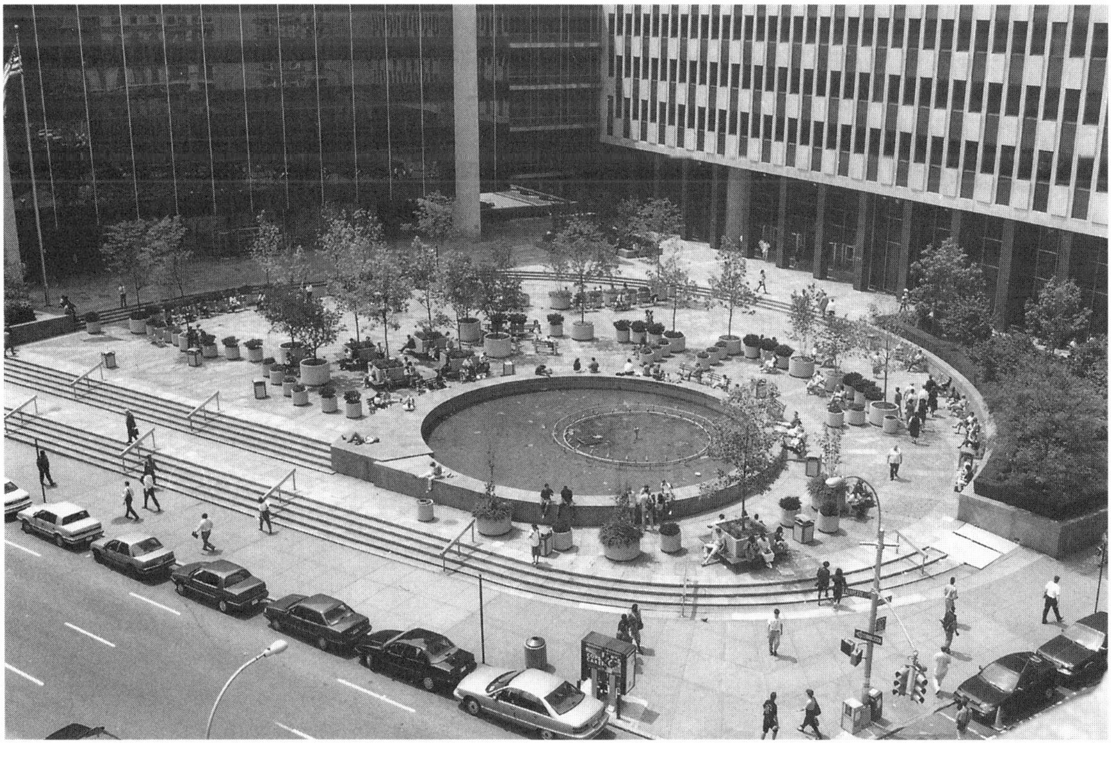

Figure 38. Federal Plaza, 1989, New York City. Photograph by Burt Roberts.

seating and planter tubs that could not in any sense be called art or even artful arrangement. The placement of the planters at all entrances to the building appeared to serve as a barricade for vehicular access. At the same time, plans were underway for the refurbishment of the entire plaza.

After Diamond's hearing, well before the ultimate removal of *Tilted Arc,* the NEA considered involving landscape architect Martha Schwartz in a modification of Federal Plaza. These plans never materialized. However, after the sculpture was removed and it became evident that Federal Plaza required major structural repairs, Schwartz's services were folded into the architecture budget, thereby obviating the need for a formal art-selection process. The GSA substituted Schwartz's work for Serra's in a unilateral manner, much as it had removed *Tilted Arc.* Only this time, it acted from Washington, not New York.

In announcing plans for the redesign of the plaza, Dale Lanzone, then head of the program in charge of GSA's art commissions, stated, "We're not trying to be more conservative, but public art has changed since the *Tilted Arc* days. These decisions are a public process. I'm not saying we can please everyone, but it's not like driving a train into a wall."[116] Lanzone's statements implied that Schwartz was selected by the same panel process that had chosen sculptor Beverly Pepper for the site facing Broadway that borders the west side of the plaza. But this was not the case.[117]

According to Lanzone, in Schwartz's design, "The plaza will be treated very much as a work of art, but it will be a usable space, the antithesis of Serra's treatment." The GSA, he said, had decided not to commission a sculpture for the plaza because it was just "too sensitive to ask an artist to design a sculpture for the same place where *Tilted Arc* was." Presumably, it would also have been much more difficult to fold a sculpture into an architectural repair budget.[118]

Initially Lanzone asked Schwartz to submit three proposals: one with the pool, one without, and one with whatever she wanted. The selected version eliminated all elements of the existing plaza (the original pool and pavement design as well as the subsequent standard-order benches and planters). Schwartz treated the area primarily as a place to sit and have lunch, using "typical New York park language with a twist." She described the benches as "luscious, with great curves." Lanzone admired their "lightness and humor" and "liked the idea of a woman treating the space" (Figure 39).[119]

Schwartz, once a great admirer of *Tilted Arc,* had no qualms about working in Federal Plaza. The controversy helped form her ideas about public art. In the end, she felt that Serra's sculpture did not work for the people in the building and that art was not above the rest of the world. The plaza and the sculpture were history. "What would Serra have done?" she asked herself. He would have done whatever he wanted. And so did she.

Schwartz transformed Federal Plaza into a maze of bright green benches circling mounds of grass occasionally emitting steam, punctuated by railings with a similar spiral motif.[120] Covering the entire space, the standard-order benches, distinguished

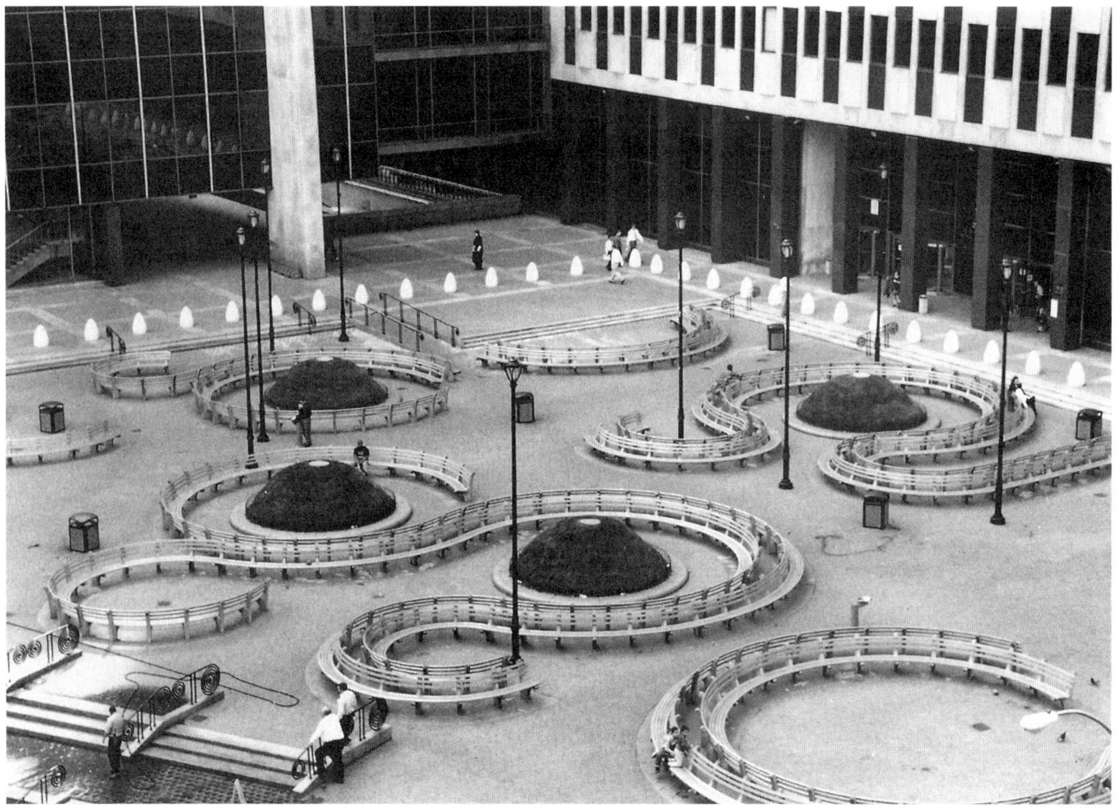

Figure 39. Martha Schwartz, Federal Plaza (detail), 1997, New York City. Photograph by Burt Roberts.

only by their acid color, rest on a ground of purple paint, already badly faded and peeling at the time of this writing. Although providing plenty of seating, the serpentine configuration of the benches prohibits any direct path across the plaza.

There were problems throughout the design process. Initially Schwartz designed the grassy mounds to be a height that would have obscured sight, but she agreed to lower them because security officers insisted that they be able to shoot over the tops. Then there was the problem of trees and grass. Schwartz allegedly refused to consider trees because they would have to be replaced periodically. However, the grass covering the mounds also proved problematic. Eventually the grass was replaced with boxwood shrubs that could survive in the city's climate (Figure 40).[121]

Schwartz thought of her design as a challenge to the paradigm of Frederick Law Olmsted's nineteenth-century parks. She saw the benches "as architectural 'hedges'" and the "grassy hemispheres" as substitutes for the "French use of shrubbery and trees."[122] She shaped the sod-covered hillocks like Hostess Snow Balls (the white or pink coconut- and marshmallow-covered chocolate cupcakes with cream centers) and imagined the concrete bollards intended for protection as slightly surreal eggs.[123]

Is any of this apparent to the using public? Apparently not, according to a small survey conducted in May 1997.[124] Although most respondents liked the plaza in

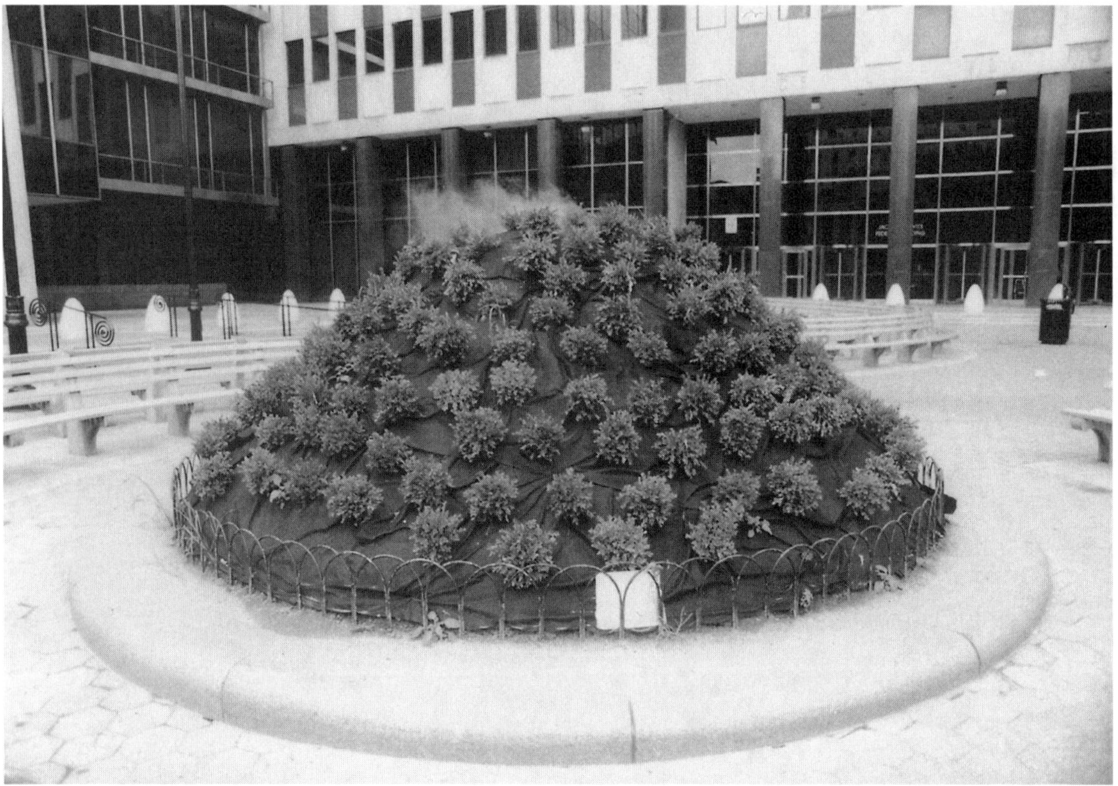

Figure 40. Martha Schwartz, replanted mound, Federal Plaza, 2000, New York City. Photograph by Burt Roberts.

general, one person wished for some shade, and another objected to the color of the benches and thought their "serpentine configuration . . . a bit too much of a maze." All were puzzled by the grass mounds; one individual had heard that the "puff smoke phenomenon" was only a rumor. Even Schwartz at one point admitted that her various references were "basically . . . a little joke for a little group of people [other landscape architects]."[125] But people had been somewhat prepared for the plaza's appearance: A display in the lobby preceded its installation.

The change to the side of the Federal Building on Broadway, the installation of Beverly Pepper's *Sentinels* (1996, Figure 41)—four cast-iron columns that follow the model of single-object-sculpture public art—also received mixed responses. Peter Koch liked that "they are not intrusive like *Tilted Arc* (don't block walking through plaza)" but objected to their form; they reminded him of "heathen idols or totem poles." Other comments indicated that quite a few individuals objected to their phallic shape, one person reported that people were upset that trees had been cut down to make room for them, and in April 1998 a security guard at the site grumbled that her taxes had been used for their purchase.

These new additions to Federal Plaza put in question the pertinence of some of the main complaints about *Tilted Arc.* Martha Schwartz's design controls one's path

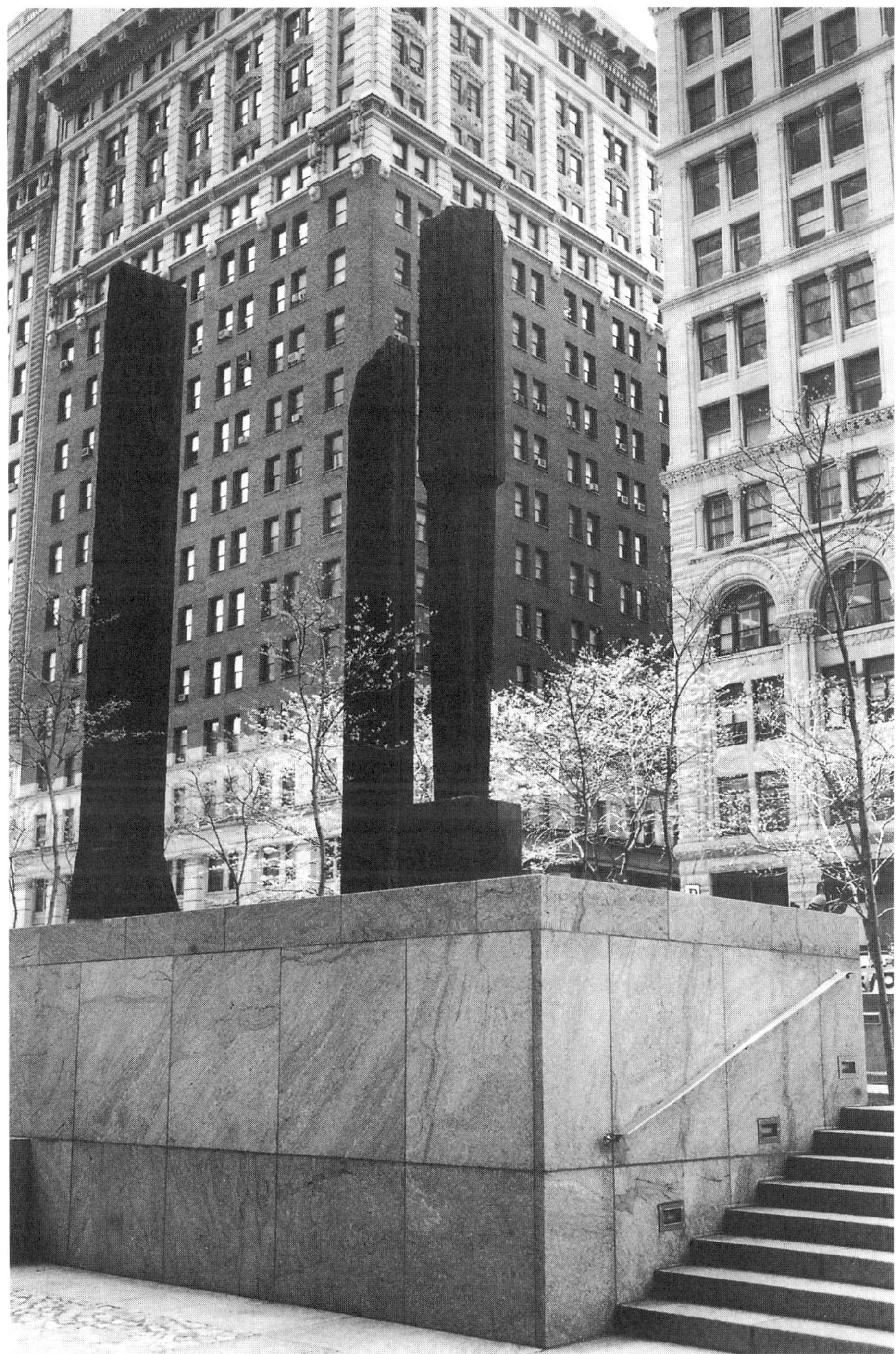

Figure 41. Beverly Pepper, *Sentinels,* 1996, New York City. Photograph by Burt Roberts.

across the plaza, precluding any direct route. And Beverly Pepper's sculptures, made of Cor-Ten steel, have a rusty surface. But Schwartz's benches can be used, and Pepper's columns can be ignored. Although the presence of the benches is pervasive and their arrangement awkward, even confusing, a pedestrian still feels in control. After all, one can see over them; the illusion of freedom of movement holds. And then there is the always seductive possibility of sitting down for a bite of lunch or just to catch the noonday rays. (Indeed, there never was and there is not now any provision for shade.) In spite of these added amenities, use of the plaza never approaches full capacity even at lunchtime on a nice day.

Is this an improvement? Initially, Federal Plaza had no design distinction, offered no pertinent historical reference, and was hardly hospitable: It provided no public seating and did nothing to encourage social interaction. It always was and continues to be an urban space used by a public with more than aesthetic needs. Certainly there were more things wrong with Federal Plaza than any single sculpture could address constructively. Serra and the GSA (here in the persona of Diamond) considered public space at Federal Plaza in a monolithic way. Neither considered the possibility, indeed the need, to address its potentially multiple uses. Today discussions of urban design and public art continue to remain alarmingly separate.[126]

Philosophical Implications

Although art critic Amy Goldin observed in 1974 that "the main reason there is so little genuine public art today is our disbelief in the reality of the public world,"[127] public space, the village green or the urban plaza, is often seen as the paradigmatic locus of democracy, where individuals may gather to express political views and organize public opinion. When public art enters a public space, it immediately becomes part of larger discussions of the definition and meaning of a public sphere.

Jürgen Habermas, in his fundamental philosophical text, *The Structural Transformation of the Public Sphere* (1962), defined the ideal (utopian, liberal, bourgeois) public sphere as a space where true public discourse occurs, without the coercion of commercial interests or state authority. At the time of its translation into English in 1989, it sparked widespread analysis and debate centering on theories of democracy, the actual inclusiveness of the public sphere, and even the possibility of its existence.[128]

Arguments as to the ideal nature of a democratic public sphere ask whether it is characterized by or whether its goal should be informed consensus or "conflict, division, and instability," as Rosalyn Deutsche suggests, an arena where "exclusions are taken into account and open to contestation." If public space is not equally open to all, if all are not equally safe, ongoing restrictions based on gender, race, ethnicity, and economic status undermine the very definition of a democratic public sphere. Indeed, J. W. T. Mitchell raises serious questions as to whether a public sphere can exist in the cultures of late capitalism, and even more basically whether it ever existed at all or whether in fact, as Bruce Robbins has suggested, it has always been a phantom.[129]

At times during Diamond's hearing, even the space at Federal Plaza before *Tilted*

Arc assumed illusionary proportions. Blaming Serra's sculpture for the destruction of an idyllic setting, people variously described this barren space with an empty pool as "a beautiful and harmonious place," "a public amenity, an oasis of light, air and space," and "a haven of an open place in a confining, crowded city . . . a pleasant and humane open space for federal employees, citizens of New York and visitors to this great city."[130]

Philosophical or theoretical definitions of the public sphere underlie the practice of public art. Most public art works toward creating a more viable or usable public space, even if that space is not defined by freedom of access, movement, and expression or by the absence of government or corporate control. Some critics are committed to fight the "growth of a new public art industry serving as the aesthetic arm of oppressive urban policies." But even though public art enters public space as part of some highly questionable urban (re)development practices, its immediate audience is composed of individuals who have to earn a living there, for whom this public space represents their everyday working environment. For them the reduction of public spaces to "harmonious leisure spots or places to eat lunch" is far from "trivializing."[131]

Clearly, different conceptions of the public sphere prompt different public art solutions. Krzysztof Wodiczko, believing in public art that is confrontational, has created structures for the homeless as well as provocative projections of institutional critique on public buildings.[132] Ukeles (in the 1985 *After Tilted Arc* exhibition discussed above) suggested a circular structure for seating at Federal Plaza to prompt civic dialogue. Although both approaches (Wodiczko's and Ukeles's) envisioned a public sphere open to free political expression and advocacy, Ukeles's left the framing of the issues up to the using public.

Serra in 1979 imagined a public sphere of critical dissension. He intended to challenge symbolically government authority and its impositions on personal freedom. A concept of the public sphere like Wodiczko's or Serra's views works like Calder's or those concerned with providing seating and other urban amenities as celebrating existing economic power structures responsible for social ills (gentrification and therefore homelessness) and the curtailment of individual freedom.

Does a critical view of the public sphere of necessity preclude public art that addresses the basic amenities of urban life rather than its philosophical underpinnings? What is the most effective way to incorporate a philosophy about the public sphere with the specific needs of private individuals using a public space?

The Public Policy Context

> For the arts, the 1980s will be a perpetual "Perils of Pauline."
>
> —**Bob Arnebeck, *New Art Examiner*, October 1981**

Throughout the decade the arts were a primary target for federal budget cuts. The rise and fall of *Tilted Arc* occurred against a background of shifting paradigms in public policy for art in general and public art in particular. Although there was no centralized or coherent national arts policy, the NEA was generally perceived as providing an umbrella for the arts, and its position was seen as a reflection of the field. When the decade began, the strong national arts coalition built by Nancy Hanks during her tenure as chair of the NEA (1969–77) was just starting to unravel. By the end of the decade, the very future of the agency was in question.

Some independent programs, like the one that commissioned *Tilted Arc,* were directly linked to the national arts agency. At the time of Serra's commission, the GSA's Art-in-Architecture selection panels were appointed by the NEA. In this way they reflected endowment thinking; often the same individuals advised both agencies. However, the NEA and GSA funded public art differently.[133] The GSA commissioned and owned art for federal buildings. The NEA's Art in Public Places matching-grant program responded to requests from communities or universities (who would select and ultimately own the commissioned works), and in its guidelines it reflected (and in turn determined) the shifting paradigms of the public-art world. While the NEA supported projects that increasingly focused on collaboration and process, the GSA continued to commission art objects.

In spite of their different missions (the NEA to support arts nationally, the GSA to contract for all goods, supplies, construction, and maintenance for the federal government), when it came to art, the work of both agencies raised basic issues of public policy and process: Should government support public art, and if so, what kind, and who should choose it? The NEA's selection process based on peer panels of arts professionals was repeatedly challenged as the national arts agency came under attack.

Public policy, whether clearly stated or not, is enforced by a process that is often mutable, open to manipulation by those who know how the system works. During the *Tilted Arc* controversy, and according to some, prompted by it, the collaboration between the national arts agency and the GSA in commissioning public art gradually eroded. By the time the sculpture was removed, the NEA no longer appointed GSA selection panels. Under GSA control these panels included a majority of members who were not art professionals, and regional administrators (like Diamond) had considerably more power. Although not mandated by public policy, this development reflected both conservative attacks on the art world and a commitment to local governance in preference to a strong centralized federal presence.

The power of a federal agency often correlates to the power of its director. At the time *Tilted Arc* was removed, there was no permanent head at either the NEA or the GSA. And furthermore, the structure and head of the Art-in-Architecture program that commissioned it had changed. This bureaucratic void left Serra completely dependent on a legal system that seemingly fails to provide visual art with the same protection as the spoken or written word, and whose ambivalence about First Amendment protection for visual art is especially apparent when it comes to abstract works. Apparently considered as being without content, abstract works technically cannot be censored.

The Rise and Fall of Recent Public Support for Art

Public policy, considered an expression of public values, is essentially determined by economic factors and political circumstances. Support for art in the United States has been the exception rather than the rule, a national anomaly. Without an established tradition of patronage or a politically savvy and cohesive constituency, the arts have been especially vulnerable to the vagaries of politics.

Prompted by the positive press that greeted poet Robert Frost's participation in John F. Kennedy's 1961 inaugural celebration, some presidential advisers began to advocate a public arts policy. Developed in an ad hoc way, based primarily on specially commissioned reports, a commitment to federal support for the arts evolved gradually, stressing the importance of good design and the need for artistic freedom.[134] Kennedy defined the arts in the United States as an expression of American liberty, as opposed to the controlled arts of the Soviet Union, thereby making support for the arts a national issue. But Kennedy was assassinated before he could establish a national policy or create the cabinet post then under consideration.

His successor, Lyndon Johnson, signed the law that created the NEA in 1965. As part of the educational policy of the Great Society, Johnson defined the arts as an expression of "the inner vision which guides us as a nation." But the real implementation of a national arts policy began when Richard Nixon appointed Nancy Hanks as the second head of the agency in 1969.[135]

With a degree in political science and a background in politics, Hanks had worked as Nelson Rockefeller's assistant in the Department of Health, Education, and Welfare and with Laurence Rockefeller as executive secretary of the Rockefeller Brothers Fund. Through her familiarity with the Rockefellers' support for art and her own experience as unpaid president of the Associated Councils of the Arts (an organization of state and community arts councils), Hanks had important connections in both the political and art worlds. Viewing herself as "an administrator and a good listener,"[136] she fostered the creation of state arts agencies nationwide and established a solid base of local support for NEA programs. Hanks's success was phenomenal. During her tenure the NEA budget rose from $8.2 million in 1970 to $123.5 million in 1978, and its staff, grant applications, and awards increased exponentially.[137]

As the agency's reauthorization cycle went from two years (1960s) to three (1970) to four (1976) to five (1980), congressional support was led in the Senate by Claiborne Pell (D.–R.I.) and Majority Whip John Brademas (D.–Ind.) in the House. In 1977 Jimmy Carter appointed Pell's former special assistant, Livingston Biddle, as third chair of the NEA. But in a shrinking economy, even with continued congressional support and with Joan Mondale, the vice president's wife, a strong and vocal supporter of the arts, the NEA was unable to build on or even maintain the power base Hanks had created.

At the time of Biddle's appointment, there were already questions about the quality and type of art funded by the NEA, whether money should be spent on advocacy as opposed to direct support, and the priority of geographical distribution.[138] Two years later (when Serra got his GSA commission), economic resources were more limited and arts institutions and programs were increasingly in competition with one another. When Reagan and a Republican Senate were elected in 1980, Pell was replaced as chair of the Senate oversight committee and several important arts advocates failed to win reelection: Senator Jacob K. Javits (R.–N.Y., for whom the building at Federal Plaza was named), Representatives John Brademas, Frank Thompson (D.–N.J.), and Fred Richmond (D.–N.Y.). In 1981 the American Council for the Arts (ACA) began organizing an annual Arts Advocacy Day in Washington, a clear signal that political support had become a serious concern. That year Frank S. M. Hodsoll was appointed fourth chair of the NEA, and *Tilted Arc* was installed.

Although the NEA was threatened with budgets cuts throughout the 1980s, funding remained static. But costs did not, as inflation became the norm. In 1985 (the year of Diamond's hearing), three Republican congressmen criticized the NEA for supporting "pornographic poetry" and accused its peer panels of "cronyism" and conflicts of interest.[139] As congressional scrutiny increased, the NEA was asked for a formal review of its selection process.

By 1989 (the year *Tilted Arc* was removed), the NEA was embroiled in the so-called culture wars that appeared to have replaced the Cold War. Sharply attacked by representatives of the religious right for supporting exhibitions that featured Andres Serrano's brilliantly colored Cibachromes of Christian images soaked in urine and Robert Mapplethorpe's black-and-white photographs of homosexual acts, the NEA became the object of a politics of diversion. Antagonism and alarm in the art world intensified when the agency's new chair, John Frohnmayer, rejected four grants to performance artists whose works he thought inappropriate and when Congress succeeded, for a brief time, in making an antiobscenity oath a prerequisite for an NEA grant.[140]

Support for art was equated with support for blasphemy and obscenity, demonstrating yet again that he who frames the issue usually wins, in this case the Reverend Donald Wildmon of the American Family Association, joined by evangelist Pat Robertson and supported by Senators Alphonse D'Amato (R.–N.Y.) and Jesse Helms (R.–N.C.). The actual facts—that the NEA had supported exhibitions for these works (i.e., institutions) and not the artists directly, that the dollar amount involved was insignificant (as was the entire NEA budget—less than support for military bands being the favorite comparison), and that the agency's track record nationwide was excellent—although often reiterated by agency supporters, seemed inconsequential. So powerful was the attack on art that in 1991 Republican politician Pat Buchanan was able to challenge President George Bush's party nomination for reelection by referring to the NEA as the "upholstered playpen of the Eastern liberal establishment" and criticizing Bush's administration for "subsidizing both filthy and blasphemous art."[141]

By the summer of 1991, as attacks on art became more common, the American Civil Liberties Union (ACLU) launched its Arts Censorship Project and People for the American Way started the publication *Artsave,* both intended to protect threatened art. The culture wars raised broad issues of artistic freedom, community standards, and the viability of public support for art. They also demonstrated art's power to trigger rage. All this was true of *Tilted Arc* as well.[142] But the *Tilted Arc* controversy was complicated not only by the difficulty of finding art-world and political support for an abstract work by an established white male artist but also by the problematic and changing concept of public art and its funding.

Public Art Policy at the NEA

The NEA's Art in Public Places program was established in 1967 to provide matching funds for public art to a variety of organizations. Its very first venture, funds for Alexander Calder's sculpture *La Grande Vitesse* (Figure 4) for Grand Rapids, Michigan, was considered a huge success. Its site was eventually renamed Calder Plaza, and an image of the sculpture was adopted as a civic logo that appeared on the mayor's stationery as well as on city garbage trucks. In 1973 then House minority leader and later president Gerald Ford told his house colleagues, "At the time I didn't know what a Calder was. It was somewhat shocking to a lot of people out home." But, he claimed, the sculpture helped regenerate the city by sparking interest in the downtown area.[143]

Art in Public Places grants responded to community requests. Initially, the NEA and the local grantee each appointed three members to selection panels; by 1979 the grantee selected the entire panel, but the agency recommended that nationally recognized professionals familiar with contemporary public art be involved. As budget categories evolved, matching grants for commissioned works went up to $50,000, and for direct purchases, to $25,000.

Although art support is ostensibly a response to practice, practice is also influenced and then to an extent determined by funding guidelines. In a 1987 press release announcing Art in Public Places grants, Richard Andrews, director of the Visual Arts program, stressed the diversity of responses to public places: "from freestanding object, sculpture which is furniture, 'site specific' art, to the creation of the place itself." The next year Michael Faubion, then acting director of the program, advocated the early involvement of artists: "Generally the panel has taken a favorable view of proposals involving the artist in the initial planning and design stages . . . work[ing] side-by-side with the overall development team." Collaboration continued to be stressed the following year when the Art in Public Places category included the Design Arts/Visual Arts Collaboration initiative for projects involving visual and design artists.[144]

By 1990 Faubion was concerned that recent proposals did not reflect more current developments in the field.[145] Peer panels had been commenting that public art applications were not as dynamic and interesting as they once had been. In 1991, in response to recent congressional budget cuts and complaints from selection panels, the NEA proposed combining the Art in Public Places and the Visual Artists Forums categories of funding.[146]

Ideally, a new focus on dialogue and education would have fostered discussions that prompted fresh ideas about public art. But the new funding categories were potentially both prescriptive and exclusionary—a shift in emphasis, if not policy. After more than two decades, the NEA abandoned its early support of independent single-object sculpture in favor of a more inclusive and collaborative approach to the creation of public art. Doubts about the viability of the type of public art that Serra made were soon encoded in national policy.

In 1991 the NEA awarded fourteen grants in the Art in Public Places category, highlighting projects "to support artists' design and construction of a neighborhood park for senior citizens in North Philadelphia, the redesign and transformation of a World War II firing range into a place of art on the campus of the University of California/San Diego, and the creation of an outdoor medieval castle–style amphitheater at the University of Nebraska in Omaha."[147]

In 1992 the same panel members recommended grants for both public art and visual artists' forums. An emphasis on social problems and multiculturalism was evident in the support for "the design of temporary billboards in Detroit with an anti-drug message; a memorial in Salem, Massachusetts to those who were persecuted and executed during the 1692 witch trials; and the final stage of a Zuni kachina murals project on the interior walls of a restored 17th-century mission in Zuni, New Mexico."[148]

By 1993 the two funding categories were officially merged, and funded projects ranged "from the creation of a mural focusing on deafness and challenges faced by the hearing-impaired to support for two artists to participate in the development of a project to preserve and improve a section of Cascade Valley Park, a 1500-acre site in an historic inner-city area along the Old Erie Canal in Akron, Ohio."[149]

This consolidation of funding categories was in place for too brief a time to evaluate.[150] But it is clear from the type of funded projects that when *Tilted Arc* was removed in 1989, it represented to the national arts agency, perhaps definitively, the old order of public art. To receive NEA funding at that time, art in a public place had to address, obviously and directly, the social situation of a site.

Public Art Policy at the GSA

The GSA's Art-in-Architecture program, based on the premise that art was a desirable part of architecture and the built environment, commissioned art for federal buildings with a small percentage of construction costs, usually 0.5 percent.[151] In 1972, after the GSA had been commissioning art for its buildings sporadically for nearly ten years, President Nixon asked the NEA "to recommend a program for including art works in new Federal buildings."[152] According to the process established early the following year, the NEA appointed panels of art professionals (peer panels) that would, with a representative of the building architect, select a number of artists appropriate to each GSA project and rank them in order of preference. The final decision on the selection of artist and all agency matters was up to the GSA administrator.[153] This practice was in place when Serra was commissioned to create a sculpture for Federal Plaza.

Tilted Arc was not the first GSA artwork to get a negative press. In 1966 a mural in Boston by Robert Motherwell proved so controversial that the Art-in-Architecture program was halted for six years. Charles Ginnever's *Protagoras* (1974) in St. Paul was compared to "a potential machine-gun nest" and the "undercarriage of a UFO-type flying saucer"; Noguchi's *Landscape of Time* (1975) in Seattle was related to the "pet rock" craze; Oldenburg's *Batcolumn* (1976) in Chicago received Senator William Proxmire's (D.–Wisc.) Golden Fleece Award for the most outrageous spending of tax dollars; and George Sugarman's *Baltimore Federal* (1977) was perceived as threatening because it "could be used to secrete bombs or other explosive objects."[154] But these initial reactions, not uncommon with public art, died down without someone committed to pursuing the controversy. As a result of Diamond's actions, *Tilted Arc* became enmeshed in the politics of both the GSA and NEA.

After Diamond's hearing in 1985, Acting Administrator Dwight Ink ruled, just before he left office, that the GSA should seek a new site for Serra's sculpture. Senator Thomas F. Eagleton (D.–Mo.), ranking minority member of the Senate committee on governmental affairs, who called Ink "a hasty executioner,"[155] and other concerned members of the Senate committee on governmental affairs had reason to think that the new GSA administrator, Terence Golden, would have acted differently. Prior to Golden's appointment, they had asked for "comments on the Art-in-Architecture program as administered by GSA; the role of the Regional Administrators as art judges and executioners; the role of the GSA in working with the NEA; [and] the role of the Regional Administrator in disposing of site-specific work."[156]

Golden's interest in art was unusual for a GSA administrator. He had taken courses in drawing and watercolor and had tried his hand at sculpture.[157] However, he did not much like *Tilted Arc* and felt it was a "disaster for the people living there. It didn't look good, was a source of graffiti, and interrupted views of the park [Foley Square]." Nevertheless, he saw the controversy as a direct result of Diamond's actions, his "personal mission from God to take out this blight." Golden, a friend of Diamond's, saw the New York regional administrator as "a control freak." But so was he, he said, and he held the higher office.

Determined that nothing would happen to the sculpture while he was head of GSA, Golden decided "to put it on a back burner and study it to death." He thought the GSA had more important issues to address than the sculpture at Federal Plaza—issues of health and environmental safety in buildings, problems of major costs, the need for reorganization, and the quality of the workforce in New York.[158] He felt strongly that *Tilted Arc* "was a low-priority matter in the public political arena and it consumed way too much time." And so he concentrated on new GSA construction in New York, Chicago, Oakland (California), and Miami, as well as the completion of the Federal Triangle in Washington, D.C., and the restoration of Blair House, the vice president's residence. He also arranged to borrow art for government offices from the National Museum of American Art.

Concurrently, Richard Andrews, director of the NEA's Visual Arts program from 1985 through 1987 and previously director of Seattle's acclaimed public art program, felt a personal mandate "to invent a capacity for on-going NEA involvement in the unprecedented process concerning *Tilted Arc*."[159] Consulting with the GSA and with the NEA chair, attorney Frank Hodsoll (who saw the controversy basically as a contract dispute), Andrews convened a panel for considering alternative sites. Golden saw the 1987 deliberation chaired by Theodore Kheel as just an "event to keep things going, just busy work because nothing was going to happen" while he was in office. And indeed, nothing did.

By the fall of 1988 the GSA leadership was again in transition, and the relationship between the GSA and the NEA became increasingly strained. Golden had resigned the previous March. When Acting Administrator John Alderson failed to receive approval by the Senate, he was followed by another acting administrator, Richard Austin. At the Art-in-Architecture program, Marilyn Farley, who had worked with Don Thalacker and who had been acting director since his death in 1987,[160] was replaced by Kenneth Anderson, previously with the National Park Service. Dale Lanzone (also from the Park Service) was named director of arts and historic preservation; he subsequently controlled the Art-in-Architecture program.

The public art selection process was also in transition, prompted in part by the requests for greater public participation that emerged at the *Tilted Arc* hearing. Before he left office, Richard Andrews at the NEA and Marilyn Farley at the GSA developed a new procedure and implemented it on a trial basis for one year. Under the Andrews/Farley plan, the NEA appointed a panel consisting of the architect-engineer, two local residents knowledgeable in the arts and serving as community representatives, two local or regional art professionals, one nationally recognized art professional with experience in public art to serve as chair, and the GSA regional administrator, ex officio. The initial meeting took place at the project site, where panel members discussed the nature of an appropriate art project, potential places for it, and possible artists. At the second meeting they selected three to five artists and ranked them in order of preference for final selection by the GSA administrator. At the final meeting they reviewed the artist's proposal. At the time of the *Tilted Arc* selection process, the panel's responsibility ended with the selection of the artist.

In the spring of 1988 the new staff at GSA proposed different guidelines giving greater control of the selection process to the GSA. Under these recommendations, the GSA appointed three of the six panel members; of these, the regional administrator designated two. The NEA appointed two local or regional art professionals and one nationally recognized art professional with experience in public art, subject to approval by the director of arts and historic preservation (who now had jurisdiction over the Art-in-Architecture program). The GSA regional administrator chaired the first meeting, outlined the criteria for the project, provided directions to the panel "indicating material, design, placement, and style of art to be considered," and prepared the pre-site report.[161]

Under the new proposal, the Public Building Services commissioner (rather than the GSA administrator) approved all commissions. For those under $50,000, the

GSA regional administrator made the final selection. This increasingly localized process reflected the Reagan administration's decentralization policies. It also gave the GSA almost complete control over the selection of art. Indeed, Michael Faubion, acting director of the NEA's Visual Arts program, observed that the GSA had been acting independently for some time,[162] and recommended that the NEA not participate in the process as outlined. Nevertheless, the GSA adopted it,[163] and in April 1989 Hugh Southern, acting director of the NEA, formally terminated the national art agency's seventeen-year relationship with the GSA.[164]

From then on, officially, the GSA's Arts and Historic Preservation Division appointed the selection panel, prepared the report of the pre-site meeting led by the regional administrator, and by matching artists' current selling prices to the art budget, identified appropriate individuals for consideration by the selection panel. Lanzone stated, "Art is viewed in the same way as real estate."[165] This process, without any checks and balances, was open to up-front and behind-the-scenes control by a single individual, the director of the Arts and Historic Preservation Division.[166]

Lanzone viewed the break with the NEA as inevitable. He felt that while the NEA treated Art-in-Architecture commissions as a grant to the artist, the GSA considered art real property, acquired in the same way as cars and air conditioners. Later Serra would characterize the decision to remove *Tilted Arc* as an example of "the priority of property rights" typical of the Reagan and Bush administrations, which supported "art only as a commodity."[167]

Lanzone's initial goal as head of the Art-in-Architecture program was to avoid controversy. Specifically, he said, he was "against imposing New York values." Toward that end, in 1991 the GSA began selecting only figural work. The first published GSA art bulletin described a commission for the Los Angeles Federal Building that included sculpture by Jonathan Borofsky, Tom Otterness, and Joel Shapiro:

> It is the energy of the figure that unifies these three artists. Each uses the space to refer to the human form and for Los Angeles this human energy translates easily into the busyness of one of America's ever-expanding cities. For visitors and employees alike these three new artworks of international significance combine to represent human experience.[168]

But Representative Edward R. Roybal, the seventy-five-year-old Democrat for whom the building was named and who was then chair of the House subcommittee that oversaw the GSA and its budget, objected vehemently to nude images in Otterness's sculpture and briefly had them removed before a compromise was reached with the artist.[169]

Clearly, a strategy of commissioning only figurative art was not the answer to avoiding controversy. Lanzone was learning on the job. He "coached" Otterness in the development of his sculpture; tried to direct Michael Heizer's project for a GSA commission in Long Beach, California; and allegedly, by interfering, caused the withdrawal of two artists selected to create art for a courthouse in Newark, New Jersey.

By 1993 Lanzone, sounding more like a seasoned public arts administrator, acknowledged that the fate of public art was unpredictable at best and that works were always vulnerable to a negative campaign by "one compulsive person" who might write to members of Congress and organize opposition. Although he was referring to a recent controversy over a sculpture by Luis Jimenez,[170] he might have been describing the saga of *Tilted Arc.*

In 1996 Dale Lanzone went to work for the Marlborough Gallery in New York as head of a new department on public art. The GSA Art-in-Architecture program was moved from the jurisdiction of the Arts and Historic Preservation Division under real estate policy to the Office of Portfolio Management in charge of asset management. Robert A. Peck, commissioner of the Public Buildings Services, a presidential appointee, initiated an extensive program review.[171] On October 15, 1996, GSA hosted a national workshop at the headquarters of the American Institute of Architects, where Peck had previously worked.

In September 1997 Peck announced the creation of the Historic Buildings and the Arts Center of Expertise under the direction of Rolando Rivas-Camp, consolidating three existing programs: the Art-in-Architecture program commissioning public art; the Fine Arts program managing GSA's entire collection of art, including nineteenth-century and WPA works; and the Historic Buildings program concerned with preservation policy, restoration, adaptive reuse issues, and the like.

The following year, revised program guidelines provided a new focus with roots in the past, "particularly during the first four decades of this century when artists and architects collaborated in the creation of lighting fixtures, gates, elevator doors and surrounds, as well as murals and sculptures." Lamenting that "such collaborations and architectural ornamentation were eliminated in post–World War II architectural design,"[172] the new guidelines sought a return to this architecture-based practice:

> The Art-in-Architecture Program strives for a holistic integration of art and architecture. Through a collaboration—from initial concept through construction—artist, architect, landscape architect, engineer lighting specialist, and practitioners of other disciplines can work as a team to create new expressions of the relationship between contemporary art and Federal architecture. By focusing the Art-in-Architecture Program in this manner, we will provide the American public with Federal buildings and courthouses that are pleasing and functional, but that will also enrich the cultural, social, and commercial resources of the community where they are located.[173]

These guidelines would in all likelihood have precluded the commissioning of *Titled Arc.*

Deaccessioning Public Art

The dangerous precedent most feared by *Tilted Arc*'s supporters was that its removal would lead to a wholesale destruction of public art.[174] It would seem that if nothing else, the fate of the sculpture would have prompted the development of an official policy to control the deaccessioning of public art, from the federal level on down.[175]

Before he left the NEA, Richard Andrews developed a procedure that required any work to be in place for ten years before it could be considered for removal and guaranteed input from art professionals for any decision involving "the quality of the work itself as representative of its style or genre, and its relation to the public context."[176] Either the sponsoring agency or the artist could request a review prompted by concerns over the safety of the public or the artwork, maintenance or condition problems, or changes in the site affecting the art.

Any review would include the artist and more than one independent professional who would consider contract issues as well as public participation in the debate.[177] If removal were deemed appropriate, a separate nonprofit organization would be asked to appoint a panel including representatives from the "visual arts (artists, curators, art historians, arts administrators); designers (architects, landscape architects, urban planners); and the broader community (preservationists, arts or public interest lawyers, social psychologists, policy analysts, community activists)." Only after exploring alternative measures would the panel consider relocation of the work or sale, loan, trade, or gift (based on professional appraisals); any resulting funds would be used for future public art projects.[178] The panel's recommendation would be final and binding, and the sponsoring agency would have to document the entire process.

The NEA submitted these guidelines to the GSA, but they were never approved. Instead, until 1998 the GSA worked under guidelines (never formally or officially approved) that included a review/deaccessioning policy that, like the commissioning process, could be controlled by a single individual at the agency. A minimum of five (rather than ten) years was necessary before review, unless "life safety risks, conservation, or preservation issues are involved." Proposals from regional administrators for removal required only "a background and issues statement, proposed action, and the advantages and disadvantages of the proposed action." The Arts and Historic Preservation Division of GSA would then submit a recommendation with "a summary of the issues; pros and cons of the proposed action; the regional proposal; and a recommendation to the Commissioner, Public Buildings Services." The final decision for or against removal would be up to the GSA administrator.[179]

In 2000 the *Fine Arts Program Desk Guide* included a chapter on relocation, removal, and deaccessioning of artworks. The section on relocation begins, "Adverse public opinion does not justify the relocation or removal of artwork." Similarly, the section on removal begins, "A work of art should not be removed simply because it is controversial or unpopular." Rather, any such action should be prompted by concerns about the safety of the artwork. Procedures stress working with the artist and include a reminder that art made after 1991 is covered by the Visual Artists Rights Act (VARA) of 1990 and that therefore any relocation requires the artist's written approval. In cases of dispute, a mediation process may be used: "Consideration for removal, relocation, or deaccessioning a work of art should involve the same degree of careful review as a decision to commission a work of art, informed by professional judgment and interests of the public, and proceeding according to set procedures." If relocation is determined, "For historical and financial reasons, artwork should be relocated as close as possible to its original location." Under these procedures the removal of *Tilted Arc* would have been highly unlikely, if not impossible.[180]

Nevertheless, many local agencies and programs, such as New York City's Art Commission, which must approve all permanent structures on city property, and the Department of Cultural Affairs' Percent-for-Art program, still have no deaccession policies at all. This curious lapse in public policy implies that public art commissions are still considered permanent and that the *Tilted Arc* case is viewed as an anomaly: It is discussed as an example of a situation to be avoided at all costs, but there are no institutional protections in place should a similar case occur.

At the time of this writing, deaccession policies are rare and the NEA no longer supports public art; and for nearly a decade after the removal of *Tilted Arc,* at the GSA, a single person could control both the selection and removal of a work of government-commissioned art. As Lanzone's experience showed, neither the selection process nor the judgment of the NEA panel alone could be blamed for the *Tilted Arc* controversy. Panels make questionable selections, and public art without institutional protection is, by virtue of its placement, vulnerable to all kinds of attacks.

Both the rise and decline of recent public support for art were products of Republican administrations. Like most policy shifts, they were directly related to the economy. In the only campaign statement he made on the arts, Reagan compared them to sports, which he thought did just fine without government subsidies (although stadium construction and repairs are routinely supported by public money, and their design is typically not open to public participation).[181] A working paper prepared by the conservative Heritage Foundation think tank considered it a given that the public audience for art was small. Reagan's appointee as head of the NEA, Frank Hodsoll, favored support for large, established cultural institutions rather than for individuals or community-based organizations. In New York City the Department of Cultural Affairs' budget was cut the same year that *Tilted Arc* was removed. Art policies throughout the Reagan years reflected far-reaching directives aimed at privatization and decentralization.[182] But to what extent did they reflect public opinion?

Public Art and the Legal System

As the process that commissioned *Tilted Arc* was unraveling through various bureaucratic maneuvers in New York and Washington, Richard Serra sought legal means to protect his sculpture, but as John J. Costonis observed, "Aesthetics and law are an odd couple, rather like spouses who come to their union from different worlds. . . . Aspirational and abstract, aesthetics and law are elusive in themselves and mercurial when joined together."[183] Serra argued initially on First and Fifth Amendment grounds[184] and then invoked the recently signed Berne Convention. Ultimately, however, the outcome was determined by a vaguely worded article in the GSA contract.

Serra was not the first artist to resort to legal remedies in conflicts with federal patrons. Nor was his the first publicly commissioned work to be removed from its intended site.[185] Serra's first lawsuit in December 1986 named GSA administrators Diamond and Ink and alleged that the GSA's decision to remove *Tilted Arc* violated his rights under the free speech clause of the First Amendment, the due process clause of the Fifth Amendment, federal trademark and copyright laws, and state law.[186]

The United States District Court for the Southern District of New York (Milton Pollock, judge) issued two opinions, both in favor of the defendants. The first dismissed Serra's claims against Diamond and Ink on the grounds that they had qualified immunity as federal employees because they represented the government (which has sovereign immunity) and that they had not acted beyond their granted authority or in an unconstitutional way.[187] Serra did not appeal this decision.

In a second opinion, the district court granted summary judgment (a decision on legal grounds, accepting all facts pleaded by Serra as being true) against the sculptor based on the premise that GSA actions were not based on the content of the sculpture. Judge Pollock ruled that the decision to relocate the sculpture was "a content-neutral determination made to further significant government interests and that the hearing provided all the process that was due."[188]

Serra appealed this decision, challenging the rejection of his free expression and due process claims.[189] The appellate court, presided over by a three-judge panel that included a former counsel to the Museum of Modern Art, upheld the lower court's summary judgment.[190] It concluded that Serra's First Amendment rights were not violated. Though assuming that *Tilted Arc* was expression "protected to some extent" by the First Amendment, the court ruled that "Serra relinquished his own speech rights in the sculpture when he voluntarily sold it to GSA; if he wished to retain some degree of control as to the duration and location of the display of his work, he had the opportunity to bargain for such rights in making the contract for sale of his work."[191]

The reference to the GSA contract raised a murky issue. It was always understood by Serra and representatives of the Art-in-Architecture program that he was being commissioned for a permanent piece. As Serra recalled at Diamond's hearing, he had been assured early in the project by Thalacker, director of the program, that "you get one chance in your lifetime to build one permanent work for one Federal building. There is one permanent Oldenburg, one permanent Segal, one permanent Stella, and one permanent Calder, and this is your opportunity to build a permanent work for a federal site in America." For Serra, "The inducement was permanency. The GSA policy was, and still is, to build permanent works by nationally recognized artists for federal sites. That was their promise to me, and that pledge has been made to upwards of 250 artists in the United States."[192] Serra's view of the commission was confirmed by Julia Brown, project manager for the Art-in-Architecture program.[193]

Article 6 of Serra's contract with the GSA, entitled "Ownership," stated,

> All designs, sketches, models, and the work produced under this Agreement for which payment is made under the provisions of this contract shall be the property of the United States of America. All such items may be conveyed by the Contracting Officer to the National Collection of Fine Arts–Smithsonian Institution for exhibiting purposes and permanent safekeeping.[194]

According to Thalacker, the word "work" had been inadvertently included in the contract. This clause was intended to ensure the conservation of preparatory studies, since the GSA did not have adequate storage space, and to provide safekeeping for portable artworks in times of national emergency. But the wording was vague. The contract did not specifically grant the government the right to remove a commissioned sculpture, nor did the contract specifically forbid the removal of such a sculpture. Serra lost the contract argument. Although he had been given verbal assurance that this was a permanent commission and that removal would be a violation of contract, the court ruled that he had, in the contract, relinquished his right to control the piece.[195]

In its own way, the appellate decision was as vague as the contract when it came to Serra's First Amendment rights. At one point the court posited, "Even assuming that Serra retains some First Amendment interest in the continued display of *Tilted Arc* . . . ," but the nature of that interest was never defined.

Instead, the court upheld a "time, place, and manner restriction" that applied to situations where content was not being suppressed, the government had a significant stake, and other channels of communication still existed. Relocating the sculpture, it was argued, met these requirements. GSA had an interest in keeping the plaza "unobstructed," and Serra had already had six years to convey his message in the plaza. Since the First Amendment "protects the freedom to express one's views, not the freedom to continue speaking forever," relocation of *Tilted Arc* at this point did not "significantly impair Serra's right to free speech." He could still exercise his right to free expression in other ways: "Notwithstanding that the sculpture is site-specific and may lose its artistic value if relocated, Serra is free to express his artistic and political views through the press and through other means that do not entail obstructing the Plaza."[196]

This opinion, however, ignored the specific nature of the commission and the fact that Serra's medium of communication is sculpture, not the press. If one accepts the premise that the site is part of the work's content, then moving it is altering it (and therefore changing its meaning). It would be unthinkable, say, to change the color of a painting or to transform the content of a written work similarly.[197] Serra's claim (Article 211) compared it to "governmental destruction or tampering with the sole copy of an author's manuscript for reasons of its content."[198]

The issue of whether this decision was "impermissibly content-based" involved the court in a discussion of the content of abstract art. In all official communications, GSA officials stated (as they had been instructed on advice of counsel) that their decision was based only on the obstruction of the plaza. Thus the appellate court decided:

> Serra is unable to identify any particular message conveyed by *Tilted Arc* that he believes may have led to its removal. In view of the uncertainty as to the meaning of *Tilted Arc* and in the face of the overwhelming evidence that it was removed solely because of its obstructive effect on the Plaza, Serra has failed to present any facts to support a claim that Government officials acted in a "narrowly partisan or political manner."[199]

But even if the GSA decision were based on a judgment of aesthetic merit (as several of the petitions in fact stated), that was also permissible, according to precedent. This ruling suggests that abstract art is considerably more at risk in the legal system than is art with recognizable subject matter.

The court's finding, as Barbara Hoffman argued, was substantially based on the premise that "the idea can be divorced from its manner of expression." For an artist, especially an abstract artist, the medium and the message are essentially one and the same. As Hoffman put it:

> The "sheer size of the sculpture" was a part of its message. . . . Moreover, there was no evidence that the sculpture prevented the social use of the plaza in any way. Serra was entitled to a trial on that issue. The court demonstrated an improper deference to the political aim of the GSA in allowing its taste claim to override Serra's artistic expression and the professional advice of its Art-in-Architecture Program's administrators and art experts.[200]

The court considered the government's rights as patron and owner paramount, incorporated in GSA's mandate to manage federal property. Art is property, and the government owns it. Property rights apply to all art ownership, not just the government's, but the government as custodian for the entire public has moral and ethical obligations that were ignored by making this primarily a property issue. It could be argued that the public's right to the material outweighed government ownership.[201]

As far as due process was concerned, the court held that even if Diamond prejudged the issue before he called the public hearing (as he demonstrably did by sending out inquiries for alternative sites for the sculpture), "without a protected property or liberty interest, Serra was not constitutionally entitled to a hearing before the sculpture could be removed. . . . Even if Diamond was not entirely impartial, Serra received more process than what was due." By dismissing the hearing, the court never directly addressed the improprieties surrounding this central element of the controversy and its subsequent impact on the outcome and public opinion.

Since Ink was not charged with partiality and he reviewed the entire case, the court decided that "the effect of Diamond's prejudgment, if any, was marginal." The court concluded that since Serra was given the opportunity to defend his position before both Diamond and Ink, "any due process requirement that might have arisen in the context of this case was clearly satisfied."[202] But Diamond lied throughout the process, and Ink knew it.

There were many vagaries and arguable assumptions in the appellate court's decision. The law, in rather alarming ways, mirrors national cultural perspectives. Currently, First and Fifth Amendment law seems to protect verbal and written forms of expression far more stringently than it protects visual forms, a clear reflection of widely held values. Even if one sees the Serra case only as a contract issue, the status of works of art under the law are far from clear or definitive. This reflects a highly ambivalent attitude toward art, especially abstract art.

Artists' Rights in Europe

Late in the legal battle to save *Tilted Arc,* Serra tried to invoke the Berne Convention, first signed in Switzerland more than a century ago, on September 9, 1886. Revised a number of times over the years, the current version dates from 1971 and has been signed by seventy-eight countries in Europe and elsewhere. Serra repeatedly called for U.S. ratification. A significant part of this doctrine protects the right to artistic integrity or *droit moral* (moral rights).

Specifically, moral rights laws extend the artist's control over a work of art after it has been sold. It maintains the artist's right "to object to any distortion, mutilation, or other modification of, or other derogatory action in relation to the work."[203] Controlling the integrity of the artwork protects the artist's reputation.

To date, eleven states, including New York, have passed legislation that includes moral rights provisions,[204] but the absence of national legislation left *Tilted Arc* unprotected because it was commissioned by the federal government. The United States incorporated a limited version of the Berne Convention providing protection for American publishing companies into copyright law on March 1, 1989, another example of the greater protection granted to written expression.[205]

Even the passage of the VARA of 1990, introduced by Senator Edward Kennedy (D.–Mass.), would not have helped Serra. Combining elements of both California and New York statutes, it sought "to prevent any intentional distortion, mutilation, or other modification of [a] work which would be prejudicial to [the artist's] honor or reputation" and "to prevent any destruction of a work of recognized stature, and any intentional or grossly negligent destruction of that work."[206] But "VARA applies only to a restricted category of visual artworks, extends only limited rights, and is subject to loopholes, exclusions, and waiver provisions that substantially erode its powers."[207] The issue of distortion or mutilation of site-specific works is complicated. And public art that takes a functional form (seating, lighting, bridges, etc.) is not easily classified as art and is therefore not clearly protected.

A continuing part of the problem of resolving artists' rights in the courts stems, as Serra and many others have argued, from this country's strong emphasis on property rights. Art is seen only as a special kind of property. This premise prevailed throughout the Serra rulings, as well as in the limited acceptance of the Berne Convention. Laws both reflect public values and influence them. It is unlikely that the United States will adopt moral rights fully anytime in the foreseeable future.

The Legal Profession and Change

Clearly, public art runs a risk in entering the legal system. Barbara Hoffman criticized contemporary legal doctrine for "its failure to accommodate or even adequately define the issues and competing values at stake in the public art context." She attributed this failure "in part to the fact that neither legal theory nor art policy have been inspired by the vision of or located in the broader context of a sociopolitical public realm." The courts may also be a perilous place to decide matters pertaining to art for a more basic reason. As John Costonis observed, legal aesthetics are problematic because of the "absence of a consensus on beauty's canons and nonverifiability of their objective character; time as a relativizer of taste; vagaries of cultural diversity and of perceptual response; and the exuberance of artistic creativity, which refuses to be immobilized by the rules or traditions of received styles."[208]

As the Serra case made its way through the courts, it became apparent that judges were forming opinions based on two antithetical principles: legal precedent and the aesthetics of contemporary art. The legal system is structured on precedent. Judicial opinions are based on previous cases that invoke issues that are similar or analogous to the one they are hearing. Thus a court's rationale for a precedent-setting opinion will explain it as evolutionary rather than revolutionary.[209]

A central premise of modern art, however, has been change, the more radical the better. One of the tenets of modernism in general is that history is not a useful model and cannot be seen as a continuous, rationally explicable progression.[210] It is no exaggeration to say that the history of modern art has been seen primarily as a history of change and overthrow, with each successive "ism" (cubism, futurism, expressionism, constructivism, etc.) replacing its predecessor with a new definition of what art is and should be.[211] One of the most scathing criticisms one could level at this constantly new art was that it was in some way derivative.

In more recent decades, with the acknowledged demise of the avant-garde,[212] change per se is no longer a prerequisite of serious art, but newness is still considered an admirable quality. In contemporary art the emphasis on new formal qualities has been replaced by an insistence on the inclusion of new subject matter, be it specific (images pertaining to previously unrepresented groups based on race, ethnicity, gender, and sexual preference) or analytic (such as a psychoanalytic or deconstructionist approach to signs and symbols). At Diamond's hearing, many recognized that the newness of contemporary art might be the problem and stressed that this newness was also part of its content and function.

Serra, as discussed above, is essentially a modernist. His intention, as manifested in his 1967–68 *Verb List,* was to redefine sculpture in terms of sculptural acts and processes that might be brought to bear on any number of materials, most of them nontraditional. His extensive use of steel merges a material of the modern industrial age with formalist concerns of a modernist esthetic. Serra's (re)definition of sculpture was, in fact, without precedent. Thus modern art in general, and perhaps Serra's work in particular, may be especially provocative, if not antithetical, to legal minds professionally set in precedent and tradition, functioning daily as antagonists in arenas of opposition.

Ideally, all art styles should be equally protected by the legal system, but we have already seen that abstract works (key to the modern movement) are particularly vulnerable. Clearly, not all members of the legal profession are insensitive to modern art. However, given the nature of legal training and practice, it is not surprising that so many lawyers and judges so often find works of modern art threatening.

The first objections to *Tilted Arc* came from a judge, and at Diamond's hearing judges were among its most passionate detractors. The recent history of public art shows that complaints, if not antagonism, from lawyers and judges has been especially vociferous. This may partially be explained because federal buildings often house their offices and because they are used to making their opinions heard. Nevertheless, it is worth exploring further whether the legal mind-set, accustomed to finding validation in precedent, is not in some basic way antithetical to a reasoned consideration of issues pertaining to new and controversial art.

4. After *Tilted Arc*

The ripple effect of the *Tilted Arc* controversy was great. By the time I became director of New York City's Percent for Art Program in 1990, there had been a reevaluation of public art in the United States. Administrators all over the country revised their procedures for commissioning. "Safeguards" were put in place to avoid the excruciating public display everyone heard about in New York City.

—Tom Finkelpearl

The impact of Diamond's hearing was immediate, a harbinger of things to come. Pending the results, GSA regional directors reportedly put works of art on hold.[1] In an action similar to Diamond's, the GSA regional director in Atlanta offered the city's Lloyd Hamrol sculpture to the High Museum. The museum refused "as a matter of principle."

Without consulting the State Arts Council, Alaska's Governor William Sheffield had Robert Murray's *Nimbus* (1978) removed from the front of the Juneau courthouse and placed indefinitely in storage. The sculpture, partially funded by the NEA Art in Public places program, had been in dispute for some time.

In August 1985, nearly six months after Diamond's hearing, the removal of Serra's *Twain* (1974–82) in St. Louis (Figure 42) was almost put to popular vote.[2] Although *Art in America* reported this incident under the headline, "Another Serra under Attack,"[3] the president of the St. Louis Board of Aldermen identified money and land development as the real issues behind objections to the sculpture.[4] Ultimately the plebescite to "recall" *Twain* was not issued, and the sculpture still stands.[5]

Diamond's hearing also had a direct impact on Serra's retrospective at MoMA in 1986. Scheduled to create a work for Doris Freedman Plaza at the entrance to Central Park at Sixtieth Street, a site used for temporary displays by the Public Art Fund, the artist created a model and raised the funds for a six-month installation. However, Parks Department Commissioner Henry J. Stern turned him down. Influenced by the controversy over *Tilted Arc* and Serra's remarks at the hearing, Stern expressed concern

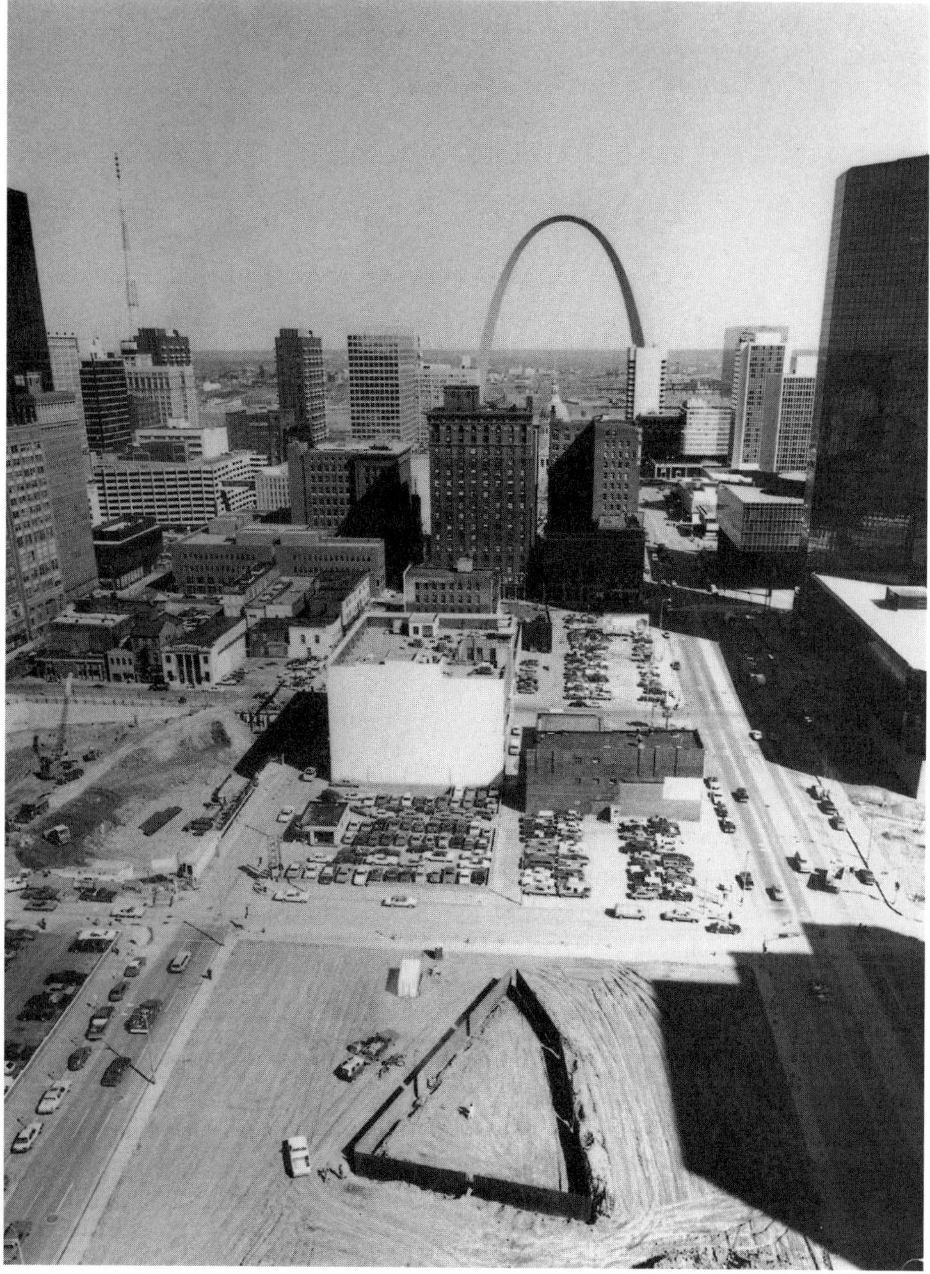

Figure 42. Richard Serra, *Twain,* 1974–82, St. Louis, Missouri. Courtesy of Richard Serra.

that the sculptor might want to keep his work at Doris Freedman Plaza and threaten to sue the city at the scheduled time of removal. Although Stern said he liked the sculpture at Federal Plaza and would be happy to find a site for it in a city park, he did not like Serra's proposed *New York, New York.*[6] Apparently without the controversy as publicized by the hearing, this sculpture would have become part of Serra's retrospective as originally planned.

Although the aftereffects of the sculpture's removal have not been as dramatic as many feared, its influence has been pervasive. While Serra has gone on making public art, primarily in Europe, the controversy has been historicized to illustrate various narratives. Sometimes seen as part of the censorship that characterized the culture wars of the later 1980s and 1990s or as a separate, isolated incident, the controversy was replayed, codifying the themes that emerged at Diamond's hearing rather than the more nuanced issues raised in some of the critical commentary (discussed in chapter 2).

Richard Serra after *Tilted Arc*

> He is unlikely to weather gracefully, like Cor-Ten steel, and it would be a shame if he did. There is a sector of artistic experience that he dominates and keeps from becoming frivolous; he is engaged in returning us to artistic forces the centuries have succeeded in repressing.
>
> **—Arthur Danto**

Although Serra threatened more than once to leave the country permanently if *Tilted Arc* were destroyed, he has not. His subsequent public commissions diverged remarkably both from the sculpture at Federal Plaza and his rhetoric during the controversy. He created at least one piece that included seating, made works for a number of corporate clients, and increasingly worked in sites with religious content. And some of his recent works, among the largest of his career, offer a more inviting, even sheltering experience.

Sculpture Plus Seating

Following the installation of *Tilted Arc,* Serra created *La Palmera* (1982–84) for Barcelona, his only public work that included utilitarian features (Figures 43, 44). Commissioned as part of a larger public sculpture program coinciding with the 1992 Olympic Games, the piece was located in a residential area defined by nondescript modern buildings. Working with the architects, Serra created two curved walls punctuated by an asymmetrically placed palm tree. He also designed a stairway to provide seating. A decade later he considered *La Palmera* successful functionally but not necessarily successful as art.[7]

A Movable Sculpture

Clara-Clara (1983), created by Serra to accompany his retrospective at the Centre Georges Pompidou in Paris, has occupied a number of different sites. After it proved too heavy for its intended location outside the museum, director Dominique Bozo suggested placing the two-part sculpture in the Jardin des Tuileries, visually framing the Egyptian obelisk on the Place de la Concorde. The siting was dramatic (Figure 45), and local response was highly enthusiastic.[8] Serra noted,

> Between five and seven on a Saturday or Sunday literally hundreds of people walk through this entrance. The piece has functioned in terms of its relation to people in a way that other pieces haven't in that people actually do walk through it, they

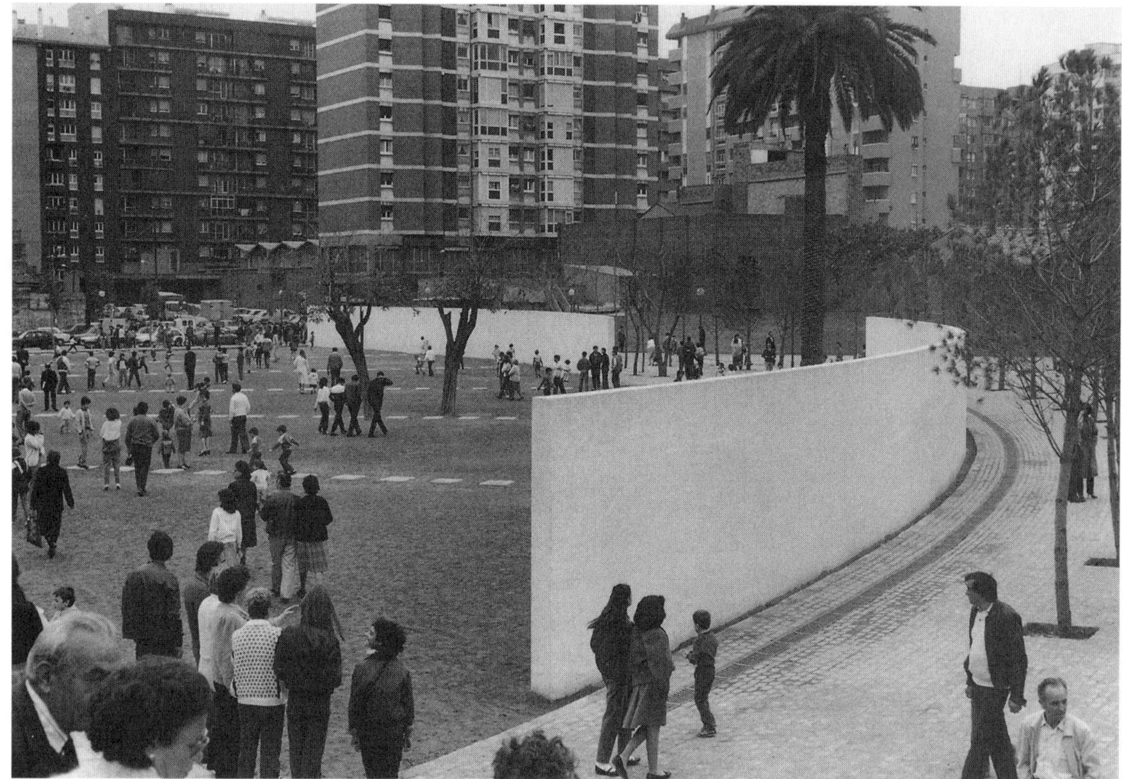

Figure 43. Richard Serra, *La Palmera,* 1982–84, Barcelona, Spain. Photograph by La Verneda, Barcelona; courtesy of Richard Serra.

> photograph it, they walk around it. Sons argue with fathers about whether it's a cone or not. People take a lot of consideration in dealing with the piece. I've met policemen who were ex-steelworkers; I've met nautical engineers; I've met a whole range of people who come and discuss the piece. That openness towards the piece, that tolerance, that inquisitiveness, is something that I've never experienced anywhere.[9]

After the Pompidou exhibition, the sculpture was purchased for the city. Responding to strong requests from the local mayor, Serra agreed to its resiting in the working-class residential neighborhood near the Square de Choisy (Figure 46). Although the sculpture was vandalized with graffiti, much to the mayor's distress, it remained there until 1996, when local dissatisfaction and an upcoming election led to its removal. Today it awaits a new site, subject to Serra's approval.[10]

Corporate Contexts

Corporate spaces, it would seem, would have been as ideologically problematic for Serra as government-defined sites. Yet the year *Tilted Arc* was removed, he installed *Fin* (1989) in the lobby of the North American headquarters of the Swiss Bank

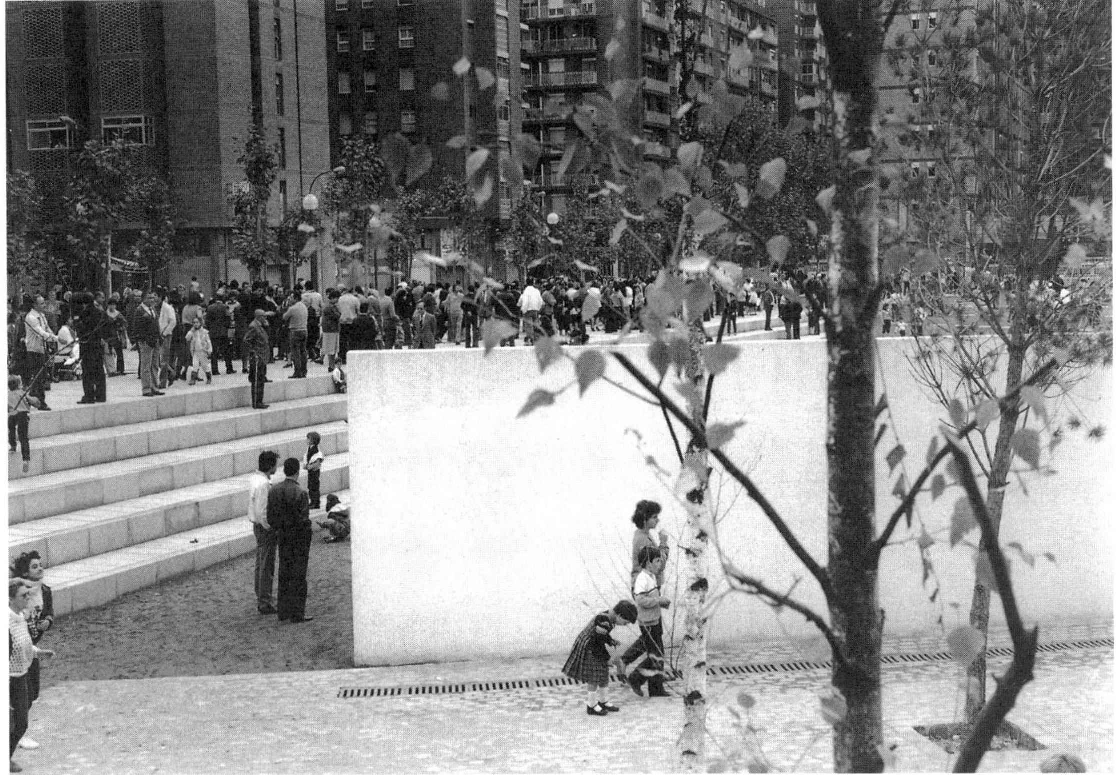

Figure 44. Richard Serra, *La Palmera* (detail), 1982–84, Barcelona, Spain. Photograph by La Verneda, Barcelona; courtesy of Richard Serra.

Corporation, located in a midtown Manhattan tower above Saks Fifth Avenue (Figure 47). The space was already defined by a row of windows facing Fiftieth Street, an elevator bank, a reception desk, and a previously designed wall with a rocky waterfall, but Serra accommodated its physical properties and use:

> It is my intention to place a sculpture in this room which augments the existing architectural character. The sculpture which has been conceived for the space is derived from the conditions and architectural measure of the space. The placement of the sculpture is based on the utility of the room, i.e., the room will remain open and accessible, allowing for an easy flow of pedestrian movement from the fountain and into the adjoining hallways and meeting areas.[11]

Serra described the welcoming gesture of the sculpture in symbolic terms, something he adamantly refused to do with *Tilted Arc:* "One has only to think of the embrace of open arms, the protective curve of a harbor or the inward expansiveness of a cave to visualize the expression and symbolism of this form."

Fin is part of an elegant corporate setting, both affirming the power of the bank and subtly redefining the place of business as a cultural space. At one end, the sculpture

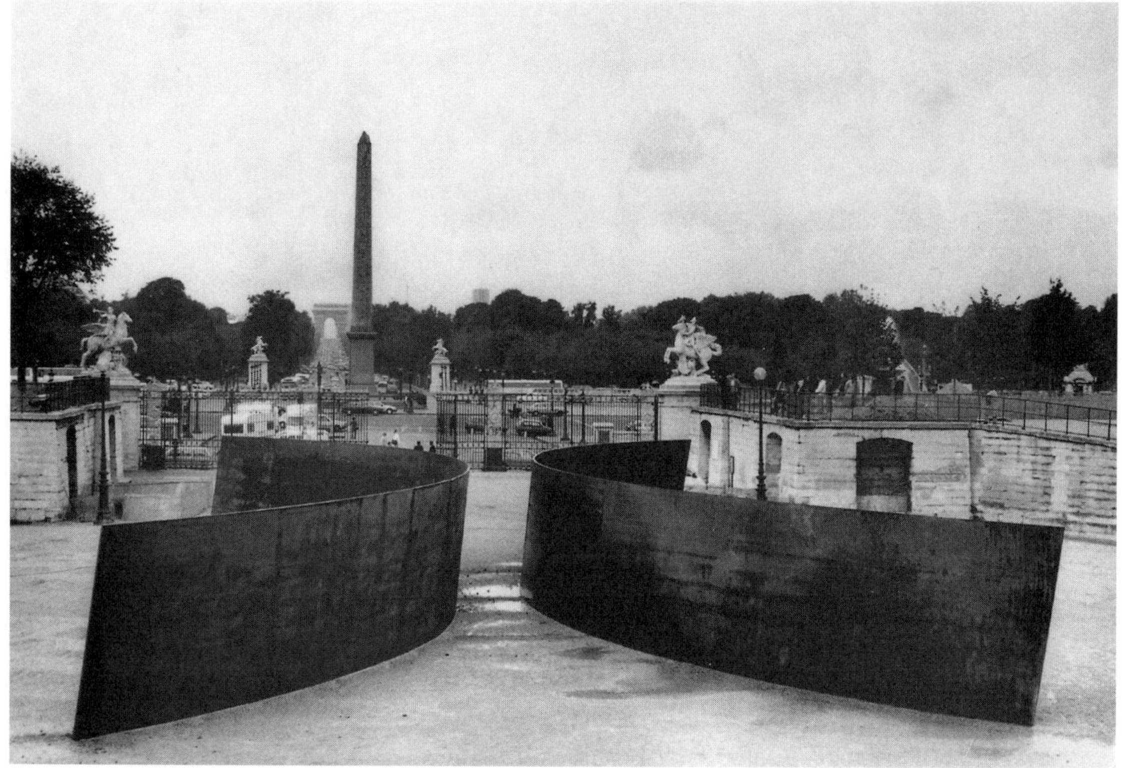

Figure 45. Richard Serra, *Clara, Clara,* 1983, Jardin des Tuileries, Paris. Photograph by Dirk Reinartz, Buxtehude; courtesy of Richard Serra.

is so close to the waterfall that visitors often perceive the entire lobby as a single piece. And in a sense it is.

Just as *Fin* enhances its corporate site, so does Serra's outdoor piece *Core* (1986) at General Mills. (Figure 48).[12] The corporate site implicitly changes the content of the piece, and it remains the responsibility of the viewer to filter out the disguising or advertising impact of the art.[13]

Religious Sites

In 1983 Serra stated that he did not think he would ever make a sculpture for a synagogue and questioned chapels by Mark Rothko in Houston and Henri Matisse in Vence.[14] Nevertheless, he subsequently accepted a number of commissions for definitively spiritual or religious sites, explaining the religious aspect as "coincidences and circumstances of the projects that were offered."[15]

In 1985 Serra created *Margeurite and Philibert* for the Cathedral in Brou, France. An interior piece consisting of two square blocks, it anchored the corners and defined the axes of the large cloister.[16] At Brou, unlike in the Yale Art Gallery where Serra later created a similar piece, the visual parameters were defined solely by the architecture.

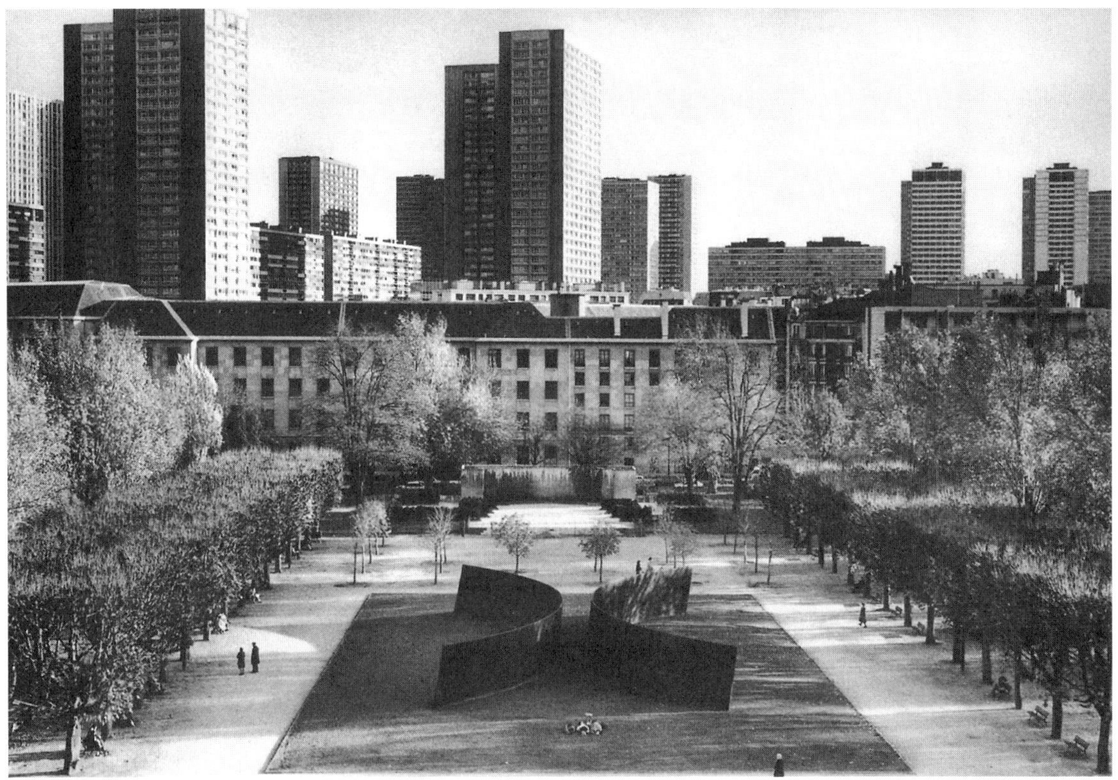

Figure 46. Richard Serra, *Clara, Clara,* 1983, Square de Choisy, Paris. Photograph by Adam Rzepka; courtesy of Richard Serra.

In 1989, the year *Tilted Arc* was dismantled, Serra accepted a commission for a site in front of the Romanesque church in Chagny, Burgundy. Installed two years later, *Octagon for Saint Eloi* (Figure 49) was the subject of numerous articles as well as a book.[17] The fifty-five-ton forged sculpture dedicated to Eloi, patron saint of iron workers, blacksmiths, and goldsmiths, is located in the town square on the axis of St. Martin's church. It is the same distance from the church door as the door is from the chancel. Its octagonal shape was suggested by the columns in Romanesque churches. Eight, one greater than the number of days it took to create the world, implies infinity and in a Christian context, "the abstract symbol of the resurrection announced by baptism."[18]

Since Serra accepted the commission in Chagny and chose the site, one may question his earlier insistence that only the physical properties of the site concern him and that other readings are irrelevant or act as a co-opting influence on art. Certainly, his commission for the Holocaust Museum in Washington, D.C., provided a highly personal context.[19]

Serra's *Gravity* (1991, Figure 22), embedded in the concourse stairs, was intended to force the viewer to choose one path over another. Today, as a result of crowd considerations, all museum tours start at the foot of the stairs next to the sculpture. Serra

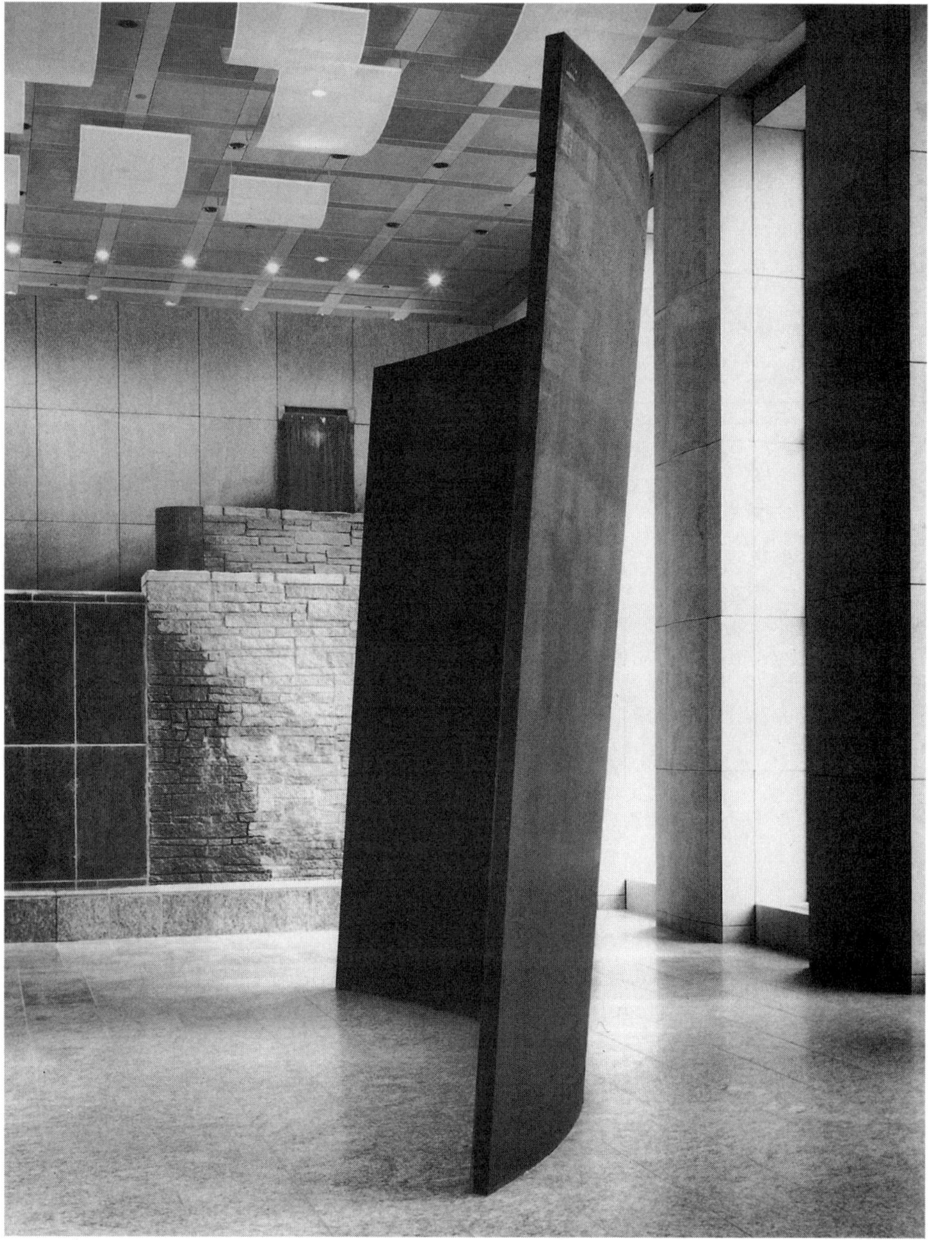

Figure 47. Richard Serra, *Fin,* 1989, Swiss Bank, New York City. Courtesy of Richard Serra.

made art for a Holocaust context again the following year when he created *The Drowned and the Saved* (1992) for an exhibition entitled *Synagogue Stommeln* (Figure 20), marking the temples destroyed during World War II. It was this commission that prompted his first public statement about his repressed Jewish identity (discussed in chapter 3 in the section "A New Interpretation"). By 1993 he talked of dealing with each site in terms of its "physical and psychological content."[20]

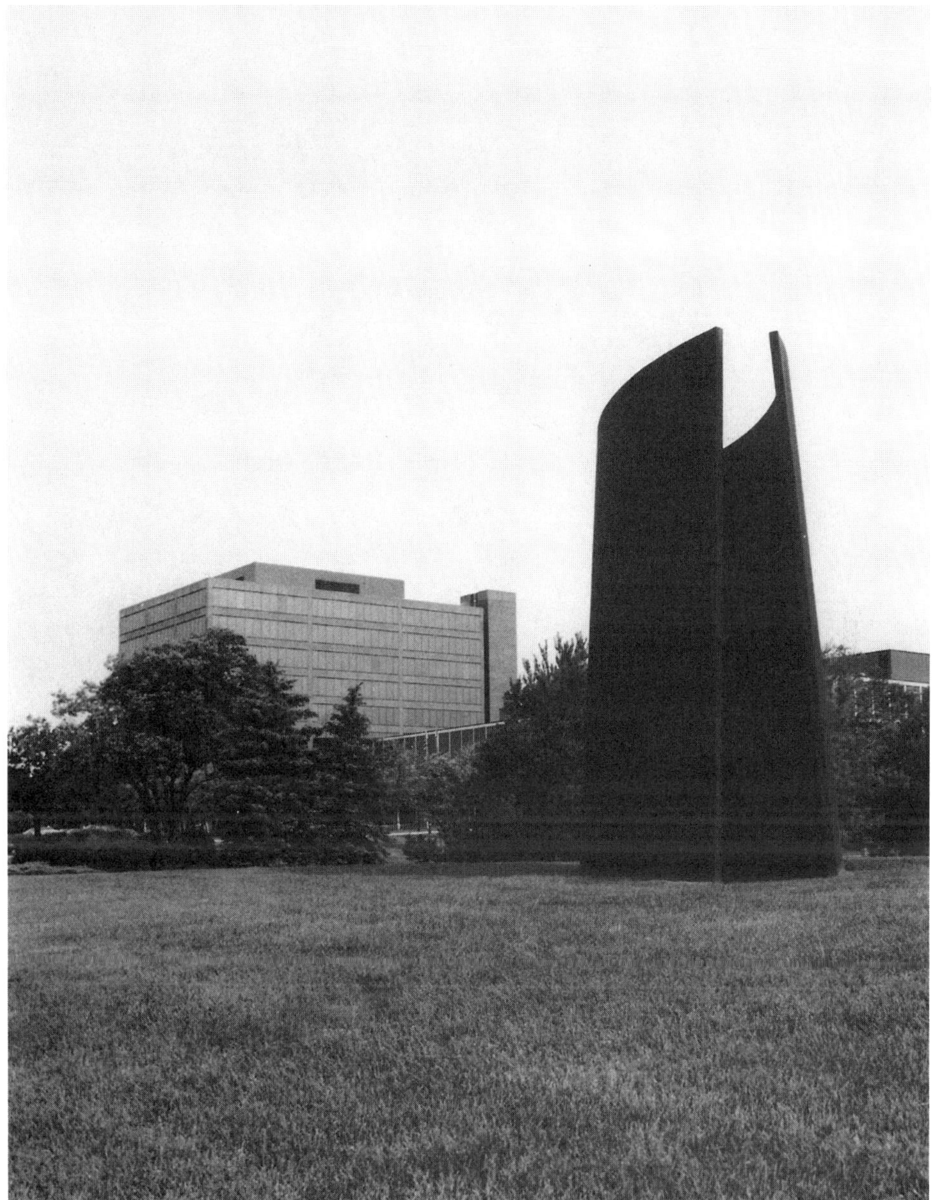

Figure 48. Richard Serra, *Core,* 1986, General Mills, Minneapolis, Minnesota. Courtesy of General Mills.

A New Direction

Concurrent with the Pulheim synagogue exhibition in the summer of 1992, *Intersection* (Figures 50, 51) was installed on the Theaterplatz in Basel as part of the *Transform* exhibition at the Kunstmuseum and Kunsthalle. The work's four curved walls created a variety of mysterious but evidently nonthreatening spaces. People walked through it, checked for echoes, read the graffiti that had already appeared, and kissed. A young man, who had no idea that it was a sculpture and had never heard of

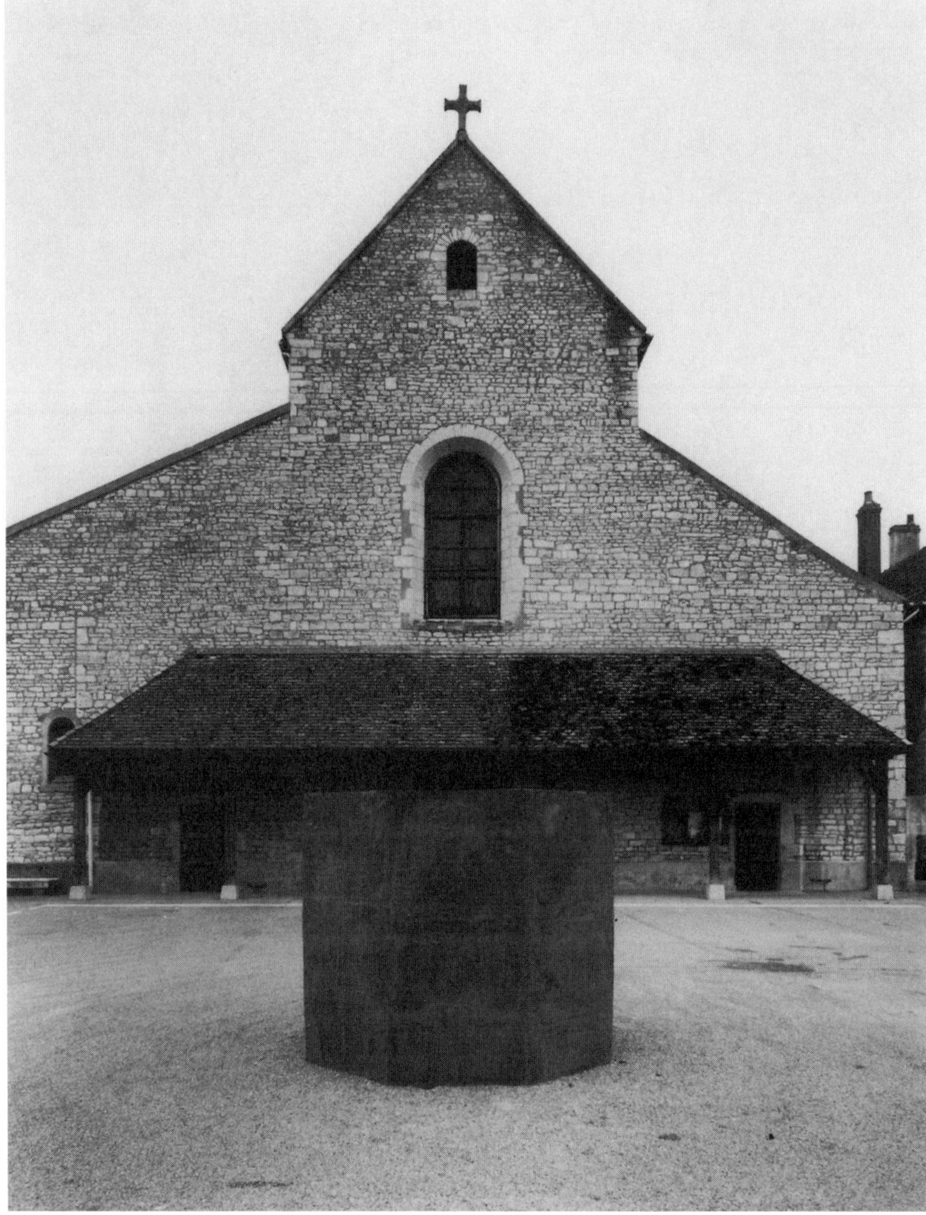

Figure 49. Richard Serra, *Octagon for Saint Eloi,* 1991, Chagny, France. Photograph by Jacques Hoepffner, Paris; courtesy of Richard Serra.

Serra, sat down in its midst to play his recorder, and what appeared to be an ad hoc dance performance by four women took place on a Saturday morning. Even the theater's architect liked it and wanted it to stay. Shortly after its installation, a local committee was formed to purchase the sculpture for the site.[21]

When *Intersection II* was displayed at the Soho branch of the Gagosian Gallery in

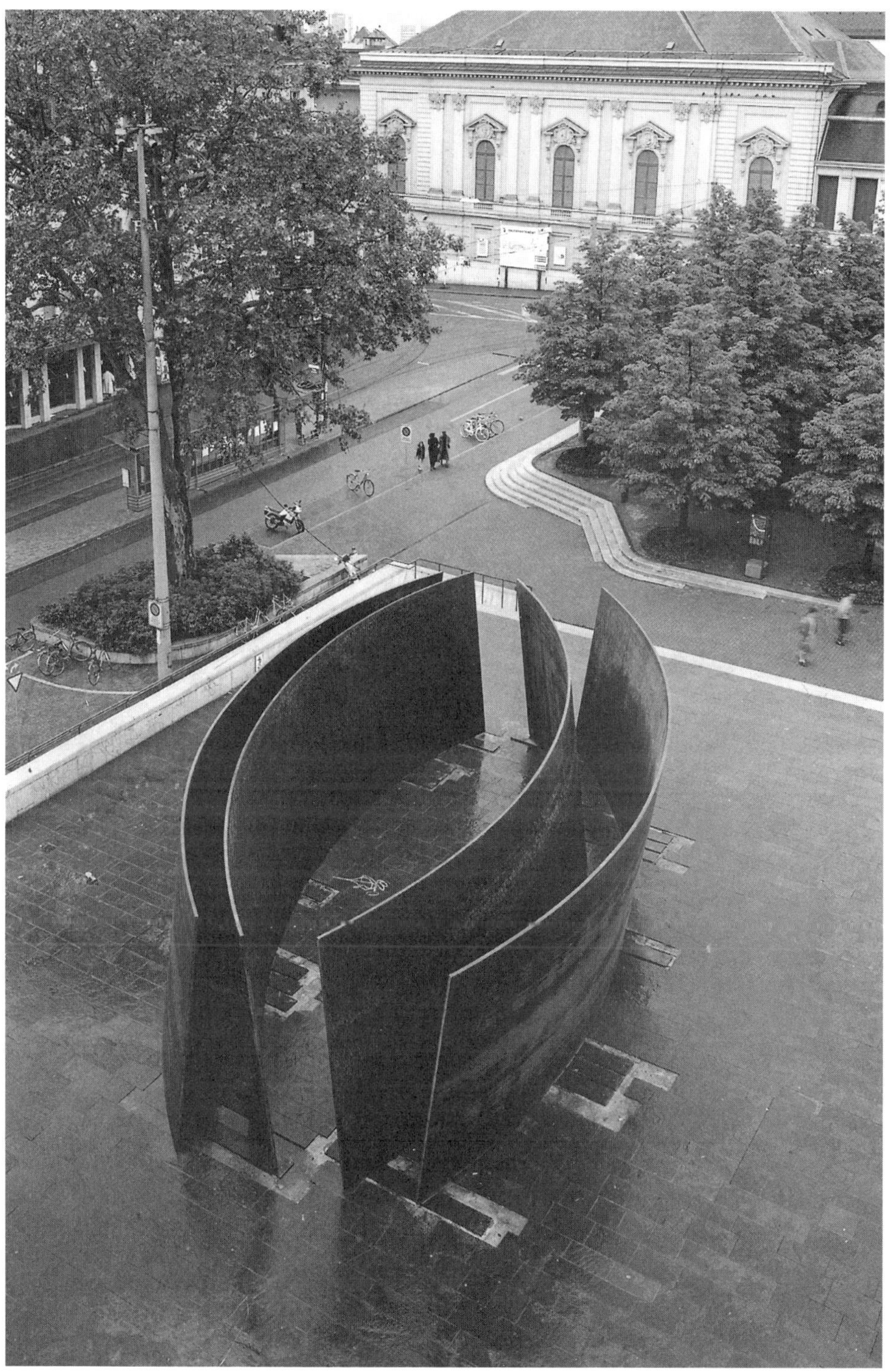

Figure 50. Richard Serra, *Intersection,* 1992, Theaterplatz, Basel, Switzerland. Photograph by Werner J. Hannappel, Essen; courtesy of Richard Serra.

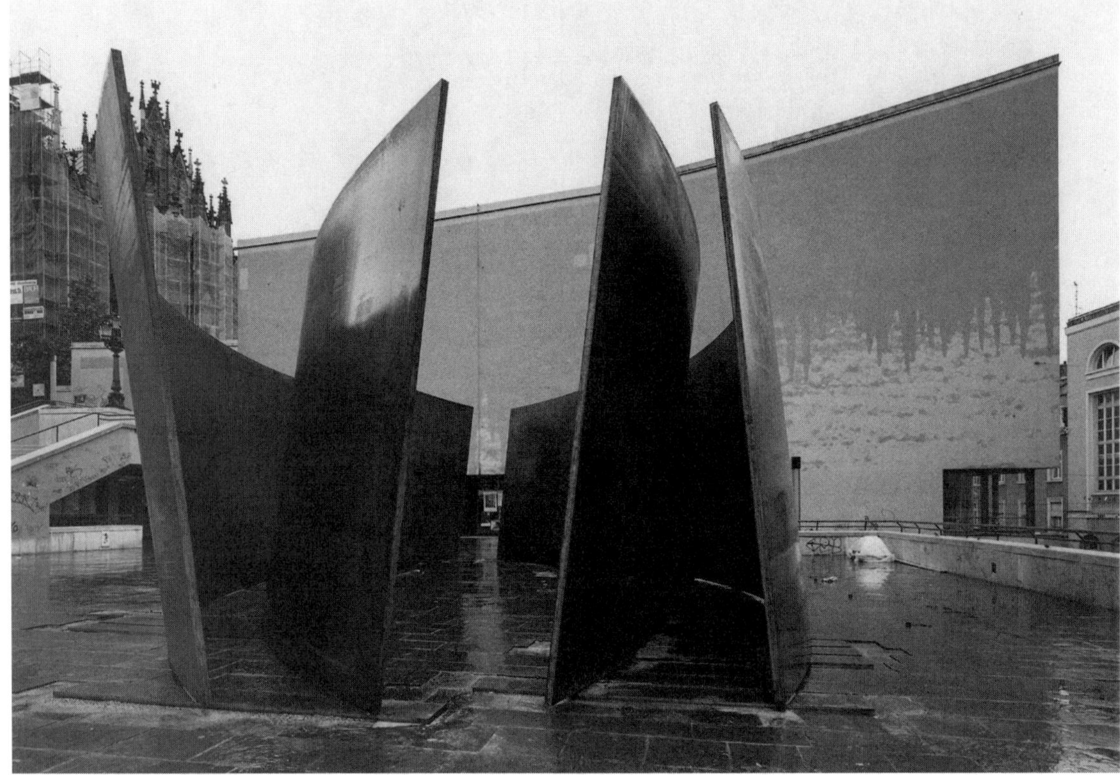

Figure 51. Richard Serra, *Intersection,* 1992, Theaterplatz, Basel, Switzerland. Photograph by Werner J. Hannappel, Essen; courtesy of Richard Serra.

New York in 1993, the year after *Intersection* was installed in Basel, it was reviewed ecstatically by *New York Times* critic Roberta Smith.[22] Hailing the piece as "one of the greatest works of abstract sculpture that New York City has seen in some time," and a monument "to the capacities of human perception," Smith invoked Greek temples, Gothic cathedrals, and Egyptian pyramids. It read like an apotheosis of the artist.

Like its predecessor in Basel, *Intersection II* suggested a new direction for Serra. Sacrificing none of its power, the work now extended an inviting gesture toward its audience. After Ronald Lauder purchased it for the Museum of Modern Art, an off-site location was sought, one that, according to the museum's president, Agnes Gund, "won't be just an extension of the museum but a reinvention."[23]

In subsequent years Serra went on to create entirely new sculptural forms, the torqued ellipses, and continued to garner widespread art-world acclaim. In 1998 the Los Angeles Museum of Contemporary Art mounted a retrospective based on his work since 1985,[24] the point where the Museum of Modern Art exhibition had stopped and the year of Diamond's hearing.

As the controversy recedes into history, it is obvious that *Tilted Arc,* far from an entry point into Serra's work, was not even typical of it. It remained his only single-wall sculpture in a publicly used site not specifically defined as an art space by a museum or cultural institution. As such, it was more vulnerable to nonart comparisons, such as to the Berlin Wall. Works that consist of two or more walls, no matter what form, are immediately perceived as art and create their own space. In that sense, they are somewhat less dependent on their site. Today, *Tilted Arc* may more usefully be seen as one statement in the complex and nuanced evolution of one of the most important sculptors of the twentieth century.

Tilted Arc and the Culture Wars

A scant three months after *Tilted Arc* was removed, Patrick R. Buchanan wrote an article entitled "In the New Kulterkampf, the First Battles Are Being Fought."[25] The implicit "old" culture war refers to Bismarck's late-nineteenth-century attempt to unify Germany and his struggle with conflicting attempts by religious and political leaders to control the content of public education. The contemporary culture wars framed a conservative attack against art that appeared to subvert "traditional values" or "community standards" of patriotism, heterosexuality, and religion.

In May 1989 the School of the Art Institute of Chicago exhibited graduate student "Dread" Scott Tyler's installation *What Is the Proper Way to Display the U.S. Flag?* A ledger for comments was placed elbow-high on the wall; above the ledger was a photomontage of coffins covered by flags being burned by South Koreans. On the floor, leading up to the display, was an American flag, apparently inviting the viewer to step on it to look more closely at the image or write comments in the book.

Tyler's installation prompted an immediate outcry from local politicians and a media field day. It was seen, according to the dean of the school, Carol Becker, as "a symbol of true violence to the American way of life."[26] The artist too was deliberately provocative: He dressed in a Che Guevara beret, a T-shirt with a portrait of Mao, and a Palestinian scarf. Identifying himself as a member of the Revolutionary Communist Party, he compared the brouhaha over the flag to the Nazi worship of the swastika. According to Becker, the controversy aroused more public hysteria than "inner-city crime, crack, homelessness, racism, toxic waste, [and] cutbacks in public education." The same could have been said about *Tilted Arc.*

This reaction to a graduate student's exhibition, something that rarely attracts attendance let alone the media, occurred nine months after objections to another student work, David Nelson's painting *Mirth and Girth* (1988), depicting the late Harold Washington, Chicago's first African American mayor, dressed in a pink bra and panties. That work prompted seventeen bomb threats to the school and museum, was physically removed and threatened with burning by nine aldermen accompanied by press and police, and was subsequently arrested by the chief himself. Nevertheless, this controversy remained largely a local issue, unlike the Tyler installation, which not only attracted national attention but resulted in proposed legislation to prohibit flag desecration, as well as Illinois State Arts Council and private funding cuts for both the School of the Art Institute and the museum.

In 1989 the NEA came under attack for its association with two exhibitions containing provocative images: *Robert Mapplethorpe: The Perfect Moment,* containing some explicit photographs of homoerotic practices, and the annual *Awards in the Visual Arts* exhibition organized by the Southeastern Center for Contemporary Art, which included Andres Serrano's *Piss Christ* (1987), a Cibachrome photograph of a crucifixion soaked in urine. The Mapplethorpe exhibition, after opening at the Institute of Contemporary Art in Philadelphia in 1988 and traveling to the Museum of Contemporary Art in Chicago, was canceled at the last minute by the Corcoran Gallery of Art in Washington, D.C., supposedly to avoid controversy over the NEA's reauthorization funding. The exhibition was shown instead at the Washington Projects for the Arts, and eventually, after appearing in Hartford and Boston, it moved to the Contemporary Arts Center in Cincinnati, where director Dennis Barrie was tried for violating obscenity laws. Senator Jesse Helms initiated legislation requiring NEA and NEH grant recipients to sign a pledge not to produce obscene art. Barrie was acquitted, and the antiobscenity oath, a content-based restriction, was eventually declared unconstitutional.[27] The NEA, however, did not emerge unscathed.

These three highly publicized cases have served to define the state of recent art censorship in the United States. But they are far from unique. What emerged in the 1980s was a growing attack on certain kinds of arts funding. Responding to a conservative agenda patterned after the 1981 Heritage Foundation's "Mandate for New Leadership," there was under Reagan an antiendowment movement, calling for private funding for the arts and a return to excellence and traditional values. *The New Criterion,* founded in 1982 by Samuel Lipman (a member of the NEA advisory council) and Hilton Kramer, became the cultural periodical of choice for the new conservatives. By 1987 the publication of Allan Bloom's *The Closing of the American Mind* provided an alarming signal of the deterioration of national culture.

This antipopulist, antimulticultural position was reflected in numerous budget cuts.[28] In 1979 the Department of Labor stopped funding the National Organizing Committee of Neighborhood Art Programs. In 1981 (coincidentally, the year the first AIDS case was reported), the Comprehensive Employment and Training Act (CETA) programs were eliminated; they had employed thousands of artists working mostly on neighborhood arts projects. In 1982 the New York City Metropolitan Transit Authority rejected Michael Lebron's anti-Reagan poster *Tired of the Jelly Bean Republic?* and the equal rights amendment died in Chicago. The following year, Frank Hodsoll, chair of the NEA, vetoed a grant to the feminist Heresies collective for a series of public forums featuring socially engaged artists and critics. In 1987 the NAMES project AIDS Memorial Quilt was first displayed during the National March on Washington for Gay and Lesbian Rights, and Hodsoll vetoed a grant to Jenny Holzer and others for an electronic billboard in Washington, D.C., that would have displayed politically provocative statements. The following year Gran Fury, an artists' collective, was formed out of the AIDS Coalition To Unleash Power (ACT UP), and the NEA demanded that the New Orleans journal *Red Bass* return a grant for an issue titled *For Palestine,* which included work by Noam Chomsky, Sue Coe, and Edward W. Said critical of the United States. In 1990, the year Dennis Barrie was brought to trial over the Mapplethorpe exhibition, the University of the District of Columbia was penalized $1.6 million for attempting to install Judy Chicago's landmark feminist work *The Dinner Party* because some House members found it obscene. The collaborative artwork, consisting of ceramic plates with vaginal imagery commemorating important women, was first exhibited in 1979, the same year Serra got his GSA commission, and had at that time toured national museums to great acclaim.

Can the controversy over *Tilted Arc* be seen as part of this larger art attack? Opinion has been remarkably divided. Some basic texts, such as Rita Gilbert's *Living with Art* (1992)and Marilyn Stokstad's *Art History* (1995) discussed the sculpture together with Mapplethorpe, while survey books on modern art contextualized it according to style (Sam Hunter as postminimal, H. H. Arnason under minimalism, Daniel Wheeler under earth and site works, Jonathan Fineberg with the work of Bruce Nauman and Eva Hesse, Edward Lucie-Smith as abstract sculpture, and Irving Sandler as postmodern art). While moderate critic Robert Hughes *(American Visions)* insisted that *Tilted Arc* had nothing to do with the controversies that followed it, conservative critic Hilton Kramer, in a 1992 essay, saw similar issues in the Serra and Mapplethorpe controversies.[29]

Writing in a public-policy context in 1993, Margaret Jane Wyszomirski thought Serra's sculpture "presaged concerns about artists rights and community standards that would arise later over publicly supported art more generally," as did Joan Jeffri, who discussed Serra in the same section as Mapplethorpe and Serrano. Sociologist Steven Dubin *(Arresting Images)* saw *Tilted Arc* as separate from controversies pertaining to race, religion, patriotism, sex, homosexuality, and AIDS, and art historian Dario Gamboni *(The Destruction of Art)* took as obvious its connection with the U.S. "political campaign against 'offensive' art strongly reminiscent of the McCarthy decade."[30]

Although critical opinion was divided on whether the *Tilted Arc* controversy was related to the identity issues and culture wars that erupted in the late 1980s, the selection panel for the next GSA project in New York was not. The two outdoor and six indoor works installed in 1989, the same year Serra's sculpture was dismantled, at the Joseph P. Addabbo Federal Building in South Jamaica, Queens, were all by African American artists. John Beardsley, chair of the selection panel (and at the time adjunct curator at the Corcoran Gallery in Washington), stated, "These commissions represent an attempt to shift away from an imperious kind of art." And Mary Schmidt Campbell, then New York City's commissioner of cultural affairs, acknowledged that *Tilted Arc* was in the "front of our minds" during the selection process.[31]

The writers who separated *Tilted Arc* from the Mapplethorpe/Serrano controversies appeared to see the former as a rejection of style (modernism or abstraction) rather than content (overtly political). Thus sociologist Judith Balfe, in a 1995 article, described Serra's sculpture as having "very little 'content'" and dismissed all the art commissioned by the GSA as "merely an attractive but socially purpose-free adornment of public space." As a corrective, Balfe suggested following what she deemed a successful compromise at the Vietnam Veterans Memorial: "A realistic bronze statue could also have been installed to establish the 'Arc' as a piece of sculpture, rather than the piece of sculpture on a site whose social utility was neither recognized nor enhanced."[32]

Equating abstract art with the absence of content or with "mere" ornament coincides precisely with the legal opinion that failed to protect *Tilted Arc* from removal. But in abstract art the form *is* the content, as evidenced by the overwhelming physical and emotional experience conveyed by Serra's work. Abstraction, as we have seen, embodies content, often of a political or spiritual nature. The art is not without content, but many, including writers who perceived the *Tilted Arc* controversy as separate from other attacks on art in 1989, apparently lack a context for understanding it.

Tilted Arc Historicized

The *Tilted Arc* controversy became official history almost at once. By the time of this writing, more than a decade after its removal, it is included in basic art-appreciation and art-history texts, books on modern art, and specialized literature on public art, controversy, and censorship. Presented variously as a symbol of the end of modernism, the failure of all or a certain type of public art, the primacy of public opinion in public art matters, and the censorship of art typical of the American 1980s, the sculpture consistently stood for more than itself, and an apparently inevitable narrative emerged that reflected both Diamond's hearing and contemporary concerns in the art world.[33]

Tilted Arc *and the End of Modernism*

During the 1980s, modern art was under attack by liberal academics as well as by the public and newly empowered conservatives. In an art world and academy increasingly committed to identity politics, modernism had come to represent a prescriptive style concerned only with producing formal innovations rather than with addressing the social concerns of previously marginal groups such as women, ethnic minorities, and homosexuals and lesbians. Modernism was now seen as representing the discredited exclusive domain of white males associated with elitism, devoid of the political content originally an integral part of the avant-garde.

Benjamin Buchloh observed that "Serra's sculpture stands at the end of that heroic tradition generally defined as the modern period."[34] Sociologist Steven Dubin saw the controversy as illustrating "the rejections of modernist assumptions and techniques. People were not angered by any overt message in the *Tilted Arc,* but they were enormously put off by what they saw as an imposing, ugly hunk of rusted steel whose artful qualities eluded them."[35] Elsewhere he further distanced the controversy from other seemingly similar controversies (discussed above), seeing the sculpture as "highlighting opposed concepts of 'good taste' instead of politically partisan disputes."[36] But if the *Tilted Arc* controversy had been "only" about taste (which has political implications in and of itself),[37] then many more sculptures would be at risk.

J. W. T. Mitchell, in his anthology *Art and the Public Sphere* (1992),[38] proposed two possible readings of the controversy, both framed by the failure of modernism. It could be seen as either "a classic instance of the high modernist transformation of a utilitarian public space into an aesthetic form (with predictable reactions from the Philistines), or as a signal that modernism can no longer mediate public and private spheres on its own terms, but must submit itself to social negotiation, and anticipate reactions ranging from violence to indifference." The first reading fails to acknowledge the atypical and quite specific nature of Serra's aesthetic forms and their transformation, and the second does not allow for the way modernist works may be converted to social use as civic logos or mascots. Whether such conversion is desirable or not is another question.

Elsewhere Mitchell states that "Serra's is a traditional work of public art; it provoked another engagement in what Michael North has called the 'tiresome battle reported in city after city . . . whenever a piece of modern sculpture is installed outdoors.'" In identifying *Tilted Arc* with traditional public art, Mitchell placed it in the same category as the now irrelevant general on horseback. Indeed, elsewhere in Mitchell's anthology art historian Virginia Maksymowicz, in her "Through the Back Door: Alternative Approaches to Public Art," described *Tilted Arc* as typical of "big steel constructions [that] have become the archetypal image" in urban plazas, with "heroes on horses"—that is, the kinds of art she is arguing against.

Dismissing all contemporary public art as a "historically bankrupt category," Benjamin Buchloh criticized the inherent contradictions of modern public art, contradictions that surfaced in Serra's (and others') rigid refusal to acknowledge the perceptual biases and limitations of its public (i.e., the losing struggle of high modern art to reach a popular audience).[39]

But Serra's sculpture cannot be considered typical of modernist abstraction. It is unique in terms of its intense physicality and emotional impact. It is nothing like, say, the Chicago Picasso, or the Grand Rapids Calder or even Noguchi's nearby *Red Cube*. Indeed, some critics have argued that it was the specific experience of *Tilted Arc* that was responsible for public reaction.

Tilted Arc *as Too Threatening*

Jonathan Fineberg, in *Art since 1940: Strategies of Being* (1995), considered *Tilted Arc* among Serra's best outdoor pieces, which "force themselves uncomfortably on the viewer. They dictate the paths of movement around, and with their monolithic massiveness feel frightening, even dangerous, with the unforgiving walls of steel overpowering anyone in range." Similarly, Edward Lucie-Smith, in *Movements in Art since 1945: Issues and Concepts* (1995), saw in Serra's work "a suppressed element of Expressionism" that prompted "the public [to] find them threatening."[40]

Robert Hughes, in *American Visions: The Epic History of Art in America* (1997), identified "the main character of Serra's work" after 1969 as "its scariness. You are never allowed to forget the weight of Serra's metal. . . . You skirt his steels walls and walk through the curving spaces they define with a degree of dread." And Anna Chave, in a 1990 article, characterized *Tilted Arc* as "a grotesque amplification of Minimalism's power rhetoric" that "doesn't simply exemplify aggression or domination, but acts it out." She described the relationship between the work and spectator as "that between bully and victim, as his work tends to treat the viewer's welfare with contempt."[41]

These critics all identified the anxiety-producing element specific to *Tilted Arc,* and Serra's work in general, as the source of the controversy. Chave interpreted it from a feminist perspective; Hughes related it to "a thoroughly legitimate though long-repressed function of sculpture at its most archaic level." And I have suggested that it derives at least in part from Serra's conflicted sense of Jewish identity (see chapter 3, the section "A New Interpretation"). All these interpretations acknowledge the uniqueness of Serra's modernist style and the experiential content it embodies.

Tilted Arc *versus the Public*

As public art evolved, the emphasis often shifted from the art to the public. Virginia Maksymowicz, finding "whether or not it [the sculpture] was good art" irrelevant, concluded, "In terms of artist-community relationships, *Tilted Arc* was an absolute fiasco." And Erika Doss, in *Spirit Poles and Flying Pigs: Public Art and Cultural Democracy in American Communities* (1995), saw Serra's sculpture as "another compelling case illustrating how artistic presumptions made about and on behalf of 'the people' can backfire."[42]

Just as Diamond framed the hearing and subsequent removal as a victory for the public, many writers after the fact historicized the controversy as a struggle between the public and art, artists, or the art establishment. Rita Gilbert's *Living with Art,* a widely used introductory text, saw the definition of art as settled by "a kind of referendum, a majority decision," a victory for the public over the art establishment. Marilyn Stokstad's *Art History* defined the central issue as "the artist's right to control what happens to a work commissioned or purchased for the public" and presented *Tilted Arc*'s removal as a government response to public demand. Daniel Wheeler in *Art since Mid-Century: 1945 to the Present* (1991), on the other hand, called the removal of *Tilted Arc* "a cultural tragedy" caused by the Philistine public (whose ignorance he illustrates by the misspellings in the hearing transcript).[43]

Suzi Gablik, in *The Reenchantment of Art* (1991), concluded, "What the *Tilted Arc* controversy forces us to consider is whether art that is based on notions of pure freedom and radical autonomy—without regard for the relations we have to other people, the community, or any other consideration except the pursuit of art—can contribute to a sense of the common good."[44] If art, per se, were perceived as a common good, this question would be moot. Even then, equal access would not automatically be provided unless this attitude were reflected in a public education system that routinely included art.

Sometimes public space was made to stand for the public. Howard Smagula, in *Currents: Contemporary Directions in the Visual Arts* (1989), framed the controversy in terms of "the right of this sculpture to aggressively assert itself upon this public plaza." And Rosalyn Deutsche, in an influential 1988 article, criticized *Tilted Arc* for remaining rooted in an aesthetic rather than urban discourse, for serving as a gloss for existing power structures when its "real social function . . . is to reify as natural the conditions of the late capitalist city into which it hopes to integrate us."[45]

These arguments presume that the public was uniform in its hatred of *Tilted Arc* and that what was expressed at the hearing somehow stood for the voice of the people. But what individual responses revealed was, rather, the preexisting rift between the public and contemporary art, much as the sculpture made obvious the worsening conditions of the urban environment. It was hardly a victory for the public that Diamond's hearing framed *Tilted Arc* as "the enemy of the people" masking harsh underlying social and economic realities. By offering no way to deal with the sculpture but to remove it, he created the illusion that the public had won and the problem(s) had been solved.

Tilted Arc *as Bad Public Art*

One way or the other, from a variety of perspectives, *Tilted Arc* was made to stand for what was wrong with all or a certain kind of public art. In defining the controversy as "the single most important test of the power of the public art establishment in its relatively short existence," Dale McConathy in 1987 equated Serra's sculpture with the old order.[46]

In a way of denigrating all contemporary public art, albeit obliquely, Robert Hughes concluded, as Arthur Danto had earlier, that the controversy "exemplified the fact that a sculpture may have genuine and even deep merit as a work of art, and yet fail in the public realm." The lesson for Howard Smagula too was that "creating public art is very different from making private sculpture that is sold to collectors and museums." But declaring *Tilted Arc* a failure (not good public art) or a potential success in another context (it would be good art if it were in an art space) implicitly diminishes a public (as opposed to art) audience, apparently precluding it from a serious art experience.[47]

Most books about public art, blaming *Tilted Arc* for failing to communicate with the public, used Serra's sculpture as an example of what not to do, a jumping-off point to develop a different type of public art, something other than the modernist art object.

Artist David Antin argued for an amorphous and ephemeral public art, for instance, a four-line poem, written in the sky, that cost $10,000: "Well, it's expensive as poems go, but it's cheap as public artworks go—if you think of something like Serra's *Tilted Arc.* But think of it this way—if an artwork is discursive—if an artwork is some kind of talk—the nice thing about this one is it goes away fast, if you don't like it.

And if you do like it, you remember it. But it takes an awful lot of energy to get rid of *Tilted Arc*."[48]

Sometimes without specific mention, the controversy seemed to lurk behind alternative approaches to public art. Mary Jane Jacob, in her 1992 Sculpture Chicago exhibition *Culture in Action,* called for "an art that fosters dialogue through communal action." The specter of *Tilted Arc* loomed large in her pointed questions "How can we enable artists to contribute reactively to the needs of society beyond the realm of esthetics?" and "How can the arts become a meaningful part of everyday experience?"[49] The foundation for integrating the arts into society must be built in the realm of public art education as well as public art itself.

The public at Federal Plaza was in no way prepared for Serra's sculpture, nor was there any program or information available after its installation to provide an art context. To a certain extent, this argument might be reframed as "the public versus public information."

The Controversy as Censorship

> If we look into the mirror one morning and see a censor staring back, there's a good chance one will soon be knocking at the door.
>
> **—Gara La Marche, executive director, Fund for Free Expression, Human Rights Watch**

Since the controversies of the late 1980s, there has been a growing body of literature on censorship in the arts; the arguments are usually framed by the culture wars with which this section began.[50] Two writers in particular characterized the *Tilted Arc* controversy as a form of censorship. In 1993 Benjamin Buchloh described it as vandalism from above initiated by several judges, comparable to Nelson Rockefeller's censoring of Diego Rivera's mural in the RCA Building and the removal of Andy Warhol's *Thirteen Most Wanted Men* (1964) from the New York State Pavilion at the 1964 World's Fair.[51] And Dario Gamboni included *Tilted Arc* in a chapter on legal abuse in his history of the destruction of art in the United States and Europe during the last two centuries.[52]

But there is also evidence of a less official form of censorship that did not come to light, cases of conscious or unconscious self-censorship on the part of artists and arts administrators before, during, and after the *Tilted Arc* controversy. Censorship is practiced within the art world in many ways. When museum director Christina Orr-Cahall canceled the Mapplethorpe exhibition shortly before its scheduled opening at the Corcoran Gallery, she was practicing censorship. That is clear.

When David Hammons's provocative piece *How Ya Like Me Now?* (1988), a 14 foot × 16 foot portrait of a white, blond, blue-eyed Jesse Jackson, was attacked (physically censored) by youths as it was being installed at a public site in Washington, D.C., in 1989, the artist decided to display it indoors with its scars intact. Part of the Washington Project for the Arts exhibition *The Blues Aesthetic: Black Culture and Modernism,* the work was accompanied by an explanatory statement. Hammons successfully co-opted this vandalism into the history of the piece, much as Marcel Duchamp had decades earlier incorporated the accidental cracks in his glass sculpture *The Bride Stripped Bare by Her Bachelors Even* (1915–23).

But when artists succumb to public opinion, are they colluding in a censorship practice or effecting a sensible compromise? Consider the following cases involving Tom Otterness, Richard Haas, and John Ahearn.

Otterness's 1991 GSA commission for the Los Angeles Federal Building named after seventy-five-year-old Democratic representative Edward R. Roybal consisted of a narrative frieze that contained an image of a crouching female nude with exposed genitals and a free-standing sculpture of a nude baby girl holding up a globe (Figure 52). When Roybal saw two boys touch the crotch of the sculpture, he complained to GSA regional director Edwin Thomas about the depiction of nudity.[53] Without notifying the artist, Thomas had the offending parts of the sculpture (one relief panel and the baby) removed during the night. The ACLU of Southern California and Mayor Tom Bradley of Los Angeles, among others, objected. The artist's attorney used the

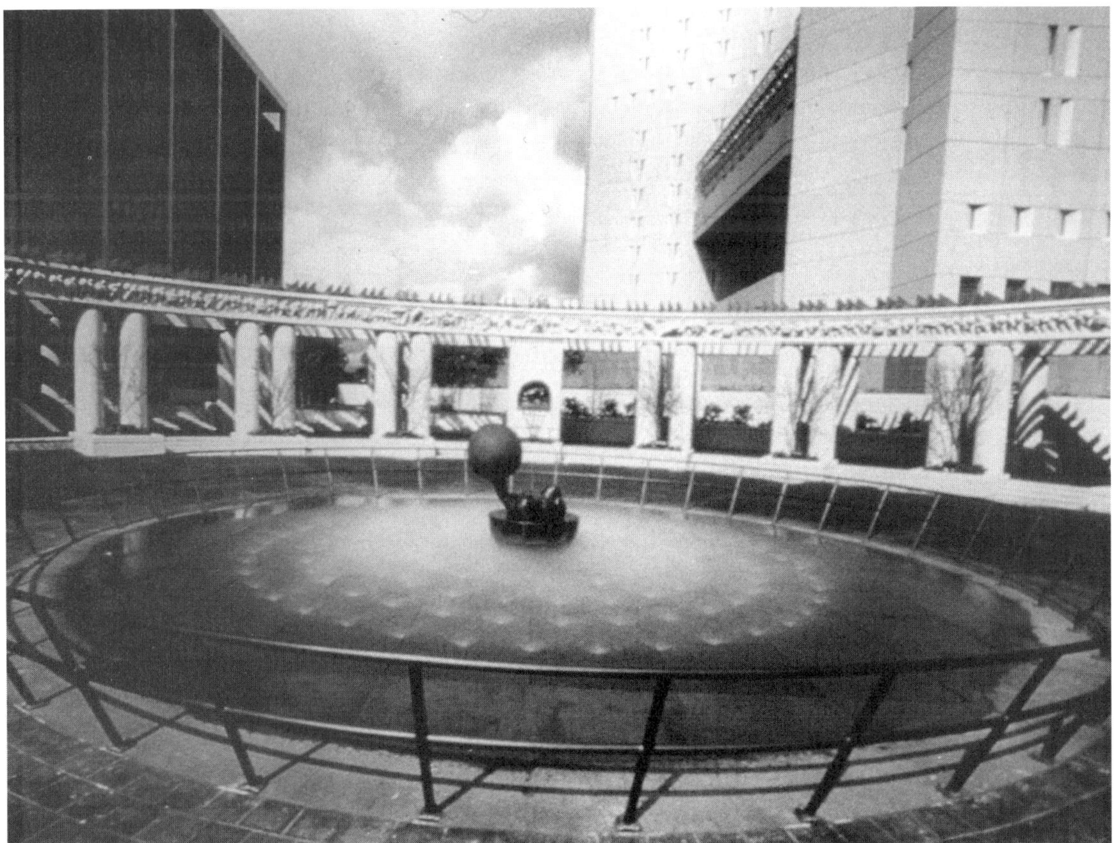

Figure 52. Tom Otterness, *The New World,* 1991, Los Angeles, California. Courtesy of the General Services Administration.

GSA's professed fear of vandalism as a negotiating point. The government agreed to restore the work, and the artist agreed to include a thirty-inch-high railing to "protect" his installation.

Richard Haas's 1989 series of narrative reliefs for the White Street Detention Center, a commission of New York City's Percent-for-Art program, consisted of seven panels depicting the history of immigration to Manhattan's Lower East Side, a multicultural, multiethnic area. This monochromatic, barely visible piece had been up for more than two years when a prison guard transferred from Rikers Island complained to the Hispanic Correction Officers Association that "what he took to be the 'Hispanic' panel did not show 'positive values.'" It depicted a man lying on the ground in front of a closed bodega and a woman in shorts whom some took to be a hooker (Figure 53). The artist, who has an adopted Hispanic son, met with a coalition of organizations coordinated by the Department of Correction's Hispanic Society and offered to change the word "bodega" to "superette." When that was not acceptable, Haas agreed to develop a new panel. The new version was subsequently reviewed and approved by the Department of Cultural Affairs and community representatives and installed in 1997 (Figure 54).[54] Two years later, Haas observed,

> I had to make compromises. I was forced to do it. When criticism comes from the community rather than from an individual sponsor or a panel of art judges, it's much more serious, if not necessarily more valid. Criticism will land in the press, and the press can take it and warp it, and you've got a battle on your hands that you know you can't win. When there is an overwhelming community reaction to your work, you know you're in trouble. In the post–*Tilted Arc* world, artists have gone to safer shores; more cutting-edge art is out.[55]

John Ahearn's much publicized 1991 public art project for a police precinct in the South Bronx consisted of three figures from the neighborhood: a black male with a basketball and a boom box; a recently released ex-con posing with his pit bull, and a teenage girl on roller skates (Figure 55). Protests emanated from two employees of New York City's Department of General Services, who had never seen the sculptures, and from local community activist Alcina Salgado, who felt the sculptures were bad for the neighborhood. Her daughter observed that if the workers at Federal Plaza in Manhattan could have a sculpture they did not like removed, the residents of the South Bronx should have the same option.

In trying to respond to Mrs. Salgado's concerns, Ahearn, who lived in the South Bronx, first repainted one of the male faces to make it less scary and then asked her to consider being the subject of a new statue, together with a fireman, garbage collector, or policeman, but she declined. Five days after the sculptures were erected, even though he had the support of the Department of Cultural Affairs that commissioned them, Ahearn asked that they be removed. As he saw it, "[I]t was the art world against the community," and he didn't want to fight with "conservative progressive" people like Mrs. Salgado, whom he respected.[56] When I discussed this case in a public art

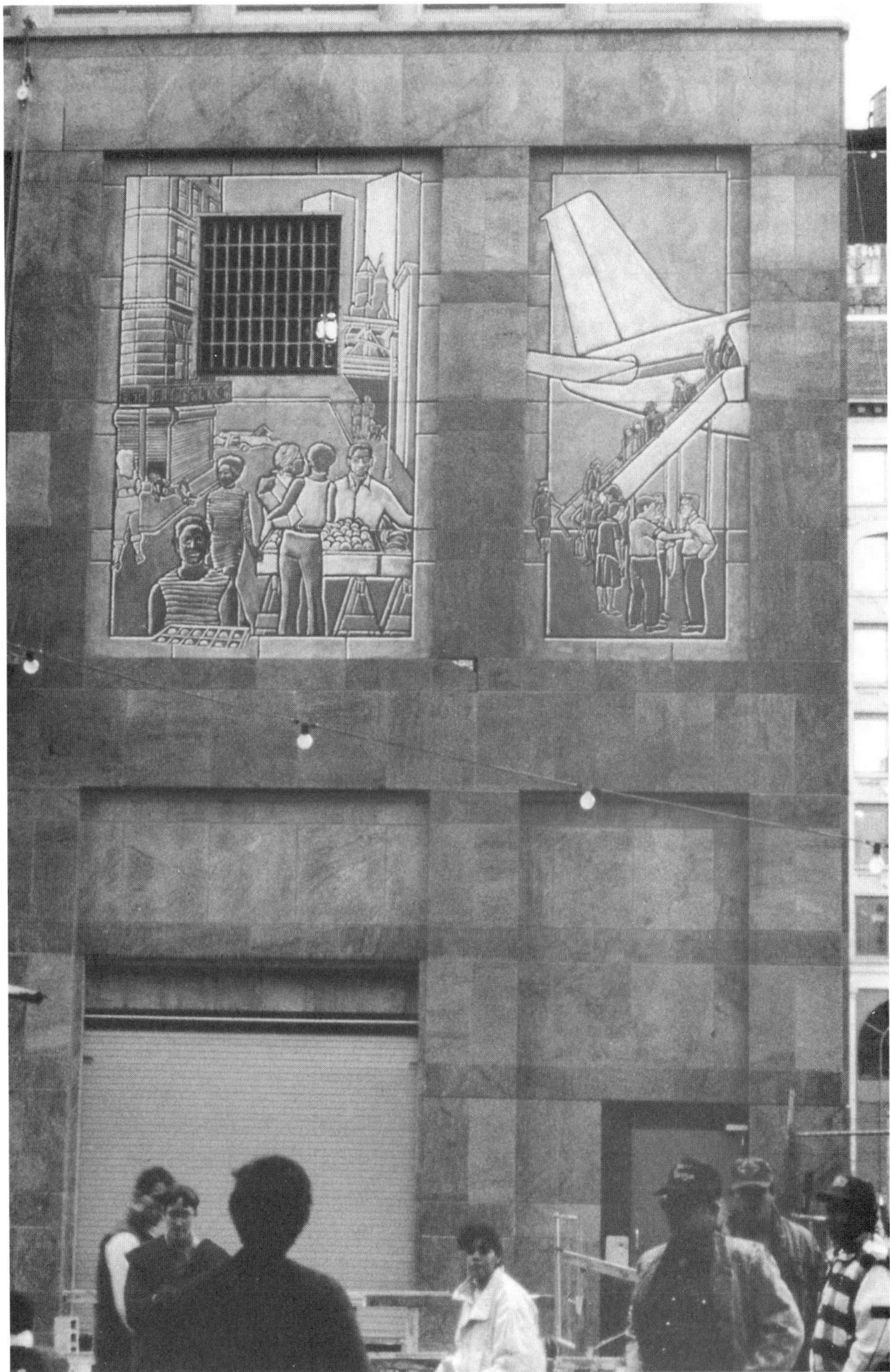

Figure 53. Richard Haas, Untitled (detail), 1989, White Street Detention Center, New York City. Photograph by Burt Roberts.

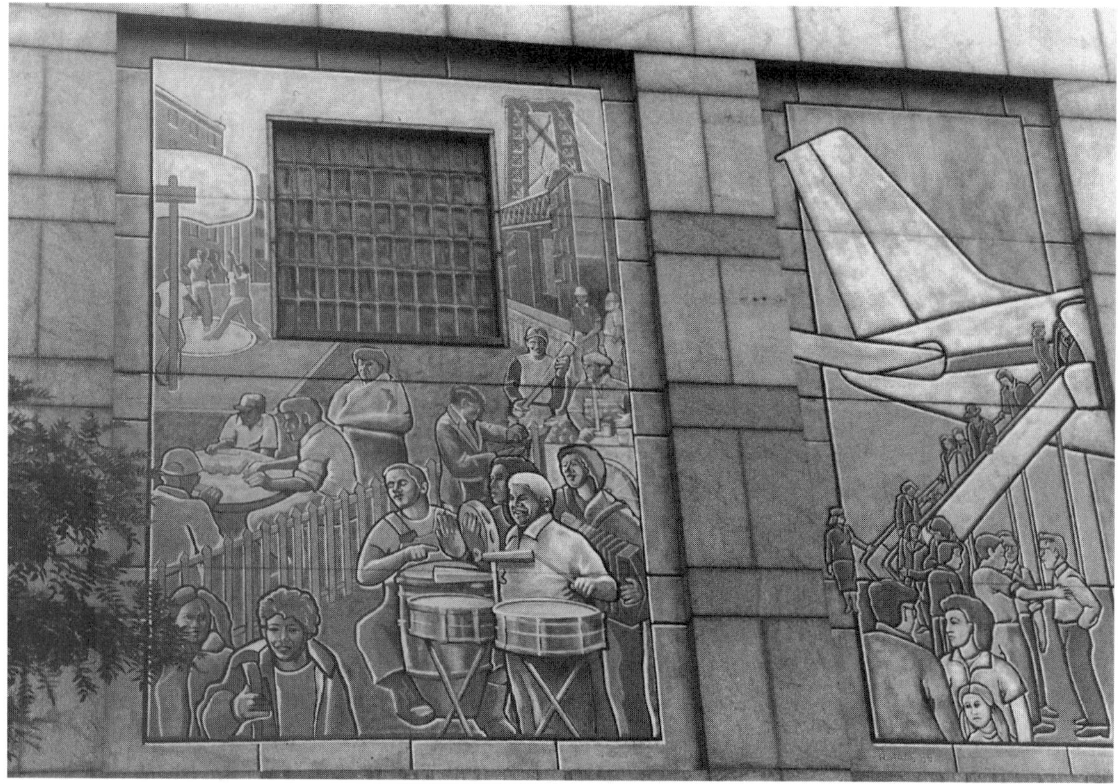

Figure 54. Richard Haas, Untitled (detail), 1997, White Street Detention Center, New York City. Photograph by Burt Roberts.

seminar at City College, one student was puzzled. "Why," he asked, "should Mrs. Salgado decide?"

In 1991 realist painter Philip Pearlstein wrote pointedly about censorship on stylistic grounds, the kind of censorship that routinely goes on at grant-selection panels and among critics. He might have added the kind that gets encoded in grant guidelines and the kind practiced by museum curators and gallery owners. The borders between censorship and selectivity are mutable. Tracing the fortunes of modern art in the twentieth century as championed, banished, and "triumphing" in postwar New York, he concluded that at the century's end "realism is out now, as is traditional abstraction, floundering in the wave-of-the-moment . . . 'politically aware conceptual art.'"[57]

It was this invisible form of censorship, revealed pointedly in the comments that saw Serra's sculpture as the end of modernism, abstract art, or a particular kind of public art, that was practiced in the *Tilted Arc* controversy by the general public, GSA judges and administrators, the lawyers who adjudicated the case, and many in the art world. This does not mean that *Tilted Arc* was the right sculpture for Federal Plaza, that the employees did not have a legitimate gripe, or that nothing should have been done. It does, however, mean that *Tilted Arc* was censored.

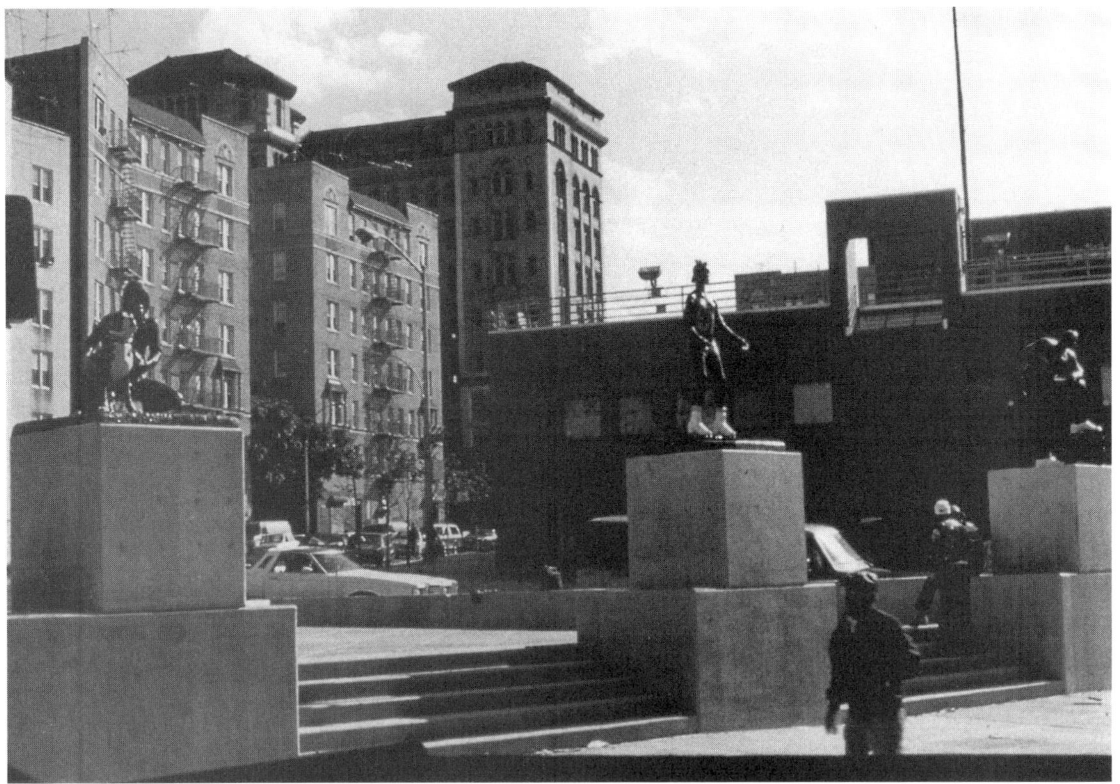

Figure 55. John Ahearn, *Bronx Sculpture Park* (Raymond Garcia, Daleesha, Corey Mann), 1991, New York City. Courtesy of the New York City Department of Cultural Affairs.

Seen as representing a recently discredited style, its status as art was challenged by some, and its relevance was questioned by others. But how much of the current art-world disdain for modernism is a response to modernism's most dogmatic white male critics and practitioners? And why is the failure of modernism (or contemporary art in general) to communicate with its audience not seen as a failure of public education to provide a context for understanding instead of the need to censure?

Conclusion

> The nineties have been a decade in which the arts community has licked the wounds it received during the eighties, but not quite recovered from them. . . . The reality is that nineties public art is much less challenging to the public—more decorative and in the background.
>
> —**Daniel Grant, *The Nation*, 1999**

The dangerous precedent feared by many—that the removal of *Tilted Arc* would lead to a wholesale destruction of public art or the end of the GSA's percent-for-art program—did not occur. The sculpture is gone, Federal Plaza has been redesigned, and most of the arguments raised at the hearing and afterward have been proved specious by what followed. Nevertheless, *Tilted Arc* remains a specter, haunting or guiding (depending on one's viewpoint) public art in this country and elsewhere, imposing a degree of self-censorship among artists and arts administrators that is both difficult to gauge and more insidious than overt acts. It continues to provoke passionate responses, striking a nerve at the root of (public) art (and artists) in our culture. Clearly, more was at stake than the fate of a single sculpture.

The *Tilted Arc* controversy fit a well-established story line: Abstract art alienates the public. In museums and in public spaces, abstract art has always been problematic, seen at various times as representing quintessential freedom or unacceptable elitism. In a 1963 speech that subsequently led to the formation of the National Endowments for the Arts and Humanities, President Kennedy identified artistic freedom as a national value and the contemporary artist (then as often as not a practitioner of abstraction) as "the last champion of the individual mind and sensibility against an intrusive society and an officious state."[1] In subsequent decades, abstraction and its uses came to be discredited by many in the art world,[2] part of the overall reaction against earlier dogmatic critics who excluded any other form of artistic expression from the hallowed canon of modern art. Seen in a socio-political context, abstract art was especially vulnerable to charges of elitism and was often equated with it.[3]

But the problem with *Tilted Arc* could not have been one of modern abstraction per se. There, on the Broadway side of the Federal Building, without noticeable protest, stand Beverly Pepper's *Sentinels,* vertical columns of Cor-Ten steel, installed by the GSA in 1996 (Figure 41). Individuals may not like the columns (or abstract art and its materials), but the work apparently has not prompted anyone to do more than vent privately. Pepper's kind of bland abstraction is much more typical of the public art revival that began in the late 1960s than is Serra's art. His work in no way exemplifies modern public sculpture that might be easily transformed into a civic emblem, such as the Grand Rapids Calder. *Tilted Arc,* with its sweeping form and precipitous tilt, could be neither "used" nor ignored, and that made its value as public art both suspect and enraging.

Like most public art, Serra's sculpture was rarely interpreted in an art context. Without an art explanation, people had only "looks like" comparisons to frame it. Serra's modernism is predicated on the notion that significant art must be oppositional to existing power structures, a concept rooted in the original definition of the avant-garde.[4] Serra's sculpture is also experiential in nature, not graspable from a visual reading alone.[5] Additionally, the precise experience of the work, its implicitly threatening quality, can be at least partially explained, I believe, in terms of Serra's conflicted Jewish identity. These contexts all contribute to an understanding, if not an appreciation, of *Tilted Arc.* Nevertheless, most public art is installed without an appropriate art explanation, is probably not understood as such, and yet continues to stand, eventually becoming invisible, absorbed into the general urbanscape.

As the 1980s evolved, it became clear that public art, like museum or gallery art, was no single entity. Artists were experimenting with different approaches, and single-object sculpture came to be considered (except by the GSA and many other publicly funded programs) a thing of the past, old-style public art, in its own way as obsolete (and elitist) as a general on horseback. Instead, public art projects that explored collaborative approaches and community involvement, emphasizing public use and public input, were favored by critics and NEA funding programs.

There has been, as yet, no documentation on whether the public likes the new-style public art any better. But as paradigms in the art and public art worlds continue to be redefined, they rarely make news and remain restricted to the art pages of newspapers and specialized journals. Neither of the new artworks at Federal Plaza, Beverly Pepper's columns and Martha Schwartz's seating arrangement, attracted media attention, certainly nothing approaching the coverage of Diamond's hearing.

Why is public art not subject to the same kind of analysis as art in galleries and museums? Was Serra's sculpture fully realized as art? Should there be different types of public art for different types of spaces? Can or should contemporary public art be considered civic art? What does its use as a municipal emblem mean? Is there a place for oppositional public art in our culture? If so, what forms should it take, and how can we measure its success? How can we accurately determine public response, and how (much) should it count in evaluating public art?

The public space setting determines much of our response to public art, and Federal Plaza was one of the worst, typical of the open spaces that had proliferated since the 1961 zoning ordinance: an empty forecourt in front of a building. Enter *Tilted Arc,* vilified as the "alien" that vanquished the cherished "icon" of open space in Manhattan. But the ideal of open space (if it ever existed) was increasingly challenged much more brutally during the 1980s by the harsh urban realities of drug addiction and homelessness and the crimes they prompted. In the media *Tilted Arc* was blamed both for not improving Federal Plaza and for rendering it useless; in the art world it was criticized for not clearly addressing the larger problems of the public sphere.

But in terms of actual space, Martha Schwartz's serpentine green benches and plant-covered mounds (Figures 39, 40) occupy more space than Serra's sculpture did. Pedestrians can no longer cross the plaza directly, and it can certainly not be used for concerts and the like. And yet there has been no protest. Nor does there seem to be any nostalgia for the original plaza, empty but for the pool, that was made so much of at Diamond's hearing.

If improving Federal Plaza had been the issue, Diamond's hearing might have been framed differently, seeking other suggestions besides removing the sculpture. The GSA might have tried to make the plaza more hospitable while *Tilted Arc* still stood. At the hearing, several noted musicians expressed interest in having their works performed at Federal Plaza, and at the 1987 NEA panel meeting Serra offered to help with any modification of the plaza.[6] None of this occurred. It is impossible to know whether using the amphitheater-like space created by *Tilted Arc* for concerts and the like, providing seating, and fixing the fountain would have made a difference in the reception of the sculpture. What is clear is that nothing of the kind was attempted. Even today there are no trees or umbrellas to provide shaded seating.

What are the essential public amenities of public space, and how do they vary from site to site? Can or should *any* public space function primarily as an art space, become a function of sculpture, as Serra intended? Does any urban space offer the kind of safe haven necessary to experience and appreciate the apparently threatening experience of *Tilted Arc*? What are the real distinctions of making art for public spaces as opposed to museum or gallery spaces? What adjustments, if any, should artists be willing to make?

Although there were problems with the public art commissioning process and eroding commitments to a public policy that supported art, this was not unique to *Tilted Arc.* True, the public had no direct input in selecting Serra, but the public had not been consulted in other public art projects in New York or elsewhere,[7] nor did the public have any say about Martha Schwartz's renovation of the plaza. And in spite of the ongoing attacks against public art, the GSA continues to commission it.

In terms of process, certainly the removal of *Tilted Arc* was far more skewed and irregular than its commission, which followed existing guidelines. The subsequent commissioning process, giving control to one individual at the GSA in Washington and more power to people who were not art professionals, had its share of controversies as well. In 1998 a new accession policy as well as a removal, relocation, and deaccessioning process were adopted at the federal level, open to periodic review and update. The removal of *Tilted Arc,* however, was accomplished by a single individual with sufficient power and bureaucratic know-how to see it through.[8] Had it not been for Diamond's persistence, it is more than likely that *Tilted Arc* would still be at Federal Plaza. And had it not been for the absence of a permanent director of the GSA and NEA in Washington (someone powerful enough to have protected the sculpture) during a critical period in 1989, Diamond might not have succeeded.

Certainly the demise of *Tilted Arc* was eased by the shifting paradigm in public policy. Support for art was under attack from the beginning of President Reagan's first term, and by the end of the decade the NEA itself was threatened. The *Tilted Arc* controversy was part of the backlash against the only program of federal funding of the arts not based on economic need—as the Depression-era programs had been—and was thus an anomaly in U.S. history. Unfortunately, Serra's sculpture came to stand for public art funding in general, representing elitism in the same way that Mapplethorpe's and Serrano's photographs later symbolized obscenity and sacrilege. But they were all exceptions, hardly typical of art created directly or indirectly with public money.

Can we have an equitable and effective public policy for supporting public art? What kinds of checks and balances should be built into the process for commissioning public art? How should the public be represented? Do we need a deaccessioning policy for public art? If so, what should it include? And why is art, especially abstract art, not protected under the First Amendment to the same extent as speech? How can we change the marginalization of art in our culture?

Criticism of Serra and his work expressed a continuing national distrust of art and art professionals. Serra himself contributed to a conflation of the *Tilted Arc* controversy (and thereby contemporary art and artists) with elitism. He was hostile to the ideas that any concerns took priority over his art or that the people should have any say in public art, that either their taste or needs mattered. He would have been better off, as one younger sculptor commented, if "he'd show a little humility."[9]

After all, this was the age of Reagan, an immensely popular president with a deceptively folksy style, garnering public approval as he emphasized individual responsibility over public welfare, framing his social laissez-faire in an anti–big government policy. Serra and some of his supporters, apparently speaking in tongues, embodied an art-world elitism that was anathema to this country, where a populist approach to art has always been in evidence, both in the emphasis on education and outreach in our museums and in recent funding demands that art prove its worth in terms of the common good in order to justify receiving government money.

But more than acting arrogantly or practicing an unpopular abstract style (as many artists do), Serra upset the conventional balance of power between art and its audience, a balance that is basic to the viewing experience, especially in an urban space. There was no way to escape *Tilted Arc;* it determined viewers' experience of the immediate environment. Apparently perceiving that their freedom was threatened, people became profoundly uneasy, if not enraged. In that basic inversion of power, Serra's sculpture easily came to represent other aspects of the democratic process run amok, came to epitomize, in fact, the pervasive experience of having no control, of being a victim, that so defines our times.[10]

As such, the *Tilted Arc* controversy might be interpreted as a "shoot the messenger" narrative. But Serra, like his public, conflated the symbolic and actual aspects of his commission; in symbolically attacking the government, his patron, he was also in reality taking on its employees. The experience implicitly intended by Serra, that the public be empowered to act in its own behalf, did not take place. Indeed, this could have happened only if one identified with the art, as few apparently did. This would have required a radically different attitude toward art, fostered by a very different kind of public education system.

One of the most serious omissions of the public art revival of the late 1960s was a public-education component. Only in 1988 did GSA adopt a policy that specifically included a directive stating, "Regional and Center staff, coordinating with GSA's public affairs offices, will be responsible for ensuring that the building and its integrated artwork are introduced to the public via media coverage, workshops, brochures, plaques, or other adequate means."[11] However, public art was and in many state and local programs still is launched into the public domain with little or no explanation—far less than is provided as a matter of course in a museum to an audience that is there specifically to look at art. This is an especially critical issue since art education in our public school system is totally absent or deficient and shows little sign of improvement. The widespread beliefs that art is not a serious subject but entertainment and that people need little or no formal education to experience, create, or comprehend it underlies both the belief that anyone is competent to select art and the belief that art requires no explanation.

Certainly Serra may be faulted for not seeing the problem or for not caring enough about the public at Federal Plaza. But Serra was hardly the only one who failed to take responsibility in this saga. The selection committee never publicly explained or defended its choice. The same could be said for high-level GSA officials in Washington, who approved the sculpture but gave no thought to preparing the public for its appearance and who, more seriously, failed to address the working conditions at Federal Plaza both outside and inside the building.

And what of the employees themselves, cited as the main victims of the sculpture? Why did taking down *Tilted Arc* arouse more passion than improving their own immediate working conditions? Getting rid of the sculpture provided a temporary catharsis for a pervasive sense of helplessness. Instead of a complex (potentially job-threatening) battle of workers against an amorphous government or an immediate boss, a clearly visible art object provided an easy and safe target.

And why were reporters and critics not prompted by the disproportionate rage to look behind the mask of controversy? The inability to listen or to suspend disrespect was the dominant motif, reinforced by a media that thrives on themes of divisiveness.

More than anything, the controversy demonstrated that a sham process was sufficient to mask real issues, preferable to problem solving and conflict resolution—a triumph of sound bites and melodrama over a sound reasoning-through of complexities. The process (the appearance of addressing issues while actually creating distractions, the practice of professional myopia, working the system through its loopholes, manipulation of and by the media) typified business as usual during the Reagan era and beyond. In the rush to claim the righteous mantle of victimhood, to affix blame, to focus on the problem rather than develop solutions, the *Tilted Arc* controversy, far from a dangerous precedent, was an example of the diversionary politics of the Reagan years and an early harbinger of the identity politics and the culture wars that continue to divide us.

The controversy has been historicized in various contradictory ways, but the polarizing art-versus-the-public frame established at the hearing remains—a destructive either/or construction. There was even a "never again" dictum: "We don't want another *Tilted Arc*" became a familiar refrain in public art circles. Always at fault was the arrogant artist, or in the less popular converse narrative, the ignorant public, or sometimes the GSA itself. But all that was ever discussed was whether the sculpture should stay or go, who was right, and who was wrong. Why was it not possible to consider the complex questions the controversy raised in various contexts?

To get beyond the elitist/populist dichotomy, one would have to ask who gains from it, what it enforces, and whether, in any real sense, it still pertains. Contemporary culture is more visual than it has ever been, and traditional high/low distinctions are increasingly mutable in an age where art and advertising so often overlap and in which popular culture informs art just as often as the reverse. Yet art (and artists) remain stigmatized as elitist, ridiculed and thereby stripped of its (their) potential power.

However, what is elitist is not so much a specific style of art but the public education system that denies equal access to it. Democracy of any sort, including cultural, assumes an educated, informed (not indoctrinated) public with the ability to think for themselves. And that requires an open, viable, and public education system that teaches tolerance and curiosity, critical as well as visual thinking.[12]

Public art often evolves from theoretical constructs of the public sphere far removed from actual realities of public space, implying expectations of public behavior and response that are increasingly difficult to define in a country whose population embraces a variety of cultural traditions. Nevertheless, both in its selection process and the range of experiences it offers, public art that considers the multiple publics and uses of a specific site has the potential to function as a catalyst for civic dialogue, creating spaces for public life, including encountering art. In the *Tilted Arc* controversy, public art emerged as a cultural oxymoron.

But although the spectacle of controversy functions as a highly successful mask, it also reveals deeply rooted hostilities, the fault lines in the fiber of society. Controversy provides an acceptable vehicle for venting opinions that polite discourse otherwise discourages. In the case of *Tilted Arc,* it revealed an apparently widespread mutual rage between the contemporary art world and its audience, and within the art world it permitted an extensive diatribe against the tenets of modernism allegedly represented by Serra's work. Controversy attracts prejudice, just as public art focuses local discontents. That is why the words of controversy and the arguments they frame are particularly revealing. They are the real subjects that need addressing because the objects (or situations) that prompt them are, for the most part, unique. If not, we would be mired in controversy all the time.

Serra's work is unique within public art, and *Tilted Arc* was unique even in his oeuvre as the only single-wall sculpture in a widely used public space. It was precisely this uniqueness that made it an easy target. As an example of art that overstepped its culturally defined boundaries of audience control, it could easily be used as a weapon against any art deemed audacious or undesirable. The real threat to democracy, however, was not Serra's sculpture but the process by which it was removed, and the way a simple spectacle so easily obscured a host of complex realities. The legacy of the *Tilted Arc* controversy that continues to haunt us is the invisible one: that of the undocumented self-censorship it prompted in artists and art agencies alike.

Notes

Preface

1. On the city, see, for example, Jack Newfield and Wayne Barrett, *City for Sale: Ed Koch and the Betrayal of New York* (New York: Harper and Row, 1988); on the country, see Haynes Johnson, *Sleepwalking through History: America in the Reagan Years,* paperback ed. (New York: Doubleday, 1992).

2. Although the federal government is not limited by New York City (or any other local) zoning law, it may voluntarily follow local precedents, as it appeared to do at Federal Plaza.

Prologue

1. See Harriet F. Senie and Sally Webster, "Critical Issues in Public Art," *Art Journal,* Winter 1989, introduction. Greenough's twelve-foot-high seated statue in classical garb was intended to conflate the likeness of the man with a symbolic personification of the new republic. See also Wayne Craven, *Sculpture in America* (Newark: University of Delaware Press, 1984), 105–9; Lillian B. Miller, *Patrons and Patriotism: The Encouragement of the Fine Arts in the United States, 1790–1860* (Chicago: University of Chicago Press, 1966), 59–65; and Vivien Green Fryd, *Art and Empire: The Politics of Ethnicity in the U.S. Capital* (New Haven, Conn.: Yale University Press, 1992), chap. 3.

2. Miller, *Patrons and Patriotism,* observed that the Greenough controversy "precipitated one of the first large-scale discussions of taste in art that took place in this country" (62). The Serra controversy also precipitated discussion on a national scale, if for no other reason than its continued coverage in the *New York Times.*

3. See Kirk Savage, "The Self-Made Monument: George Washington and the Fight to

Erect a National Memorial," and Susan Larkin, "From Scapegoats to Mascots: The New York Public Library Lions," both in *Critical Issues in Public Art: Content, Context, and Controversy,* ed. Harriet F. Senie and Sally Webster (New York: HarperCollins, 1992; reissued Washington, D.C.: Smithsonian Institution Press, 1998).

4. For an excellent summary of government funding for the arts, see Milton C. Cummings Jr., "Government and the Arts: An Overview," in *Public Money and the Muse,* ed. Stephen Benedict (New York and London: W. W. Norton, 1991).

5. The existing bibliography on New Deal art is extensive and growing. Of special interest are Richard D. McKinzie, *The New Deal for Artists* (Princeton: Princeton University Press, 1973); Francis V. O'Connor, *Art for the Millions* (Boston: New York Graphic Society, 1973); Marlene Park and Gerald E. Markowitz, *Democratic Vistas: Post Offices and Public Art in the New Deal* (Philadelphia: Temple University Press, 1984); Karal Ann Marling, *Wall-to-Wall America: A Cultural History of Post-Office Murals* (Minneapolis: University of Minnesota Press, 1982).

6. The organization of the Public Works of Art Project (PWAP) was actually determined in 1933 at Bruce's home. It was set up within the Treasury Department initially because Secretary of the Treasury Henry Morgenthau and his wife were very interested in the project. After one year, PWAP was succeeded by two independent programs, the Section of Fine Arts, directed by Bruce, and the WPA/FAP, under Holger Cahill, which included drama, music, and historical survey projects as well as art. For a good analysis of Bruce's role and influence, see Erica Beckh, "Government Art in the Roosevelt Era," *Art Journal,* Fall 1960, 2–8.

7. See Park and Markowitz, *Democratic Vistas,* 130ff.

8. For a discussion of the evolution of this support, see John Wetenhall, "Camelot's Legacy to Public Art: Aesthetic Ideology in the New Frontier," in Senie and Webster, *Critical Issues in Public Art,* 142–57.

9. These basic conflicts in art patronage in the United States are discussed by Kevin V. Mulcahy, "Government and the Arts in the United States," in *The Patron State: Government and the Arts in Europe, North America, and Japan,* ed. Milton C. Cummings Jr. and Richard S. Katz (New York: Oxford University Press, 1977), 311–32.

10. For a discussion of federal legislation affecting cities, see Mark I. Gelfand, *A Nation of Cities: The Federal Government and Urban America, 1933–1965* (New York: Oxford University Press, 1975), 348–87.

11. In an unpublished "Report on Public Art to the Chairman of the National Endowment for the Arts" (1973), art historian Irving Sandler observed, "Increasingly, the public (including artists) cares about renewing our cities and our environment, and is becoming aware of the role that art can play. Art can be used to enrich the environment. Moreover, city planners agree that one way to provide a neighborhood with an identity is through the introduction of a landmark, and some recognize that artists can be employed to create such monuments" (3).

12. A complete study of the commission is found in Patricia Balton Stratton, "Chicago Picasso" (M.A. thesis, Northwestern University, 1982).

13. William B. Chappell, "The Chicago Picasso Reviewed a Decade Later," *Art International,* October/November 1977, 61–63, presents convincing evidence that the sculpture is a conflation of the artist's wife, Jacqueline Roque, and his pet Afghan hound, Kaboul. This private image has obvious sexual connotations as well.

14. For a discussion of this program, see John Beardsley, *Art in Public Places* (Washington, D.C.: Partners for Livable Places, 1981).

15. For documentation and discussion of the art commissioned by the GSA during this time, see Donald W. Thalacker, *The Place of Art in the World of Architecture* (New York and London: Chelsea House Publishers and R. R. Bowker Company, 1980).

16. One notable exception to this modernist approach to contemporary public sculpture was George Segal, who followed a tradition of figurative sculpture that was also often commemorative. For his GSA commission, Segal did a freestanding tableau in bronze, *The Restaurant* (1976), in Buffalo, New York, discussed in Thalacker, *The Place of Art,* 14–17. Segal's sculpture was not always without controversy, however. See, for example, Joseph Disponzio, "George Segal's Sculpture on a Theme of Gay Liberation and the Sexual-Political Equivocation of Political Consciousness," in Senie and Webster, *Critical Issues in Public Art,* 199–214.

17. For a review of Serra's life and career before *Tilted Arc,* see my article "The Right Stuff," *Artnews,* March 1984, 50–59. All subsequent quotes, unless indicated, are from this article or the two 1983 interviews with Serra that preceded it. A biography, list of exhibitions, and bibliography are included in the catalog of Serra's 1986 retrospective at the Museum of Modern Art. See Rosalind E. Krauss, *Richard Serra/Sculpture* (New York: Museum of Modern Art, 1986), 167–79. For more recent work, see *Richard Serra: Sculpture, 1985–1998,* ed. Russell Ferguson, Anthony McCall, and Clara Weyergraf-Serra (Los Angeles: Museum of Contemporary Art, 1999), 217–37.

18. For a discussion of arte povera, which includes an amazingly varied body of work, see Germano Celant, *Arte Povera* (Milan: Gabriele Mazzotta Editore, 1969). Characterized by attempts to link art and life in form and attitude, arte povera includes the work of both American and European artists.

19. Richard Serra, "Interview: Richard Serra and Bernard Lamarche-Vadel" (May 1980), in *Richard Serra: Interviews, Etc., 1970–1980* (Yonkers, N.Y.: Hudson River Museum, 1980), 134–35.

20. Ibid., 136.

21. Serra also created such a piece for his retrospective at the Museum of Modern Art in 1986.

22. In 1983 Serra started showing with Larry Gagosian, and three years later he joined the Pace Gallery. Today he also shows with Matthew Marks, who opened a second gallery in Chelsea, allegedly in part to accommodate Serra's work.

23. Serra describes this evolution in "Interview: Richard Serra and Liza Bear" (1976), in *Richard Serra: Interviews,* 70.

24. Earthworks and environmental art are discussed by John Beardsley, *Earthworks and Beyond,* 2nd ed. (New York: Abbeville Press, 1989).

25. For an interesting account of this trip and Serra's thinking at the time, see Philip Leider, "How I Spent My Summer Vacation," *Artforum,* January 1970, 40–48.

26. "Rigging" (text based on an interview between Gerard Hovagymyan and Richard Serra, January 1980), *Richard Serra: Interviews,* 123.

27. Information about the Wesleyan commission was provided by Martin Waters of the public information department at the university in a telephone conversation in December

1993. Serra's principal supporters were John Martin, director of the center in its formative years; Richard Field, a curator there; and John Paoletti, a junior faculty member at the time.

28. Richard Serra, "Extended Notes from Sight Pond Road," in *Richard Serra: Recent Sculpture in Europe, 1977–1985* (Bochum, Germany: Galerie m, 1985), 175.

29. "Richard Serra's Urban Sculpture: An Interview, Richard Serra and Douglas Crimp" (July 1980), in *Richard Serra: Interviews,* 175.

30. Quoted in Jo Ann Lewis, "Completing, L'Enfant," *Artnews,* March 1978, 110, 112, 114.

31. The panel consisted of Irving Sandler (professor of art history at the State University of New York (SUNY), Purchase, and an initial consultant to the NEA in the creation of its Art in Public Places program), Diane Vanderlip (educator and director of the art gallery at Moore College of Art), John Neff (curator of modern art at the Detroit Art Institute and director-designate of the Museum of Contemporary Art in Chicago), and James Elliott (director of the art museum of the University of California, Berkeley).

32. See Grace Glueck, "A Tale of Two Pylons," *New York Times,* April 7, 1978.

33. Quoted in Glueck, "A Tale of Two Pylons."

34. "Terminus," *Artnews,* March 1978, 112.

35. Quoted in Crimp, "Richard Serra's Urban Sculpture," 167.

36. Von Berswordt's role is discussed in *Terminal von Richard Serra: Eine Dokumentation in 7 Kapiteln* (Bochum, Germany: Museum Bochum, 1980), 23ff.

37. The vagaries of the civic process are related in exemplary detail in *Terminal von Richard Serra.* At one crucial meeting, the SPD voted against purchasing the sculpture in the morning, only to reverse itself in the afternoon. The issue of rust, which figured prominently in the complaints against *Tilted Arc,* is given a whole chapter in the account of the *Terminal* controversy.

38. The history of *Terminal* and the reasons for the controversies in Kassel and Bochum are analyzed in Harald Kimpel, ed., *Aversion/Akzeptanz* (Marburg, Germany: Jonas Verlag, 1992), 43–54.

39. *Terminal von Richard Serra,* 130.

40. For a discussion of Serra's films, see "The Films of Richard Serra: An Interview [with] Annette Michelson, Richard Serra, and Clara Weyergraf" (first published in *October* 10 [Fall 1979]), in *Richard Serra: Interviews,* 93–117.

41. Quoted in Crimp, "Richard Serra's Urban Sculpture," 175.

42. Both works are illustrated in Steve Cannon, Kellie Jones, and Tom Finkelpearl, Curator, *David Hammons: Rousing the Rubble* (New York: Institute for Contemporary Art, P.S. 1; Cambridge: MIT Press, 1991), 52, 84–85, respectively. They are discussed in an essay by Tom Finkelpearl, "On the Ideology of Dirt," 85ff.

43. Serra made this comment in an interview with Alfred Pacquement, "Entretien avec Richard Serra," in *Richard Serra* (Paris: Centre Georges Pompidou, 1983), 39. Translated by Jane Marie Todd in *Richard Serra: Writings Interviews* (Chicago: University of Chicago Press, 1994), 157–64. In contrast to his work in the landscape, Serra stated: "In most urban sites, I prefer verticality because it corresponds better to the scale of the surrounding architecture. My main concern is the approach to the space. In an urban site, I take into account the traffic, the streets, and the surrounding architecture. I construct a kind of disjunction with a structure that will locate the place, that relates to and at the same time separates itself from the surrounding architecture" (160).

44. Richard Serra, "St. John's Rotary Arc," *Artforum,* September 1980, 53.

45. Kim Levin, "Richard Serra's Arch Angle," *Village Voice,* March 25–31, 1981, 94; Elizabeth Frank, "Richard Serra at Castelli Greene St." *Art in America,* Summer 1981, 126.

1. Commission, Installation, Removal

1. More than thirty articles appeared in the *New York Times* in 1979 reporting the scandals. GSA administrator Jay Solomon ran into trouble personally when he dismissed Robert T. Griffin, deputy administrator of the agency and a close friend of House Speaker Thomas P. O'Neill Jr., without informing the speaker. It was this gaff of protocol that earned Solomon President Jimmy Carter's disfavor. Articles pertaining to these circumstances appeared in the *New York Times* on January 24, 1979, and January 27, 1979.

2. Donald W. Thalacker, *The Place of Art in the World of Architecture* (New York and London: Chelsea House Publishers and R. R. Bowker Company, 1980).

3. Freeman, who had extensive experience in the management and procurement of large weapons, was charged with continuing Solomon's investigation of agency fraud. Freeman's "superlative tact" was cited as a significant factor in his appointment. See "Admiral Called Likely G.S.A. Head," *New York Times,* March 23, 1979; Edward C. Burks, "New Man Minding Federal Store," *New York Times,* March 26, 1979.

4. The guidelines in place when Serra was commissioned by the GSA were established in 1973 and subsequently modified. The operative guidelines in 1979 were: "1) The project architect is encouraged to submit an art-in-architecture proposal as part of his overall design concept. This proposal includes a description of the location and nature of the artwork(s) to be commissioned, such as a sculpture in the plaza or a tapestry in the lobby; 2) GSA and the NEA appoint a panel of qualified art professionals to nominate three to five artists for each proposed commission. This panel is constituted on an ad hoc basis for each specific project. The panelists, at least one of whom must be from the geographical area of the project, meet with the project architect and representatives of GSA and NEA at the project site to review visual materials on artists whose work would be appropriate for the proposal commission(s); 3) The panel's nominations are submitted to GSA by formal letter from the NEA. After evaluation of the nominees' existing work by a design review panel in GSA's Public Buildings Services (PBS), the GSA Administrator selects the artist; 4) A fixed-price contract is negotiated with the artist for the design, execution, installation, and photography of the artwork. Artists' concepts are reviewed and approved by the design review panel."

5. This information is included in the GSA project file for *Tilted Arc* in an unpaginated document entitled "Chronology of Events" (hereafter referred to as "Chronology"). There is no indication who prepared this detailed document. It is much more detailed than the chronology that appears in Attachment A to Dwight Ink's final decision document *Decision on the "Tilted Arc"* (May 31, 1985, unpublished, available at GSA). The project file is in the GSA office of the Art-in-Architecture program in Washington, D.C. At the time of this writing, it could be consulted by appointment.

6. While director of the Institute of Contemporary Art at the University of Pennsylvania, Delehanty had served on three selection panels, one in 1973 and two in 1974. Licht had also been a member of two selection panels in 1974, one while an art historian at the University of Rochester and one later that year as a curator at the Museum of Contemporary Art in Chicago. The following year he was also on two GSA panels. Robert Pincus-Witten's

essay, "Richard Serra: Slow Information," first published in 1969, is included in Pincus-Witten, *Postminimalism* (New York: Out of London Press, 1977).

7. Panel meetings are not public. However, the GSA project file on *Tilted Arc* contains notes taken by an unidentified GSA staff member.

8. GSA project file; handwritten notes taken at the meeting.

9. Interview with Marilyn Farley, January 1992.

10. See Michael Weizenbach, "Ex-GSA Director Washes Hands of Rusty Sculpture," *Washington Times,* June 11, 1985. In an interview with the author in March 1993, Terence C. Golden, administrator of GSA after Dwight Ink, also expressed the opinion that he had more important issues to deal with than the art commissioned by the agency.

11. NEA memorandum dated June 10, 1985, to Frank Hodsoll from Richard Andrews on *Tilted Arc* selection process. Private NEA files.

12. "Richard Serra's Urban Sculpture: An Interview, Richard Serra and Douglas Crimp" (July 1980), in *Richard Serra: Interviews, Etc., 1970–1980* (Yonkers, N.Y.: Hudson River Museum, 1980), 168.

13. Alfred Pacquement, "Entretien avec Richard Serra," in *Richard Serra* (Paris: Centre Georges Pompidou, 1983), 41. Translated by Todd in *Richard Serra: Writings Interviews,* 157–64. Shortly after the installation of *Tilted Arc,* Serra stated, "Someone asked me recently about the Federal Plaza. I must say it was a problematic site, excessively defined by the presence of government and representative of the American justice system. I hope the work will not become a symbol of that plaza" (163). Omitted from this translation of the interview is a reference to the Federal Plaza as a "ridiculous place," a concern that the sculpture not serve capitalism, and a sentence discussing the site as an entry point for all immigrants to the United States, who would have to pass in front of the sculpture.

14. Conversation with the author in 1983 in preparation for *Artnews* profile.

15. Ibid.

16. Ibid.

17. A memo of March 19, 1980, from Cecilia Horovitz, contracting officer in New York, specified these concerns (some of which had been raised previously by the design-review panel):

1. The load this sculpture will superimpose on the existing structure supporting the Plaza requires a complete structural analysis of the area. Submit your details and calculations for GSA's approval before advancing in the development of this project.
2. Extreme care must be applied to the detailing and execution of waterproofing in the installation of this sculpture, to avoid future problems of leaks through the Plaza.
3. How do you propose to resolve the problem of rust stains that may affect the existing pavement surrounding the sculpture?
4. An already critical wind tunnel effect exists around the building. How will the sculpture modify this condition, affecting the safety of pedestrian traffic?
5. This sculpture will present a large vertical surface which will attract graffiti and ball playing. This would create problems of security, maintenance and even possible irreparable damage to this art piece. The cost of cleaning and maintenance must be considered, since it may be very substantial through the life of this sculpture.

6. This sculpture introduces a screen effect in the presently wide open Plaza. Visual control will no longer be effective.
7. Submit your recommendations on how to approach security and crime control in the area.
8. Also, related to safety of pedestrian traffic, security and crime control, is the need for adequate illumination of the sculpture and its surroundings. This critical element should be made part of your design and submitted for approval by GSA before further project development.

On condition of anonymity, several individuals at GSA expressed the feeling that Serra was made to go to inordinate lengths to accommodate engineering requirements. In a letter to Cecilia Horovitz dated June 18, 1980, Malcolm Graff responded in detail to her concerns and submitted preliminary drawings and engineering calculations. He provided evidence that the sculpture would actually improve drainage in the plaza and act as a windbreak for pedestrians. He also demonstrated that *Tilted Arc,* after a slight reorientation, would "not interfere with any of these existing traffic patterns or significantly alter pedestrian circulation on the plaza." At the time, weathering steel was thought to require no maintenance.

18. Handwritten memo by GSA staff member Marilyn Farley in GSA's *Tilted Arc* file, dated February 23, 1981.

19. Conversation with the author in 1983 for *Artnews* profile.

20. Richard Serra, "Introduction," in *The Destruction of "Tilted Arc": Documents,* ed. Clara Weyergraf-Serra and Martha Buskirk (Cambridge: MIT Press, 1991), 5 (hereafter referred to as *Destruction*).

21. Grace Glueck, "An Outdoor-Sculpture Safari in the City," *New York Times,* August 7, 1981.

22. *Destruction,* 26.

23. Quoted in Grace Glueck, "Serra Work Stirs Downtown Protest," *New York Times,* September 25, 1981.

24. "Chronology."

25. Dwight Ink, acting administrator of GSA, stated, "The process in place at the time of the artist's nomination and selection did not include soliciting public and community views and reactions to the artwork prior to its commissioning. Although representatives of the New York art community were on the Artist Nomination Board, there was no relationship perceived between the community and employees in the office building, and the goals and procedures of the Art-in-Architecture program. As a consequence, the community, being largely a non-participant in the art selection process, was not properly prepared to receive the work of art and was not in a position to provide even minimal public understanding and acceptance of the work. The lack of community support was first evidenced when the artwork was installed and may have resulted, in part, from this failure" (*Decision on the "Tilted Arc,"* 6). However, the current GSA selection procedures, in which community representatives outnumber art professionals, have not eliminated controversies.

26. Both versions are included in "Chronology." This document is the primary source for the events discussed below, unless otherwise noted.

27. This event is included in the official, though abbreviated, chronology found in Ink, Attachment A.

28. Copies of these letters may be found in *Destruction,* 33–40.

29. Susan Heller Anderson and David W. Dunlap, "*Arc* under Scrutiny," *New York Times,* December 29, 1984.

30. U.S. District Court, Southern District of New York, *Richard Serra, Plaintiff, v. United States General Services Administration . . . ,* December 17, 1986, Docket No. 86 Civ. 9656, J. Pollack presiding, 21n79. This document was reviewed by several GSA employees at the time and deemed accurate. (Hereafter cited as Serra Complaint.)

31. *Destruction,* 45.

32. *Destruction,* 48.

33. *Destruction,* 49.

34. GSA Region 2 news release, R2-85-M004, dated March 5, 1985.

35. *Destruction,* 65.

36. A complete list of speakers and sample testimonies are included in *Destruction,* 59–129. For a contemporary summary of the issues raised at the hearing, see the Summer 1985 issue of the *Public Art Fund Newsletter* by the author. An interesting analysis of the hearing is provided in Casey Nelson Blake, "An Atmosphere of Effrontery: Richard Serra, *Tilted Arc,* and the Crisis of Public Art," in *The Power of Culture: Critical Essays in American History,* ed. Richard W. Fox and T. J. Jackson Lears (Chicago: University of Chicago Press, 1993), 264–68.

37. Serra Complaint, 26n95, 33n122, notes that although Diamond stated that more than twenty public events were held at Federal Plaza between 1976 and 1981 when Serra's sculpture was installed, he could not document any of them.

38. *Destruction,* 142–49.

39. Undated memo from GSA General Counsel Latimer to Acting Administrator Ink. The memo informs Ink: "If you should determine that the sculpture, for appropriate reason, is not suitable for continued viewing at the plaza, you have the authority to require its removal to another Federal location, or to declare the property excess to the needs of GSA, with potential for sale or disposal to non-Federal entities."

40. From a confidential conversation with a member of Community Board 1 at the time. Serra Complaint notes that Diamond "failed to disclose: that prior to the Board's vote there was discussion about *Tilted Arc* only in a sub-committee . . . ; that subsequently the presence of a quorum at the vote of the Board was questioned; [that] this Community Board has few members who live and work in the immediate vicinity of the plaza; that the plaza is on the fringe of the Board's geographical jurisdiction; that people who live in the community rarely used the plaza; and that Serra, who lives within the Board's jurisdiction, was not informed of its proposed resolution, nor invited to appear before the Board" (33).

41. A draft of a memo entitled "*Tilted Arc,* Arguments for Relocation," dated April 17, 1985, states, "(1) The unpopularity of *Tilted Arc* has spilled over into the program, making all future placements of modern art in Federal Buildings suspect; and (2) The weakness in the current regulations . . . did not allow community participation in the initial selection of *Tilted Arc.* These regulations are currently being rewritten to expand community participation in the selection process in the future."

42. *Destruction,* 152–56.

43. The letter is reproduced in *Destruction,* 150–51. It was signed by Senators Howard M.

Metzenbaum and Edward M. Kennedy and Representatives Tom Downey, Frank Horton, Hamilton Fish Jr., and Jim Jeffords.

44. Ink's decision is reproduced in full in *Destruction,* 157–73.

45. Conversation with Richard Andrews, March 1993.

46. Memo titled "Meeting between GSA and NEA," dated June 5, 1985. There was apparently no attempt to take Serra up on his offer to help design improvements to Federal Plaza. In a conversation with the artist in December 1993, he recalled that what he had in mind was a more open dialogue and removal of the inoperative fountain. The fountain was removed in 1996.

47. Adele Chatfield-Taylor, "Re: The *Tilted Arc*—Next Steps" (memo to Frank Hodsoll, June 17, 1985).

48. Adele Chatfield-Taylor, "Re: *Tilted Arc*" (memo to Frank Hodsoll, September 16, 1985). Apparently the initial idea was to make these changes without fanfare but, as Chatfield-Taylor noted, "Diamond had later decided publicity was appropriate to any undertaking having to do with the 'Tilted Arc.'"

49. Memorandum of Agreement between the General Services Administration and the National Endowment for the Arts Regarding the *Tilted Arc* Site Review Advisory Panel (GSA project file).

50. This account is based on personal notes taken at the NEA panel meeting in New York. Unless otherwise noted, quotations from the panel meeting are from these notes.

51. *Destruction,* 188–90.

52. All quotations in this paragraph are from Daniel B. Schneider, "The Homeless Arc," *New York Times,* April 9, 2000. The Maryland building also contains a summary of the history of *Tilted Arc,* prepared for potential art pilgrims. My thanks to William Caine at the GSA for this information.

2. Public Opinion

1. Hearing, 2:451.

2. Judith H. Balfe and Margaret J. Wyszomirski, "Public Art and Public Policy," *Journal of Arts Management and Law,* Winter 1986, defines "1) the artists, who desire artistic freedom, recognition, and security for their work; 2) the commissioning public agency, which is responsible for the promotion of the long-term aesthetic welfare of society, while confronting immediate political and procedural constraints upon its actions; and 3) the public, which must assent to the funding and give community acceptance to the particular works installed in its midst" (5).

3. Casey Nelson Blake, "An Atmosphere of Effrontery: Richard Serra, *Tilted Arc,* and the Crisis of Public Art," in *The Power of Culture: Critical Essays in American History,* ed. Richard W. Fox and T. J. Jackson Lears (Chicago: University of Chicago Press, 1993), 247–89.

4. Robert Storr, "*Tilted Arc:* Enemy of the People?" *Art in America,* September 1985, 90–97.

5. John Lindell, in "On Site Specificity," *Documents,* Spring 1994, observed, "I say the gay community all the time, but there really isn't one. I'm supposed to represent a community that in fact doesn't exist. I'm an individual in relationship to a very conflicting group of subcultural people. This idea that we assign people to groups is false but still very operative" (21).

The construction of the art world is, if anything, even more complex than that of the gay community.

6. Wendy Harris, interview with the author, April 1997.

7. An insightful first-person account of the rise and decline of Wall Street is Michael Lewis, *Liar's Poker* (New York: W. W. Norton, 1989). Rosalyn Deutsche, "Uneven Development: Public Art in New York City," *October,* Winter 1988, 3–52, is a detailed account of the direct relationship between homelessness and the spending policies of the 1980s as well as public art's implication in the process.

8. For a succinct summary and critique of the effects of Reagan politics on life in the 1980s, see Haynes Johnson, *Sleepwalking through History: America in the Reagan Years* (New York: Doubleday, 1991); for a rundown of the foibles of Ed Koch's administration, see Jack Newfield and Wayne Barrett, *City for Sale: Ed Koch and the Betrayal of New York,* paperback ed. (New York: Harper and Row, 1989).

9. Quoted in Johnson, *Sleepwalking through History,* 189.

10. Responses to Diamond's questionnaire "For Relocation." In GSA project file, Washington, D.C.

11. For a general discussion of rising anger in the United States, see Susan J. Tolchin, *The Angry American: How Voter Rage Is Changing the Nation* (Boulder, Colo.: Westview Press, 1996). Art critic Michael Brenson characterized the thirty-eight letters he received as possibly the most immediate and angry of any elicited by his columns in the *New York Times.* For example, Fred L. Mayer addressed him as "dear art expert" and referred to his article on *Tilted Arc* as "lengthy bullshit"; and F. W. Liander wrote, "I wonder at your sensibilities. To call this monstrosity a work of art is lunacy" (correspondence lent to the author).

12. *In the Matter of a Public Hearing for the Relocating of "Tilted Arc" at the Plaza of 26 Federal Plaza* (New York: GSA. Nation-Wide Reporting Service, 1985). Available at the Museum of Modern Art (MoMA) library. (Hereafter referred to as Hearing.) Hirsch, Hearing, 1:200. Paris, Hearing, 2:354.

13. Segal, Hearing, 1:99. Sugarman, Hearing, 1:90.

14. In 1975 Sugarman's *Baltimore Federal* (1975), also a GSA commission, was the object of intense controversy as judges complained about the sculpture's appearance and perceived it as threatening, a place for muggers and rapists to hide. See, for example, Meyer Raphael Rubinstein, "Outdoor Eye: George Sugarman's Public Sculpture," *Arts,* January 1990, 76–77. The controversy over Segal's *Gay Liberation* (1980) in New York City's generally liberal Greenwich Village centered on its subject matter, with opposition coming from a variety of sources, including members of the gay community. See Joseph Disponzio, "George Segal's Sculpture on a Theme of Gay Liberation and the Sexual-Political Equivocation of Public Consciousness," in *Critical Issues in Public Art: Content, Context, and Controversy,* ed. Harriet F. Senie and Sally Webster (New York: HarperCollins, 1992; reissued Washington, D.C.: Smithsonian Institution Press, 1998), 199–215.

15. "Interview: Richard Serra and Liza Bear," in *Richard Serra: Interviews, Etc., 1970–1980* (Yonkers, N.Y.: Hudson River Museum, 1980), 76.

16. "Interview: Richard Serra and Bernard Lamarche-Vadel," in *Richard Serra: Interviews,* 149.

17. Patricia C. Phillips, "Forum: Something There Is That Doesn't Love a Wall," *Artforum,* Summer 1985, 100–101.

18. See Storr, *"Tilted Arc."*

19. An important analysis of the relationship between class and taste is Pierre Bourdieu, *A Social Critique of the Judgment of Taste,* trans. Richard Nice (Cambridge, Mass.: Harvard University Press, 1984). See also Paul Dimaggio and Michael Useem, "Social Class and Arts Consumption: The Origins and Consequences of Class Differences in Exposure to the Arts in America," *Theory and Society,* 1978, 141–61.

20. See, for example, Monroe C. Beardsley, "Aesthetic Welfare, Aesthetic Justice, and Educational Policy," in *Public Policy and the Aesthetic Interest,* ed. Ralph A. Smith and Ronald Berman (Chicago: University of Chicago Press, 1992), 40–51.

21. *Coming to Our Senses: The Significance of the Arts for American Education* (New York: McGraw-Hill, 1977), p. 248.

22. See *Beyond Creating: The Place for Art in America's Schools* (Los Angeles: J. Paul Getty Trust, 1985). An earlier but much less widely circulated or accessible survey, *Course Offerings and Enrollments in the Arts and the Humanities at the Secondary School Level* (Washington, D.C.: National Center for Education Statistics, 1984) reported slightly higher figures.

23. National Endowment for the Arts, *Toward Civilization: A Report on Arts Education* (Washington, D.C.: NEA, 1988). Figures in this report indicated a slightly higher percentage of instruction devoted to the visual arts than did the Getty report.

24. Laura Chapman, "Arts Education as a Policy Issue: The Federal Legacy," in Smith and Berman, *Public Policy,* 119–36. This article provides an interesting critique of the 1977 Rockefeller panel report initially suggested by Nancy Hanks and of art education programs sponsored at the NEA.

25. Margaret Jane Wyszomirski, "From Accord to Discord: Arts Policy during and after the Culture Wars," in *America's Commitment to Culture,* ed. Kevin Mulcahy and Margaret Jane Wyszomirski (Boulder, Colo.: Westview Press, 1995), 25.

26. For insightful critiques of television in general and its effects see Jane Feuer, *Seeing through the Eighties: Television and Reaganism* (Durham, N.C.: Duke University Press, 1995); Todd Gitlin, *Inside Prime Time* (New York: Pantheon Books, 1985); and especially Jeffrey Scheuer, *The Sound Bite Society: Television and the American Mind* (New York: Four Walls, Eight Windows, 1999). See also Johnson, *Sleepwalking through History,* 139–52.

27. Clara Weyergraf-Serra and Martha Buskirk, eds., *The Destruction of "Tilted Arc": Documents* (Cambridge: MIT Press, 1991), 9–10. (Hereafter referred to as *Destruction*).

28. Scheur, *The Sound Bite Society,* 161.

29. John Ryan and Deborah A. Sim, "When Art Becomes News: The Portrayal of Art and Artists on Network Television News," *Social Forces,* March 1990, 869–89. This paper demonstrates the need and provides an excellent model for further studies on this provocative topic. All subsequent quotes in this paragraph are from this source.

30. With newspaper coverage it is always interesting to consider where in the paper an article appears and the impact of headlines, both as information for those who read only them and also as a frame for the article. For *Daily News* coverage, see Jennifer Caldwall and James Harney, "Sculpture Foes Call that Metal Scrap," March 7, 1985, 23; cartoon of March 8, 1985, 6; "Give the Thing a Useful Purpose," March 9, 1985, 19; and Beth Fallon, "Lacing into the Iron Curtain Downtown," 36. In the *New York Times,* see Grace Glueck, "An Outdoor-Sculpture Safari in the City," August 7, 1981, C1; Grace Glueck, "What Part Should the Public Play in Choosing Public Art?" February 3, 1985, section 2, p. 1; Douglas C.

McGill, "Office Workers and Artists Debate Fate of a Sculpture," March 7, 1985, B1, B6; Douglas C. McGill, "Art People," April 5, 1985, C24; Esther B. Fein, "Panel Backs Removal of Foley Square Sculpture," April 19, 1985, C4; Eleanor Munro, "For an Art Truce in Foley Square," May 18, 1985, 25; "Public Sculpture Is Symbolic First and Pleasurable Only Second," May 24, 1985; "Intrusive Arc," May 31, 1985, A26; Joseph Berger, "*Tilted Arc* To Be Moved from Plaza at Foley Square," June 1, 1985, 25, 28; Douglas C. McGill, "TA Removal Draws Mixed Reaction," June 6, 1985, C21; Douglas C. McGill, "Art People," December 18, 1987, 36; David W. Dunlap, "Moving Day Arrives for Disputed Sculpture," March 11, 1989, 29, 32; "Without TA, a Plaza Bustles," September 21, 1989, B2; and Carol Vogel, "The Art Market," May 28, 1993, C23 (announcing Martha Schwartz's plans for Federal Plaza). In the *Washington Post,* see Margot Hornblower, "New Yorkers, Artists Tilt over Arc," March 7, 1985, D1; "Twisted Art," September 19, 1987, A22; "Serra's Arc of Defeat," March 15, 1989; "The Arc Comes Down," March 24, 1989, A22. And in the *Washington Times,* see Suzanne Fields, "Waiting for the Eloquence," March 14, 1985.

31. I invoke here Michel de Certeau, *The Practice of Everyday Life,* trans. Steven Rendall (Berkeley and Los Angeles: University of California Press, 1984).

32. Tavolaro and Crawford in responses to Diamond's questionnaire "For Relocation." Lawrence stated, "The one by the Holland Tunnel, no one really goes up next to it. You can't. You are not allowed in that space and to me it looks lovely and it gives a wonderful sweep to an area which otherwise is rather hideous for all the exhaust fumes that go by. For us, though, around here in the building, we can testify again and again it's no longer a living space near that piece" (Hearing, 3: 597–98). Steven Faust made a similar observation, adding *T.W.U.* to his list of Serra sculptures appropriate to their urban sites (Hearing 3: 602–3).

33. U.S. District Judge Gerard L. Goettel stated, "While views of what constitutes art can be subjective, that piece of rusty metal could not be characterized as being art by even the greatest leap of the imagination" (letter to Diamond, February 19, 1985, GSA project file). Judge of the U.S. Court of Appeals for the Second Circuit, William Hughes Mulligan, observed, "The concept that it is art . . . is incomprehensible to any visitor who views it." More succinctly, one federal employee declared, "It isn't art. It's junk" (response to Diamond's questionnaire, GSA project file). And much more of the same . . .

34. Dario Gamboni, *The Destruction of Art* (London: Reaktion Books, 1997), 304–5. In the chapter titled "Mistaking Art for Refuse," Gamboni observes that much modern art consists of the "systematic questioning of the line between art and non-art" (292). A compelling analysis of the confusion of art with reality is David Freedberg, *The Power of Images: Studies in the History and Theory of Response* (Chicago: University of Chicago Press, 1989).

35. Brownstein, Hearing, 2:352. Kim Levin, "Richard Serra's Arch Angle," *Village Voice,* March 25–31, 1981, 94. Paris, Hearing, 2:353–55. Slizys, in responses to Diamond's questionnaire, "For Relocation," GSA project file.

36. In a conversation in July 1993, artist Melinda Hunt, an immigrant from Canada and an admirer of Serra's sculpture, found *Tilted Arc* especially appropriate for the experience of obtaining citizenship.

37. Responses to Diamond's questionnaire.

38. Serra, public lecture at the Ninety-Second Street Y, New York, 1993.

39. Arthur Danto, "Richard Serra," in *The State of the Art* (New York: Prentice Hall, 1987), observed that in a museum, "in a curious way the surfaces seem as oddly elegant as

those of travertine marble," but outside there are other associations due to the work's "proximity to the unavoidable flotsam of urban life with which rust symbolically belongs" (179–80).

40. Carman, letter to Diamond, February 26, 1985, in GSA file. Other quotations from responses to Diamond's questionnaire.

41. Kilbourn, Hearing, 1:72, 65. Haggerty, Hearing, 3:659.

42. See Gamboni, *Destruction of Art,* chapter 9: "The Degradation of Art in Public Places," 170–89.

43. John Dornberg, "Art Vandals: Why Do They Do It?" *Artnews,* March 1987, 103, notes that between 1970 and 1979 the number of reported cases of art vandalism in the United States increased 70 percent.

44. Anonymous quotes, unless otherwise indicated, were taken from the numerous responses on the form distributed by Diamond's office soliciting workers' opinions on the relocation of the sculpture.

45. Letter to Diamond, February 15, 1985, GSA project file.

46. Hearing, 1:78.

47. Hearing, 1:208.

48. For an analysis of this country's at best ambivalent attitude toward culture and the intellectual professions, see Andrew Ross, *No Respect: Intellectuals and Popular Culture* (New York: Routledge, 1989).

49. To cite just one example, the 1993 movie *Dave,* starring Kevin Kline, posited that the director of a temp employment agency could step into the job of U.S. president and do it quite well, better than the elected official. The appeal of Ross Perot in the political campaign of 1992 reflected another aspect of the premise that a nonprofessional outsider can show the pros a thing or two.

50. Mondale, Hearing, 2:17. Highstein, Hearing, 1:160.

51. Johnson, Hearing, 3:623. Rubin, Hearing, 1:15.

52. Javits, hearing testimony, reproduced in *Destruction,* 98. St. Clair, Hearing, 2:503, reproduced in *Destruction,* 106.

53. Letter to Diamond, March 9, 1985, GSA project file.

54. Ganz, Hearing, 2:319; Metzenbaum, Letter to Ink, May 31, 1985, GSA project file, reproduced in *Destruction,* 174. Serra, Hearing, 1:45, reproduced in *Destruction,* 68.

55. Solomon-Godeau, Hearing, 3:567. Harrow, Hearing, 1:52, 54.

56. Letter to Dwight Ink, May 2, 1985, GSA project file.

57. Glueck, "Outdoor-Sculpture Safari." As discussed in chapter 2, Glueck's article provided ammunition for Judge Re. Peter Schjeldahl, "Artistic Control," *Village Voice,* October 14–20, 1981, 100. Schjeldahl's vituperative article prompted a barrage of responses for and against the sculpture, a mini preview of the testimony later given at the hearing. See "Letters: Defenders of the *Tilted Arc,*" *Village Voice,* November 4–10, 1981, 118. The title is misleading, since not all the letters defend the sculpture; several in fact applaud the article.

58. Paul Goldberger, "Critic's Notebook," *New York Times,* May 2, 1985; Phillips, "Forum," 100–101.

59. Gary Indiana, "Debby with Monument: A Dissenting Opinion," *Village Voice,* April 18, 1985, 94.

60. Michael Sorkin, "Que Serra Sera," *Village Voice,* March 5, 1985, 85.

61. Michael Brenson, "The Case in Favor of a Controversial Sculpture," *New York Times,* May 19, 1985.

62. Arthur Danto, "*Tilted Arc* and Public Art," in *The State of the Art,* 90–94.

63. Calvin Tomkins, *"Tilted Arc," The New Yorker,* May 20, 1985, 95ff.

64. See Harriet F. Senie, *Contemporary Public Sculpture: Tradition, Transformation, and Controversy* (New York: Oxford University Press, 1992), 175–77.

65. Robert Hughes, "The Trials of *Tilted Arc,*" *Time,* June 3, 1985, 78. Storr, *"Tilted Arc,"* 90–97.

66. Quoted in Hollis Clayson, "Materialist Art History and Its Points of Difficulty," *Art Bulletin,* September 1995, 370.

3. Reframing the Controversy

1. See, for example, Renato Poggioli, *The Theory of the Avant-Garde* (Cambridge, Mass.: Harvard University Press, 1968).

2. The definition of modernism in terms of its self-reflexiveness is closely associated with Clement Greenberg, especially his often reprinted "Towards a Newer Laocoon," *Partisan Review,* July–August 1940, 296–310. See also Robert Hughes, *The Shock of the New* (New York: Alfred A. Knopf, 1981).

3. See, for example, Barnett Newman, "The Sublime Is Now," *Tiger's Eye,* December 1948, 51–53, for his often quoted statement: "Instead of making cathedrals out of Christ, man, or 'life,' we are making [them] of ourselves, out of our own feelings."

4. Andreas Huyssen, *After the Great Divide: Modernism, Mass Culture, Postmodernism* (Bloomington: Indiana University Press, 1986).

5. See, for example, Kim Levin, "Farewell to Modernism," *Arts Magazine,* October 1979, 90–92; Douglas Davis, "Post-Everything," *Art in America,* February 1980, 11–14; Clement Greenberg, "Modern and Post-Modern," *Arts Magazine,* February 1980, 64–66; Irving Sandler, "Modernism, Revisionism, Pluralism, and Post-Modernism," *Art Journal,* Fall 1980, 345–47.

6. Hal Foster, ed., *The Anti-Aesthetic: Essays on Postmodern Culture* (Port Townsend, Wash.: Bay Press, 1983), ix. Contributors included Jürgen Habermas (who saw modernity as an incomplete project rather than as one that was permanently flawed), Kenneth Frampton, Rosalind Krauss, Douglas Crimp, Fredric Jameson, Jean Baudrillard, and Edward W. Said. On the East Village, see, for example, Anne E. Bowler and Baline McBurney, "Gentrification and the Avant-Garde in New York's East Village," in *Paying the Piper: Causes and Consequences of Art Patronage,* ed. Judith Huggins Balfe (Urbana and Chicago: University of Illinois Press, 1993), 161–82.

7. Brian Wallis, ed., *Art after Modernism: Rethinking Representation* (New York: New Museum of Contemporary Art, 1984); Lucy Lippard, *Get the Message? A Decade of Art for Social Change* (New York: E. P. Dutton, 1984).

8. Suzi Gablik, *Has Modernism Failed?* (New York: Thames and Hudson, 1984). Marcia Tucker, preface to Max Almy et al., *Difference: On Representation and Sexuality* (New York: New Museum of Contemporary Art, 1985). The exhibition, guest curated by Kate Linker and Jane Weinstock (film and video), was accompanied by a catalog containing essays by Craig Owens, Lise Tickner, Jacqueline Rose, Petter Wollen, and Jane Weinstock. All explored questions of posing, the gaze, sexuality, and vision, linking their analysis to psychoanalytic theory

in the work of Sigmund Freud, Roland Barthes, Michel Foucault, and, most importantly, Jacques Lacan.

9. Rosalind Krauss, *The Originality of the Avant-Garde and Other Modernist Myths* (Cambridge: MIT Press, 1984).

10. In most standard histories of modern art, Serra is included among the minimalists. See, for example, Sam Hunter and John Jacobus, *Modern Art* (Englewood Cliffs, N.J.: Prentice Hall, 1992). Robert Pincus-Witten, *Postminimalism* (New York: Out of London Press, 1977), begins with "Richard Serra: Slow Information."

11. First published in 1972, Serra's *Verb List* has been frequently reprinted in publications dealing with his work, most recently in *Richard Serra: Writings Interviews* (Chicago: University of Chicago Press, 1994), 3.

12. Clement Greenberg's essay "Modernist Painting," originally published in 1965, serves as the introduction to Francis Frascina and Charles Harrison, eds., *Modern Art and Modernism: An Anthology* (New York: Harper and Row, 1986), 5–10.

13. *Serra: Writings,* 277. This 1992 comment is typical of many comparable statements made throughout his career.

14. Rosalind E. Krauss, "Richard Serra, a Translation," in Krauss, *Originality of the Avant-Garde,* 270. Included in this essay for the catalog accompanying Serra's retrospective at the Musee National d'Art Moderne, Centre Georges Pompidou, published in 1983, is this phenomenological description of the experience of *Shift,* a six-part landscape piece of 1970–72 in King City, Canada: "From being the lines along which one sights as one stands above them and looks down, thereby establishing one's connection to the distance, *the walls change as one 'descends' the work to become an enclosure that binds one within the earth.* Felt as barrier rather than as perspective, they then heighten the experience of the physical place of one's body" (267, emphasis added). What is the precise nature of this heightening of body awareness and the physical experience of descending? It sounds very much like a burial experience (see my emphases above).

15. See Armin Zweite, "Evidence and Experience of Self: Some Spatially Related Sculptures by Richard Serra," in *Richard Serra,* ed. Ernst-Gerhard Güse (New York: Rizzoli Books, 1988), 8ff. See also David Craven, "Richard Serra and the Phenomenology of Perception," on *St. John's Rotary Arc,* in *Arts,* March 1986, 49–51.

16. Morris's influential three-part series, "Notes on Sculpture," was first published in *Artforum,* February 1966; October 1966; Summer 1967. It is excerpted in Charles Harrison and Paul Wood, *Art in Theory: 1900–1990* (Oxford: Blackwell, 1992), 813–22. Kenneth Baker, *Minimalism* (New York: Abbeville, 1988), 123.

17. In a review of Serra's exhibition, *Richard Serra: Weight and Measure Drawings* at the Drawing Center in New York City, Michael Kimmelman observed, "The drawings are slow and measured, and their intensity, not to say format, brings to mind Rothko and Newman, even though those connections are not the ones Mr. Serra intends" ("Powerful Rectangles by Serra," *New York Times,* June 10, 1994).

18. Michael Kimmelman, "At the Met and the Modern with Richard Serra," *New York Times,* August 11, 1995.

19. Philip Leider, "How I Spent My Summer Vacation," *Artforum,* January 1970, 40–48. The cover of the issue featured Newman's sculpture *Broken Obelisk.*

20. See Zweite, "Evidence and Experience," 14. Serra's comment first appeared in a

review of his work by Rosalind Krauss, "Richard Serra: Sculpture Redrawn," *Artforum,* May 1972. In 1980 Robert Pincus-Witten wrote, "The broad face of the *Rotary Arc* symbolizes painting. One could be even more specific: the very edges of the arc enact the 'zips' of Newman" ("Entries: Oedipus Reconciled," *Arts Magazine,* November 1980, 130–33). And in a 1991 interview Serra invoked Newman as an example of an artist whose work defied language (Heinz Peter Shwerfel, "Ein Mann, der Gern aneckt," *Zeitmagazin,* November 22, 1991, 80).

21. *Serra: Writings,* 280. These comments were made in an interview with Nicholas Serota and David Sylvester on May 27, 1992.

22. E. A. Carmean Jr. and Eliza R. Rathbone with Thomas B. Hess, *American Art at Mid-Century: The Subjects of the Artist* (Washington, D.C.: Washington National Gallery, 1978), 34–35.

23. Rosalind Krauss, *Richard Serra/Sculpture* (New York: Museum of Modern Art, 1986), suggests, "In some sense . . . all sculpture configures the human body; that is, it operates as a model—of widely divergent kinds—of the human subject. . . . Further, it does this no matter how reduced it might be in the manner of its actual likeness to the human body." Krauss saw Serra's primary concerns throughout the 1970s as "a problem in the domain of perception—perception, that is, grounded in a living, moving, reacting body." She suggests that sculpture might variously convey "an image of ideal repose or of the purposiveness of action; of the centeredness of reason or the abandon to feeling" (22, 28).

Donald Kuspit, "Material as Sculptural Metaphor," in *Individuals: A Selected History of Contemporary Art, 1945–1986,* ed. Howard Singerman (New York: Abbeville, 1986), observed: "When a sculpture—even an abstract sculpture—carries the kind of conviction we call 'presence,' we are unconsciously reading it as a metaphoric symbolization of the body's emotional meaning. . . . Sculpture may renounce the overt illusion of the body, but covertly it represents the most intimate conception of the body" (106).

Kate Linker, "Abstraction: Form as Meaning," in Singerman, *Individuals,* argues, "Whether as expressive subject or Hegelian mind, the self is the great abstraction of the modernist period" (30).

The interpretation in this section appeared as an essay, "Perpetual Tension: Considering Richard Serra's Jewish Identity," in *Complex Identities: Jewish Consciousness and Modern Art,* ed. Matthew Baigell and Milly Heyd (New Brunswick, N.J.: Rutgers University Press, 2001), 206–22.

24. Kenneth Baker, *Minimalism* (New York: Abbeville, 1988), 114.

25. Interview with Liza Bear, March 30, 1976, in *Richard Serra: Interviews, Etc., 1970–1980* (Yonkers, N.Y.: Hudson River Museum, 1980), 67.

26. Gerhard Dornseifer, *Richard Serra, The Drowned and the Saved* (Pulheim, Germany: Synagogue Stommeln, 1992), n.p. An interesting review of the exhibition, Ursula Bode, "Denkmal auf Zeit," *Der Zeit,* July 24, 1992, notes that Serra waived his fee for this commission and that the artist wished the catalog to serve as a memorial.

27. Brooks Adams, "Richard Serra: The Art World's Man of Steel," *Elle Decor,* June/July 1995, 52.

28. The suggestion that he read Levi came from Serra's therapist, whom he consulted about conflicts over taking the commission for a site with such specific content. Conversation with the artist in April 1998.

29. Simon N. Herman, *Jewish Identity: A Social Psychological Perspective* (New Brunswick, N.J.: Transaction Publishers, 1989), 87. David Theo Goldberg and Michael Krausz, eds., *Jewish Identity* (Philadelphia: Temple University Press, 1993), 11.

30. Helen Epstein, *Children of the Holocaust* (New York: Bantam Books, 1980), 1, 4–5. The therapeutic community has increasingly paid attention to the plight of children of survivors and the heritage of silence they inherited. See, for example, Douglas Martin, "When Holocaust Lives with Parents," *New York Times,* April 29, 1995.

31. Ziva Amishai-Maisels, *Depiction and Interpretation: The Influence of the Holocaust on the Visual Arts* (Oxford: Pergamon Press, 1994), 366.

32. Yehudit Shendar, "And the Lion Shall Dwell with the Fish," in *Witness and Legacy,* ed. Stephen C. Feinstein (Minneapolis: Lerner Publications, 1995), 20. Shendar also observed, "Holocaust ghosts haunt one's life not only as embodiments of lost family members. They transform to feelings of hate and anger" (22).

33. Herman, *Jewish Identity,* 34. Alan Montefiore, "Structures of Personal Identity and Cultural Identity," in Goldberg and Krausz, *Jewish Identity,* 213. Jean Paul Sartre, *Antisemite and Jew* (New York: Schocken, 1965), 100.

34. This pattern was observed in the life of Benjamin Disraeli and Karl Marx, whom Isaiah Berlin described as among those "whom history and social circumstances had cut off from their original establishment—the once familiar, safely segregated Jewish minority—[and who tried] to replant themselves in some new and no less secure and nourishing soil." Quoted in Herman, *Jewish Identity,* 36, from Isaiah Berlin, "Benjamin Disraeli, Karl Marx, and the Search for Identity," *Midstream,* August 1970, 29–49.

35. Stephen C. Feinstein, "Witness and Legacy," in Feinstein, *Witness and Legacy,* 11.

36. *Serra: Writings,* 179–80.

37. Primo Levi, *The Periodic Table* (New York: Schocken, 1984), 87.

38. *Serra: Writings,* 184–85, part of an essay entitled "Weight," which appeared in 1988 (the year after Primo Levi committed suicide) in the catalog for an exhibition of his sculpture at Galerie m in Bochum, Germany.

39. An interesting discussion of this and other films by the artist is "The Films of Richard Serra: An Interview," *October,* Fall 1979, 69–164. The interview with Annette Michelson, Serra, and Weyergraf is reprinted in *Serra: Writings,* 61–95. *Steelmill/Stahlwerk* is arguably Serra's most political film. Serra has always identified with workers, one of society's perpetually victimized groups.

40. *Serra: Writings,* 225–27.

41. R. H., *25 Jahre Philharmonie Berlin: Festschrift zum 15 Oktober 1988* (Berlin: Enka-Druck GmbH, 1988), 59–60. According to the author, even though the sculpture was designed for another site, Serra supplied a belated formal interpretation of the relationship of the sculpture to this location. Nevertheless, German art historian and public art administrator Stefanie Endlich, in a conversation in August 1992, stated that Serra's acceptance of this site generated much ill will for the artist in Berlin.

42. Conversation with author, December 1993.

43. Conversation with author in preparation for March 1984 *Artnews* article. Serra also thought it helped that the mayor of Barcelona at the time was named Serra.

44. *Serra: Writings,* 183.

45. Amishai-Maisels, *Depiction and Interpretation,* 355.

46. Casey Nelson Blake, "An Atmosphere of Effrontery: Richard Serra, *Tilted Arc,* and the Crisis of Public Art," in *The Power of Culture,* ed. Richard Wightman Fox and T. J. Jackson Lears (Chicago: University of Chicago Press, 1993), 247–89, discusses this aspect of Serra's history in some detail.

47. Serra appeared to confront these identity issues only later with commissions that addressed the Holocaust, discussed earlier in this chapter.

48. *Public Art Review* was created precisely for this purpose in 1989.

49. See Harriet F. Senie, *Contemporary Public Sculpture: Tradition, Transformation, and Controversy* (New York: Oxford University Press, 1992), 106–10.

50. For an expanded discussion of this development see ibid., chap. 3; and Donald Thalacker, *The Place of Art in the World of Architecture* (New York: Chelsea House and R. R. Bowker, 1981).

51. Patricia C. Phillips, "Forum: Something There Is That Doesn't Love a Wall," *Artforum,* Summer 1985, observed, "As a device to catalogue the flight from the gallery or a reformed involvement with it, the concept of site-specific work was an embryonic idea which later was inflated into an explanation, an apology, and occasionally a defense. The term 'site specific' became so overused that it often codified dissimilar ideas, romanticized some very bad work, and misled serious inquiry" (100–101).

52. See Senie, *Contemporary Public Sculpture,* chap. 2.

53. Donald Judd, "Specific Objects," *Arts Yearbook,* no. 8 (1965): 74ff., articulated this concept by stating that what was now included in the perception of art was the "spectator, artwork, and the place inhabited by both," which, in turn, was dependent on the "viewer's temporal movement in the space with the object." This is a simplified, more general version of Serra's later definition of site specificity, which extended well beyond gallery confines.

54. See Anna C. Chave, "Minimalism and Biography," *Art in America,* January 1990, 44–63.

55. See Maurice Tuchman, ed., *American Sculpture of the Sixties* (Los Angeles: Los Angeles County Museum, 1967). For a critical discussion of the *Scale as Content* exhibition, see A. Hudson, "Scale as Content," *Artforum,* December 1967, 45–47; Lucy Lippard, "Escalation in Washington," in *Changing: Essays in Art Criticism* (New York: E. P. Dutton, 1971), 237–54. The exhibition *Nine at Castelli* was discussed by Douglas Crimp, "Serra's Public Sculpture: Redefining Site Specificity," in Krauss, *Richard Serra/Sculpture* (New York: Museum of Modern Art, 1986), 41. It was reviewed by Max Kozloff, "Nine in a Warehouse: An Attack on the Status of the Object," *Artforum,* February 1969, 38–42.

56. Doris Freedman, daughter of builder Irwin Chanin, was crucial to the development of public art in New York City in her later role as founder and director of the Public Art Fund. The exhibition catalog, *Sculpture in Environment* (New York: Department of Cultural Affairs, 1967), contains a foreword by August Heckscher, then commissioner of cultural affairs, and an essay by Irving Sandler.

57. Earthworks officially entered the art world in an exhibition organized by Smithson at the Dwan Gallery in 1968, including works by Robert Morris, Michael Heizer, Dennis Oppenheim, Walter de Maria, and Claes Oldenburg. For a good general introduction to earthworks, see John Beardsley, *Earthworks and Beyond* (New York: Abbeville, 1989). For the relationship of earthworks to the development of recent public art, see Senie, *Contemporary Public Sculpture,* chap. 4. Robert Scull, for example, commissioned one of Heizer's early exca-

vation pieces in Nevada. In a sense, the remote location of these earthworks actually made them, if not more elitist than gallery art, at least directly accessible only to much smaller audiences.

58. See John Coplans, "Robert Smithson, The *Amarillo Ramp*," in Robert Hobbs, *Robert Smithson: Sculpture,* ed. Robert Hobbs (Ithaca, N.Y.: Cornell University Press, 1981), 47–55.

59. Unless otherwise noted, Serra's comments here and below are taken from his formal statement at Diamond's hearing.

60. Other artists defined site specificity differently. For example, Robert Irwin, the selection committee's first choice, outlined the parameters of a site-conditioned/site-determined response for art in the public realm in *Being and Circumstance: Notes toward a Conditional Art* (Larkspur Landing, Calif.: Lapis Press, with the Pace Gallery and the San Francisco Museum of Art, 1985): "Here there are numerous things to consider; what is the site's relation to applied and implied schemes of organization and systems of order, relation, architecture, uses, distances, sense of scale? For example, are we dealing with New York verticals or big sky Montana? What kinds of natural events affect the site—snow, wind, sun angles, sunrise, water, etc.? What is the physical and people density? the sound and visual density (quiet, next-to-quiet, or busy)? What are the qualities of surface, sound, movement, light, etc.? What are the qualities of detail, levels of finish, craft? What are the histories of prior and current uses, present desires, etc.? A quiet distillation of all of this—while directly experiencing the site—determines all the facets of the 'sculptural response': aesthetic sensibility, levels and kinds of physicality, gesture, dimensions, materials, kind and level of finish, details, etc.; whether the response should be monumental or ephemeral, aggressive or gentle, useful or useless, sculptural, architectural, or simply the planting of a tree, or maybe even doing nothing at all" (27).

61. Statement made to NEA advisory committee, December 15, 1987, reproduced in Clara Weyergraf-Serra and Martha Buskirk, eds., *The Destruction of "Tilted Arc": Documents* (Cambridge: MIT Press, 1991), 183–85. (Hereafter referred to as *Destruction.*)

62. *Destruction,* 12–13.

63. Lecture at the Ninety-Second Street Y in Manhattan, January 21, 1993.

64. Rosalyn Deutsche, "*Tilted Arc* and the Uses of Public Space," *Design Book Review,* Winter 1992, 25. Tom Crow, "Site-Specific Art: The Strong and the Weak," in *Modern Art in the Common Culture* (New Haven, Conn.: Yale University Press, 1996), 131–50. James Meyer, "The Functional Site; or, The Transformation of Site Specificity," in *Space, Site, Intervention: Situating Installation Art,* ed. Erika Suderburg (Minneapolis: University of Minnesota Press, 2000), 23–37. Other interesting expanded definitions are found in "On Site Specificity: A Discussion with Hal Foster, Renee Green, Mitchell Kane, Miwon Kwon, John Lindell, Helen Molesworth," *Documents,* Spring 1994, 11–22. Miwon Kwon, "One Place after Another: Notes on Site Specificity," *October,* Spring 1997, 85–110, reprinted in Suderburg, *Space, Site, Intervention,* 38–63. Dario Gamboni, "Deplacer egale detruire? Notes historiques sur un argument theorique," *Annales d'Histoire de l'Art et d'Archeologie,* vol. 19 (Brussels: Université Libre de Bruxelles, 1997), 33–46.

65. Albert Elsen, text for a debate on the future of *Tilted Arc* held at the School of Law, University of Texas at Austin, in 1988.

66. Crimp, "Serra's Public Sculpture," 53, 55. By 1997 Crimp had modified his views, stating that "it seems clear now that the art that makes the critique is not necessarily the art that goes on to construct a means of sociality, or of constructing a public sphere. In other

words, I think that you could say that *Tilted Arc* functioned as a critique of the falsity of that plaza. . . . But it is not able to move beyond that critique, and offer any sort of solution for the way that public sphere gets constructed." See Tom Finkelpearl, *Dialogues in Public Art* (Cambridge: MIT Press, 2000), 75.

67. For a discussion of some attempts at site-specific art that worked or did not, see Erika Doss, *Spirit Poles and Flying Pigs: Public Art and Cultural Democracy in American Communities* (Washington, D.C.: Smithsonian Institution Press, 1995).

68. The pamphlet that accompanied the exhibition, *After Tilted Arc: The Aesthetic Quest and Public Life* (New York: Storefront for Art and Architecture, 1985), includes statements by curator Tom Finkelpearl and director Glenn Weiss. All quotes, unless otherwise noted, are taken from this source. The artists included in the exhibition were Bill and Mary Buchen, Dina Bursztyn, Rosemary Cellini, Dan Coma, Green Market CENYC, David Hammons, Hera, Kristin Jones and Andrew Ginzel, Tadashi Kawamata, Kazuko, Jeffery Kipness, Sandford Kwinter and Françoise Schein, Ed McGowin, Deborah Ossoff, Robert Parker, Scott Pfaffman, Toshio Sasaki, Carolee Schneeman, Vernon Shetley, Leonid Sokov, Michael Sorkin, Nancy Spero, Mierle Laderman Ukeles, Allan Wexler, Hannah Wilke, Steven Woodward, and anonymous.

69. Undated press release issued by the Storefront for Art and Architecture, Glenn Weiss and Kyong Park.

70. Gellis elicited the following associations with rust: STEEL STRUCTURES URBAN DECAY COLD STURDY INDUSTRIAL RUSTING AGING SHELTERS HARD DOORWAYS BRITTLE BEAMS SHINY STRONG DECAY CORROSION MELTING SOFT MALLEABLE HIGH RISE SKELETONS ANGULAR CONTORTED REFINED MILITARY DESTRUCTION UNEMPLOYMENT TECHNOLOGY CAPITALISM FIRM CONFINEMENT RIGID SLAB PRISON MACHINERY BARRIER FENCE VEHICLE IRREVERSIBLE INDELIBLE RUST STAINS POWDER OLD BRIDGES BOILERS PASSING TIME. She believed that if the sculpture were changed to a glass arc, open-fence arc, pole arc, copper arc, or moss arc, "the viewers' experience would change, affirming that the violent reaction to the piece is from its material rather than its formal sculptural qualities."

71. In a review of the exhibition, Nancy Princenthal, "After *Tilted Arc* at Storefront for Art and Architecture," *Art in America,* February 1986, 126–27, found Wexler's "the most enchanting and intelligent" proposal, "suggesting participatory theater, Berlin Wall politics, and the nature of the debate over *Tilted Arc* itself."

72. Letter to Dwight Ink, June 4, 1985, GSA project file. Other quotations from reponses to questionnaire.

73. See Senie, *Contemporary Public Sculpture,* chap. 4, "Landscape into Public Sculpture."

74. See ibid., chap. 5, "Sculpture with a Function: Crossing the High Art–Low Art Barrier."

75. Patricia Phillips, "Public Art's Critical Condition," *On View,* Spring/Summer 1990, 9–14. See Suzanne Lacey, ed., *Mapping the Terrain: New Genre Public Art* (Seattle, Wash.: Bay Press, 1995); J. W. T. Mitchell, ed., *Art and the Public Sphere* (Chicago: University of Chicago Press, 1992); Arlene Raven, ed., *Art in the Public Interest* (Ann Arbor: UMI Press, 1989).

76. Eleanor Heartney, "The Dematerialization of Public Art," *Sculpture,* March–April 1993, 44–49. Using *Tilted Arc* to mark the turning point, she observed that the new breed of public artists "tend to speak in terms of community participation, temporariness and the limitation of the authorial role of the artist" (44). Gallery art had "dematerialized" much earlier,

with the conceptual art of the 1970s. See Mary Jane Jacob, *Places with a Past: New Site-Specific Art at Charleston's Spoleto Festival* (New York: Rizzoli Books, 1991).

77. See Mary Jane Jacob, Michael Brenson, and Eva M. Olson, *Culture in Action* (Seattle, Wash.: Bay Press, 1995).Heartney, "The Dematerialization of Public Art," 49. Michael Kimmelman, "Of Candy Bars and Public Art," *New York Times,* September 26, 1993. Kimmelman raises many problematic issues with regard to this kind of approach, which included "block parties and parades, paint charts, chocolate bars and hydroponically grown leafy vegetables." On Jacob's exhibitions, see Mary Jane Jacob and Michael Brenson, eds., *Conversations at the Castle: Changing Audiences and Contemporary Art* (Cambridge: MIT Press, 1998).

78. See Marlene Park and Gerald E. Moskowitz, *Democratic Vistas: Post Offices and Public Art in the New Deal* (Philadelphia: Temple University Press, 1984), 8–9, 14.

79. Hearing, 1:86.

80. The brochure is first cited in an unsigned memo prepared for Dwight Ink (acting administrator of GSA) and Frank Hodsoll (chairman of the NEA), referring to a meeting held on June 5, 1985, between representatives of the GSA and NEA.

81. These comparisons are discussed in more detail in Senie, *Contemporary Public Sculpture,* 225–26.

82. For a discussion on the various modes of community participation in the public art process, see Marie Gee, "Yes in My Front Yard," *High Performance,* Spring/Summer 1995, 60–65.

83. Successful education programs are discussed in Jeffrey L. Cruikshank and Pam Korza, *Going Public: A Field Guide to Developments in Art in Public Places* (Amherst, Mass.: Arts Extension Service and NEA, 1988), 103–15.

84. A newspaper editorial, "The Arc Comes Down," *Washington Post,* March 24, 1989, summed up the controversy in terms of conflicting ideas about the appropriate use of Federal Plaza: "Mr. Serra had argued in essence that if the sculpture interfered with the plaza's use, that was because it was itself 'using' the area. . . . The employees had other uses of the space in mind: they wanted to be able to walk across the courtyard, to eat lunch outdoors and to be free of the sight of something they considered hideously ugly."

85. *The WPA Guide to New York City* (New York: Random House, 1982), 102. Elliot Wilensky and Norval White, *AIA Guide to New York City,* 3rd ed. (New York: Harcourt Brace Jovanovich, 1988), 65, describe Foley Square as a "chaotic irregular subdivided excuse for a public space."

86. Currently the area around Federal Plaza and Foley Square is being redesigned to form a more coherent civic center. See, for example, David W. Dunlap, "Around City Hall, the Past Is New: Rediscovery and Reclamation Are the Themes in Manhattan's Civic Center District," *New York Times,* April 19, 1998.

87. See Kenneth T. Jackson, ed., *The Encyclopedia of New York City* (New Haven, Conn.: Yale University Press, 1995), 411.

88. "Foley Square from Gangs to Gawkers," *New York World Telegram,* July 23, 1949.

89. Paul Goldberger, *The City Observed: New York* (New York: Vintage Books, 1979), observed: "The term 'civic center' is a bit formal for the City Hall–Foley Square area, but it does sum up the neighborhood's prime function, the housing of government. Moreover, it suggests the aspirations, generally misguided, which bureaucrats have had for generations to give the area more coherence" (26).

90. When evidence of the Negros Burial Ground, which dates back to the 1750s, was unearthed in 1992 during excavation for a new GSA office building, Mayor David Dinkins requested that work on that part of the building site be suspended. Although Diamond initially rejected the mayor's request, he was overruled by GSA officials in Washington. See Alan Finder, "U.S. Suspends Digging at Site of Cemetery," *New York Times,* July 30, 1992. There has been speculation that Diamond subsequently lost his job as GSA regional administrator as a result of his decision. Eventually the city's Landmark Preservation Commission created "the African Burial Ground and Commons Historic District, from the southern tip of City Hall Park to the north side of Duane Street, including part of Foley Square." See David W. Dunlap, "African Burial Ground Made Historic Site," *New York Times,* February 26, 1993.

91. During the building boom of 1959–1973, office space increased by 50 percent. What most of these modern buildings had in common stylistically, distinguishing them from the architecture that had previously characterized the area, were flat roofs, steel and glass curtain-wall construction, and blank facades that lacked decorative detail.

92. Goldberger, *The City Observed,* 34–35. Goldberger contrasted the dismal buildings at Federal Plaza with Chicago's contemporary Federal Center, which was designed by Mies van der Rohe and whose forecourt was subsequently defined by the Chicago Picasso.

93. J. B. Jackson, "The American Public Space," *The Public Interest,* Winter 1984, 54.

94. The shift of open space to private ownership is documented and analyzed by Herbert I. Schiller, *Culture, Inc.: The Corporate Takeover of Public Expression* (New York: Oxford University Press, 1989). Shopping malls, regardless of their private ownership, have to a certain extent replaced main streets. As Margeurite Villecco, "The Renewed Importance of the Public Realm," *Architecture,* December 1985, observes, "With mannequins as monuments, these controlled . . . and supervised environments provide a place for public participation that many downtowns cannot. . . . The shopping mall is not our image of the public realm, but for many it is the 'experience' of the public realm our environment provides" (47).

95. The city's first zoning resolution was adopted in 1916 in response to the thirty-two-story Equitable Building at 120 Broadway, which obstructed light in its immediate environment to an unconscionable degree. As a result, there was a profusion of so-called wedding cake or ziggurat-shaped towers that did not block light as much. An excellent discussion of various approaches to zoning and their effects is Donald H. Elliott and Norman Marcus, "From Euclid to Ramapo: New Directions in Land Development Controls," *The Hofstra Law Review,* Spring 1973, 56–91.

96. See for example, George McCue, "Plazas and Pleasures," *Art in America,* January 1972, 92–95.

97. Robert Hughes, "The Trials of *Tilted Arc,*" *Time,* June 3, 1985, 78. Paul Goldberger, "Critic's Notebook," *New York Times,* May 2, 1985. Goldberger also felt that Serra understood "the nature of urban space and Foley Square, in a way that the architects . . . did not. The arc, in its long, gentle sweep, reaches out to embrace the two great classical courthouse buildings across the square, pulling the civic buildings around Foley Square together, where the Federal Plaza building tries to stand apart." Michael Sorkin, "Que Serra Sera," *Village Voice,* March 5, 1985. "Notes and Comments," *The New Yorker,* March 27, 1989, 33.

98. These comments were taken from forms distributed by Diamond at Federal Plaza.

99. For the "malling of America" see, for instance, Margaret Crawford, "The World in a Shopping Mall," in *Variations on a Theme Park: The New American City and the End of Public*

Space, ed. Michael Sorkin (New York: Hill and Wang, 1992), 3–30. See also Margeurite Villecco, quoted in note 94. Since today's malls may include public facilities (libraries, museums, social services agencies), their definition as either private or public is further muted. See Witold Rybczynski, *City Life* (New York: Simon and Schuster, 1995), 208ff.

100. According to architect and planner Michael Kwartler, in conversation with the author, the rationale behind these changes was to reinforce the public space of the street. Randomly located plazas, at the time seen as destructive to the spatial definition of the street, could still be built on avenues, which were wider, already more open.

101. Jack Newfield and Wayne Barrett, *City for Sale: Ed Koch and the Betrayal of New York,* rev. ed. (New York: Harper and Row, 1989), 4.

102. Stephen Carr, Mark Francis, Leanne G. Rivlin, and Andrew M. Stone, *Public Space* (Cambridge and New York: Cambridge University Press, 1991), 3, 3, 272.

103. William H. Whyte, *The Social Life of Small Urban Spaces* (Washington, D.C.: Conservation Foundation, 1980), 96.

104. These projects are discussed in Senie, *Contemporary Public Sculpture,* chap. 3.

105. Interview with Gordon Bunshaft, February 1978.

106. Quoted in Russel Ferguson, Anthony McCall, and Clara Weyergraf-Serra, eds., *Richard Serra: Sculpture, 1985–1998* (Los Angeles: Museum of Contemporary Art, with Steidl, Göttingen, 1998), 33.

107. In addition to Serra's descriptions of his studies of the space, see Penelope Walker, "The Trial of *Tilted Arc,*" *International Sculpture,* June/July 1985, 4, 17.

108. John J. Costonis, *Icons and Aliens: Law, Aesthetics, and Environmental Change* (Urbana and Chicago: University of Illinois Press, 1989). Although Costonis discusses a number of neighborhood disruptions, such as fruit stands on Park Avenue, many of his observations apply to *Tilted Arc* as well. I thank Michael Kwartler for this reference.

109. Goldstein, Hearing, 1:206. Gattuso, Hearing, 3:574–75.

110. La Basi, Hearing, 3:634. Wagner, Hearing, 2:485.

111. O'Dougherty, Hearing, 1:139ff. Blake, "An Atmosphere of Effrontery," 276–77.

112. Serra still finds this a spurious complaint, questioning what people wanted to see and arguing that many things block one's sight in Manhattan; interview with the artist, April 1998.

113. For a discussion of this aspect of spatial experience, see Michel de Certeau, *The Practice of Everyday Life,* trans. Steven Rendall (Berkeley and Los Angeles: University of California Press, 1984), chap. 7, "Walking in the City," 99–110.

114. GSA press release, June 30, 1989.

115. The "new" look of Federal Plaza received only cursory recognition in the local press. The news brief "Open Space Replaces 'Arc,'" *New York Times,* June 15, 1989, took up a scant fraction of a column.

116. Lanzone quoted in Carol Vogel, "Where an Arc Once Ruled," *New York Times,* May 28, 1993.

117. Pepper was originally selected by a panel to make a piece for a nearby federal site, and the budget was transferred to Federal Plaza when that site proved to be inappropriate.

118. Lanzone, quoted in Vogel, "Where an Arc Once Ruled."

119. Conversation with Schwartz, November 23, 1993. Conversation with Lanzone, June 1993.

120. In May 2001 no one in Schwartz's office could explain the significance of the steam, and the landscape architect was unavailable for comment.

121. According to an unnamed source close to the project, in conversation with the author, July 2000, Schwartz failed to obtain an agronomist's report on the feasibility of the grass. According to Schwartz's office, "the decision to replace the grass with boxwood has to do with maintenance issues of the mounds" (e-mail, May 16, 2001).

122. Undated press release obtained from GSA Public Affairs Office at Federal Plaza.

123. See Karrie Jacobs, "Site Lines: Que Serra, Serra," *New York,* January 20, 1997, 16.

124. In May 1997, with the assistance of Wendy Harris, I distributed a questionnaire to the staff of the Army Corps of Engineers. In the interest of obtaining an unguarded response, I did not ask for a signature, although some signed it anyway. This summary is based on a small sample of four responses. I have no idea whether it is typical, but it is honest.

125. Quoted in Jane Brown Gillette, "Self Portrait," *Landscape Architect,* February 1997, 92.

126. A panel on the future of the Civic Center held at the Urban Center in midtown Manhattan on November 15, 1995, dismissed as unimportant the role of art both in general and in Federal Plaza specifically, the latter perhaps because the plaza is outside the city's control. Titled "Defining the Civic Center—Debating Its Future," the panel was chaired by Kenneth T. Jackson, chair of Columbia University's Department of History and editor of *The Encyclopedia of New York City.* Panelists were William E. Davis, American Institute of Architects (AIA), New York City landmarks preservation commissioner and chair of the African Burial Ground Competition Coalition; Carole DeSaram, public member of Manhattan Community Board 1; William J. Diamond, now commissioner of New York City's Department of General Services; and Carl Weisbrod, president and CEO of the Alliance for Downtown New York, Inc. During the question period that followed the presentations, an architect observed that Martha Schwartz's new design looked as if *Tilted Arc* had split and was running around all over the place.

127. Amy Golden, "The Esthetic Ghetto: Some Thoughts about Public Art," *Art in America,* May/June 1974, 34.

128. Jürgen Habermas, *The Structural Transformation of the Public Sphere: An Inquiry into a Category of Bourgeois Society,* trans. Thomas Burger with Frederick Lawrence (Cambridge: MIT Press, 1989). For an excellent summary of the critical issues, see Craig Calhoun, ed., *Habermas and the Public Sphere* (Cambridge: MIT Press, 1991).

129. Rosalyn Deutsche, *Evictions: Art and Spatial Politics* (Cambridge: MIT Press, 1996), 289. For gender issues in the public sphere, see Nancy Fraser, "Rethinking the Public Sphere: A Contribution to the Critique of Actually Existing Democracy," in Calhoun, *Habermas and the Public Sphere,* 109–42. Mitchell, *Art and the Public Sphere,* 2, asks, "Are we witnessing the liquidation of the public sphere by publicity, the final destruction of the possibility of free public discussion, deliberation, and collective determination by a new culture of corporate, military, and state media management, and the emergence of a new world order in which public art will be the province of 'spin doctors' and propagandists? Or does the internationalization of global culture provide opportunities for new forms of public solidarity to emerge, and leave openings for the intrusion of new forms of public resistance to homogenization and domination?" (2). Bruce Robbins, ed., *The Phantom Public Sphere* (Minneapolis: University of Minnesota Press, 1993).

130. Hearing, respectively, Margo Jacobs, architect's wife, 1:139; Shirley Paris, neighborhood resident, 2:354; and Judge Re, 2:361–62.

131. Deutsche, *Evictions,* 291, 267.

132. Rosalyn Deutsche, "Krzysztof Wodiczko's *Homeless Projection* and the Site of Urban 'Revitalization,'" *October,* Fall 1986, 63–98.

133. Judith H. Balfe and Margaret J. Wyszomirski, in "Public Art and Public Policy," *Journal of Arts Management and Law,* Winter 1986, 5–29, discuss in detail the differences in commissioning practices.

134. The ad hoc evolution of this support is analyzed in John Wetenhall, "Camelot's Legacy to Public Art: Aesthetic Ideology in the New Frontier," in *Critical Issues in Public Art: Content, Context, and Controversy,* ed. Harriet F. Senie and Sally Webster (New York: HarperCollins, 1992; reissued Washington, D.C.: Smithsonian Institution Press, 1998), 142–70.

135. Johnson quoted in Edward Rothstein, "You Can't Please All of the People . . ." *New York Times,* July 26, 1992. For a detailed discussion of Nancy Hanks's accomplishments, see Margaret Jane Wyszomirski, "The Politics of Arts Policy: Subgovernment to Issue Network," in *America's Commitment to Culture: Government and the Arts,* ed. Kevin V. Mulcahy and Margaret Jane Wyszomirski (Boulder, Colo.: Westview Press, 1995), 47–76.

136. Quoted in Malcolm N. Carter, "The NEA: Will Success Spoil Our Biggest Patron?" *Artnews,* May 1977, 35.

137. These statistics are taken from Wyszomirski, "The Politics of Arts Policy."

138. See, for example, Robert Brustein, "Whither the National Arts and Humanities Endowments?" *New York Times,* December 18, 1977, and Carter, "The NEA."

139. See Wyszomirski, "The Politics of Arts Policy," 65ff.

140. There has been extensive press coverage of the Corcoran Gallery's cancellation of the exhibition of works by Mapplethorpe in Washington; the trial of the Contemporary Art Center in Cincinnati for showing the same exhibition, which had venues in five cities; the passage and repeal of Jesse Helms's so-called decency amendment; and John Frohnmayer's tenure as head of the NEA. For an insightful study of these and other censorship issues, see Steven C. Dubin, *Arresting Images: Impolitic Art and Uncivil Actions* (New York: Routledge, 1992).

141. Quoted in Margaret Jane Wyszomirski, "From Accord to Discord: Arts Policy during and after the Culture Wars," in Mulcahy and Wyszomirski, *America's Commitment to Culture,* 13.

142. There were few to link the *Tilted Arc* controversy with Mapplethorpe and Serrano. Wyszomirski, "The Politics of Arts Policy," observed that the controversy "presaged concerns about artists rights and community standards that would arise later over publicly supported art more generally" (64). Dario Gamboni, *The Destruction of Art: Iconoclasm and Vandalism since the French Revolution* (London: Reaktion Books, 1997), observed that the "end of *Tilted Arc* coincided with a political campaign against 'offensive' art strongly reminiscent of the McCarthy decade" (161).

143. Ford is quoted in Ronald G. Shafer, "A Touch of Class? Washington Planners Beset by Critical Public over Their Efforts to Put Art into Architecture," *Wall Street Journal,* September 21, 1976. For a more complete discussion of *La Grande Vitesse,* see John Beardsley, *Art in Public Places* (Washington, D.C.: Partners for Livable Places, 1981), 14–24; and Senie, *Contemporary Public Sculpture,* 100–104. See also Robert Sherrill, "What Grand Rapids Did for Jerry Ford—and Vice Versa," *New York Times Magazine,* October 20, 1974, 31–33, 72–92.

144. Andrews: NEA press release, September 1987. Faubion: NEA press release, October 17, 1988. On Art in Public Places category: Press release, October 2, 1989.

145. Conversation with the author, October 20, 1993.

146. These were the reasons for the change of policy according to Susan Lubowsky, then director of the Visual Arts program, in a telephone interview, November 26, 1991. Valuable information regarding NEA public art policies and directions was also provided by Bert Kubli, then NEA program specialist for visual artist public projects, special projects, and challenge grants.

147. NEA press release, "Grants to Support Public Art and Visual Art Discourse Announced," August 30, 1991. Awards totaling $596,000 were made in both categories.

148. NEA press release, "NEA Support for Public Art and Visual Art Discourse Announced," September 4, 1992. Forty grants were made, for a total of $430,000.

149. NEA press release, "Grants to Support Public Art and Encourage Public Discourse Announced," August 23, 1993. A total of forty-five grants, totaling $475,000, were awarded.

150. In 1995, under Jane Alexander, agency categories and funding guidelines were completely revamped in response to increased budget cuts and widespread lobbying for the agency's demise.

151. For a further discussion of the basis of percent-for-art programs, see Senie, *Contemporary Public Sculpture,* chap. 2.

152. Official White House statement, known colloquially as Nixon's design message, dated May 16, 1972.

153. Letter dated February 14, 1973, from Arthur F. Sampson, acting administrator for GSA, to Nancy Hanks, chair of the NEA.

154. For a more detailed discussion of the reception of earlier GSA commissions, see Thalacker, *The Place of Art.*

155. In a letter to Ink dated May 31, 1985, Eagleton wrote, "It was well known to you that various Senators had inquired of Mr. Golden as to how he would handle the *Tilted Arc* matter once he was in office. Yet, at one minute to midnight, you decided to act without giving Mr. Golden a chance to give the issue a fresh and independent judgment.

"While I agree that the Art-in-Architecture program may need procedural changes which would allow more local involvement and a closer working relation between artists and architects, I do not feel an existing sculpture, erected pursuant to all applicable review standards, should now be removed by an acting GSA administrator because he deemed earlier procedures inadequate."

156. Letter from Eagleton to Golden dated May 3, 1985. Reproduced in *Destruction,* 174.

157. I am indebted to Terence Golden for a candid interview in May 1993; quotations from Golden are from this interview.

158. Problems at the GSA were reported in the *New York Times* throughout the *Tilted Arc* controversy. In 1979, the year of the commission, there was a growing scandal involving GSA employees' taking kickbacks from private contractors (articles appeared in the *New York Times* on January 5, March 10, April 26, May 12, May 27, and July 31, 1979); this was followed by the forced resignation of GSA Administrator Solomon (January 24, January 27, and March 3, 1980); allegations of mismanagement, inappropriate spending, fraudulent billing, and lax financial controls (July 16, July 20, September 27, and December 18, 1980). A new GSA administrator, Gerald P. Carmen, made changes in staff, instituted some reforms, and in 1982

named a new advisory board to help the agency improve efficiency and operation (January 10, 1982). In 1983 there were reports of rats and robberies at the GSA (June 6 and November 15, 1983), and the National Academy of Public Administration said the GSA was doing a poor job of keeping buildings clean and safe. A GSA employee, Bertrand G. Berube, who was dismissed that year for saying many federal buildings posed health hazards because maintenance had been deferred to save money, subsequently won a lawsuit and was awarded $560,000 (September 4, 1988). In 1984 GSA buildings had problems with asbestos (April 14, 1984), and the deputy regional administrator in New York, Edward H. Wyatt Jr., was arrested for taking bribes that went back to 1980 (August 10, 1984), and subsequently pleaded guilty (November 21, 1984). The same year, the former GSA commissioner of public buildings was sentenced to four years in federal prison for attempted extortion (August 15 and November 22, 1984), and two GSA officials were involved with private funds set up in 1980 to help finance Reagan's campaign (June 9, 1984). In 1985, a few weeks after the *Tilted Arc* hearing, Wyatt was sentenced to two years in prison (March 22, 1985). By 1988, the year Golden resigned, the GSA was being investigated by a federal grand jury over allegations that a middle-level official had disclosed sensitive bid information from AT&T to competitors for telephone-switching contracts (March 5, 1988). Golden was not implicated in any way.

159. Telephone interview in March 1993.

160. Thalacker had been a strong director and public advocate of the Art-in-Architecture program and a key player in the *Tilted Arc* controversy as it unfolded, providing agency support and guidance. There are many who feel that the outcome might have been different had Thalacker lived and continued as head of the GSA program.

161. The history of the relationship of the NEA and GSA in the panel process, as well as current concerns about current changes, is outlined in a memo from Michael Faubion to Frank Hodsoll, through Jack Basso, Hugh Southern, Fred Kellogg, and Art Warren, dated October 28, 1988, "Re: GSA Art-in-Architecture Program Proposed Changes in Selection Procedures." The internal GSA document is referred to as "Chapter 15."

162. In the memo cited in note 161, Faubion noted, "Three out of five artists selected for projects over the last year have called the Endowment with concerns about conflicts between Endowment panel recommendations and GSA requests for changes in their proposals. Recently, an artist called to say he had just found out his GSA-commissioned piece had been removed from its site several months ago, without his knowledge or permission. After requesting advice from the Endowment regarding *Tilted Arc,* GSA has never responded with a decision and is, in fact, still planning to remove the sculpture, counter to the Endowment's advice. And after requesting advice from us in conservation and deaccessioning policies, which was transmitted, GSA has chosen not to include that information in Chapter 15."

163. A letter dated April 13, 1989, from George P. Cordes, acting commissioner of Public Buildings Services, informed Hugh Southern, acting chairman of the NEA, that "GSA's Regional Administrators are accountable within their regions for all aspects of our program activities, and therefore, they represent a significant Federal presence. The responsibilities vested with the Regional Administrator are such that both the short and long term effects of accepting particular works of art into our property inventory must accommodate basic GSA management needs.

"The modification to the Chapter 15 [the section of a larger document that outlined GSA's new selection process] that you cannot accept is one that is essential to us and allows

Regional Administrators to chair or co-chair the initial pre-site panel. It is critical for our regions to communicate fundamental issues that affect the character of the artwork for our projects. We believe this modification clarifies GSA's project requirements without affecting the independence, integrity and professionalism of the nomination process."

164. Letter from Hugh Southern to Richard Austin dated April 27, 1989, indicating that up until that point Southern still believed it would be possible to maintain a working relationship with the GSA and continued to hope it might still be so in the future.

165. Quoted in Mary Sherman and Stanley Collyer, "Should Public Art Be Treated as a Real Estate Investment?" *Competitions,* Spring 1994, 17.

166. On May 20, 1993, Senator Jeff Bingaman (D.–N.M.) introduced the Art-in-Architecture Act of 1993 (S.998), which would grant the GSA Art-in-Architecture program formal congressional authority and incorporate all selection procedures within that agency. No mention is made of the NEA. The act was referred to the Committee on Environment and Public Works, where it still resides as of spring 2001.

167. Lanzone's comments were made in an interview with the author in January 1992. Serra's remarks are from his introduction to *Destruction,* 5.

168. "Borofsky, Otterness, and Shapiro Create Figures for Los Angeles Federal Building," *GSA Arts,* Summer 1991, 4.

169. The controversy and Otterness's response is discussed in chapter 4, in the section "The Controversy as Censorship."

170. The controversy surrounding Jimenez's *Fiesta Jarabe*—which was installed at the U.S. border station at Otay Mesa, California, in 1992 and depicts a Mexican couple dancing a traditional Mexican hat dance—was over appropriate representation of cultural identity, a growing area of debate in public art controversy. The sculpture was announced in *GSA Arts,* Winter 1992, 1, 4, in rather condescending language—for example, "Slick, colorful, and boisterous, the sculpture combines the Spanish and the Indian, representing the region's multiculturalism. . . . Jimenez's art successfully combines traditions for a distinctive festive flavor full of color and movement that celebrates and embraces the border culture." The controversy, in this case, eventually subsided.

171. I am grateful to William R. Caine, fine arts specialist, Art-in-Architecture program, for an update and explanation of the most recent GSA policies.

172. Robert A. Peck, "Changes to the Art-in-Architecture Program," memorandum for regional administrators, March 15, 1998.

173. *Art-in-Architecture Program Guidelines,* March 1998.

174. *Tilted Arc* is only one of a long list of publicly commissioned works that were dismantled or destroyed arbitrarily. People for the American Way puts out a publication entitled *Artsave* that lists works considered to have been censored. For a while, abstract works seemed particularly vulnerable. More recently, works that appear to consider ethnic identity seem more at risk. See, for example, Sylvia Hochfield, "The Moral Rights (and Wrongs) of Public Art," *Artnews,* May 1988, 143–46.

175. All museums have a policy that allows them, under strictly defined circumstances, to remove art from their collection. Such deaccession policies usually require that if the art is sold, the money earned must be used only to purchase art. Although dispersed throughout the country, GSA's public art constitutes a collection, and yet the only policy referring to its re-

moval is predicated on perceived danger to it, stipulating that it be stored elsewhere on federal property for protection.

176. See Cruikshank and Korza, *Going Public,* 168–69 for an annotated version of this review process, highlighting points of particular concern. Quotations of procedures are from this version.

177. The specific conditions for review were as follows.

1. The condition or security of the artwork cannot be reasonably guaranteed.
2. The artwork requires excessive maintenance or has faults of design or workmanship and repair or remedy is impractical or unfeasible.
3. The artwork has been damaged and repair is impractical or unfeasible.
4. The artwork endangers public safety.
5. No suitable site is available, or significant changes in the use, character, or design of the site have occurred which affect the integrity of the work.
6. Significant adverse public reaction has continued unabated over an extended period of time.
7. The quality or authenticity of the artwork is called into question.
8. The sponsoring agency wishes to replace the artwork with a more appropriate work by the same artist.
9. Removal is requested by the artist.

The review process would also consider and include:

1. Review of the artist's contract and other agreements which may pertain.
2. Discussion with the artist of the concern prompting review.
3. Opinions of more than one independent professional qualified to recommend on the concern prompting review (conservators, engineers, architects, critics, art historians, safety experts, etc.).
4. Review of written correspondence, press, and other evidence of public debate.

178. Under the last stipulation, whenever feasible, the artist would be given first option to purchase; any sale would be through auction, gallery resale, or direct bidding by individuals; and trade would be through artist, gallery, museum, or other institutions.

179. *Art-in-Architecture Program Procedures* (Washington, D.C.: U.S. General Services Administration, 1998) 10.

180. "Chapter 10: Relocation, Removal, and Deaccessioning," *Desk Guide 2000, Fine Arts Program* Office of Chief Architect (Washington, D.C.: U.S. General Services Administration, 2000), 60, 62, 63, 61.

181. My thanks to Michael Kwartler and Burt Roberts for this observation.

182. For a more detailed analysis, see Gerald Marzorati, "The Arts Endowment in Transition," *Art in America,* March 1983, 9–13; Carole S. Vance, "Restructuring the NEA," *Art in America,* November 1990, 49–55.

183. Costonis, *Icons and Aliens,* 1. An abbreviated version of this section appeared as "Public Art and the Legal System," *Public Art Review,* Fall/Winter 1994, 13–15.

184. The First and Fifth Amendments read as follows:

I. Congress shall make no law respecting an establishment of religion, or prohibiting the free exercise thereof; or abridging the freedom of speech, or of the press; or the right of the people peaceably to assemble, and to petition the Government for a redress of grievances.

V. No person shall be held to answer for a capital, or otherwise infamous crime, unless on a presentment or indictment of a Grand Jury, except in cases arising in the land or naval forces, or in the militia, when in actual service in time of war or public danger; nor shall any person be subject for the same offense to be twice put in jeopardy of life or limb; nor shall be compelled in any criminal case to be a witness against himself, nor be deprived of life, liberty, or property, without due process of law; nor shall private property be taken for public use, without just compensation.

185. For a discussion of other works of art that have been removed or destroyed, see Cruikshank and Korza, *Going Public,* 123–31; Barbara Hoffman, "Law for Art's Sake," *Critical Inquiry,* Spring 1991, 544–48. Hoffman published a later version of this essay (with the same title) in *Columbia-VLA Journal of Law & the Arts,* Fall 1991, providing more examples, 44–52. See also *Artistic Freedom under Attack,* vol. 1, published by People for the American Way, a nonpartisan constitutional-liberties organization (Washington, D.C., 1992).

186. *Richard Serra v. United States General Services Administration,* United States District Court, Southern District of New York, Docket No. 96 Civ. 9656, December 17, 1986. An edited version of Serra's complaint is reproduced in *Destruction,* 199–205.

187. *Richard Serra v. United States General Services Administration,* United States District Court, Southern District of New York, Docket No. 33, 86 Civ. 9656, opinion 61441, decision by Judge Milton Pollock, August 31, 1987. An edited version of this decision is reproduced in *Destruction,* 206–18.

188. *Richard Serra v. United States General Services Administration,* 667 F. Supp. 1042 (S.D.N.Y. 1987). Judge Pollock's decisions are summarized in Circuit Judge Jon O. Newman's ruling on Serra's appeal.

189. The appeal filed by Serra on December 15, 1987, United States Court of Appeals for the Second Circuit, Docket No. 87-6231, is reproduced in *Destruction,* 219–38. An edited version of the brief filed by the defendants on January 26, 1988, Docket Nos. 87-6231, 87-6251, is found in *Destruction,* 239–45. The arguments and issues are analyzed by Hoffman, "Law for Art's Sake," 540–73, and in a later version with more legal detail in *Columbia-VLA Journal of Law & the Arts,* Fall 1991, 39–96. All subsequent quotes, unless otherwise noted, are taken from the earlier article.

190. The decision by Judge Jon O. Newman, United States Court of Appeals for the Second Circuit, Nos. 822, 823—August Term 1987, dated May 27, 1988, is reproduced in *Destruction,* 246–53, from which all quotations from this ruling are taken.

191. *Richard Serra v. United States General Services Administration,* 847 F. 2d 1045, 1048, 1049 (2nd Cir. 1988).

192. Hearing, 1:41–42; 1:42.

193. Brown stated, "In all stages of the decision making process it was understood by Serra, and by the government, that Serra was making a permanent work for that specific space. That principle is one of the foundations of the GSA Art-in-Architecture Program. It is a national program that seeks to commission works of art of the highest quality for federal build-

ings across the country that will be, to as large an extent as possible, integral to the sites and spaces in question. . . . To remove this work would counter an agreement that was made between the artist and the government, which was entered into in every stage with careful and responsible deliberation" (Hearing, 1:167).

194. The contract is reproduced in its entirety in Dwight Ink, Attachment J to *Decision on the "Tilted Arc"* (May 31, 1985, unpublished, available at GSA). Article 6 appears on page 6 of the twenty-nine-page contract. In 1977, the GSA did organize a traveling exhibition, entitled *Art in Architecture,* that was very well received.

195. Attorney Jack Guthman, in conversation and correspondence with the author (December 1997), saw this as a clear contract issue, while attorney Jean Reed Haynes, in correspondence with the author (September 1997), stressed that "there was a powerful contractual argument that, for whatever reason, did not prevail." Barbara Hoffman, in conversation with the author (October 1993), suggested that the contract remains the best place to protect public sculpture.

196. *Destruction,* all quotes from 250.

197. Hoffman took issue with the court's interpretation of the First Amendment as applied to artistic expression. She saw "a hostility to according full protection to nonpolitical artistic expression" ("Law for Art's Sake," 127) and argued that "artistic expression in the public context should be accorded full First Amendment protection" (129). Most definitively, she felt that Serra's claim was not given "the same careful analysis and protection that courts have traditionally reserved for other forms of speech" (129). She also challenged the court's opinion that Serra had other venues for free expression, especially in this commission: "The court's view that destroying an artist's past work does not suppress speech if the artist can create new work does little to promote one objective of public art programs: the creation of a cultural legacy" (131).

198. *Destruction,* 203.

199. *Destruction,* 251–52.

200. Hoffman, "Law for Art's Sake," 136, 137.

201. The most frequently cited precedent is *Pico v. Board of Education,* which ruled in 1980 that the removal of books from a high school library because their content was deemed by the board of education to be "anti-American, anti-Christian, anti-Semitic and just plain filthy" was a violation of students' First Amendment rights. Hoffman argues, "Even if the Pico standard of 'partisan or political motive' arguably affords public school administrators discretion in removing books based on criteria of civility and taste in the public school environment, to afford such deference to government bureaucrats or, worse, to politicians does not seem to further any identifiable goals of public art programs" (131).

202. *Destruction,* 253.

203. Article 6*bis* of the Berne Convention reads as follows:

1. Independently of the author's economic rights, and *even after the transfer of said rights* [emphasis added], the author shall have the right to claim authorship of the work and to object to any distortion, mutilation, or other modification of, or other derogatory action in relation to, the said work, which would be prejudicial to his honor or reputation.
2. The rights granted to the author in accordance with the preceding paragraph, after his death, shall be maintained, at least until the expiry of the economic rights, and shall be

exercisable by the persons or institutions authorized by the legislation of the country where protection is claimed. However, those countries whose legislation, at the moment of their ratification of or accession to this Act, does not provide for the protection after the death of the author of all the rights set out in the preceding paragraph may provide that some of these rights may, after his death, cease to be maintained.

3. The means of redress for safeguarding the rights granted by this Article shall be governed by the legislation of the country where protection is claimed.

204. Hoffman discusses the state versions of *droit moral* legislation, most of them modeled after the legislation of California and New York. She summarizes: "The New York model, though it does not prohibit destruction of art, does prohibit the display or publication of, or making accessible to the public in any way an altered, defaced, mutilated, or modified work of fine art without the artist's consent if damage to the artist's reputation is likely to result" (568). The various state statutes that address artists' moral rights are also discussed in Cruikshank and Korza, *Going Public,* 133–34.

205. Excerpts from the Berne Convention Implementation Act of 1988, as they modify U.S. copyright law, are reproduced in *Destruction,* 267–68. Specifying those rights not affected, the act states, "The provisions of the Berne convention, the adherence of the United States thereto, and satisfaction of United States obligations thereunder, do not expand or reduce any right of an author of a work, whether claimed under Federal, State, or the common law—(1) to claim authorship of the work; or (2) to object to any distortion, mutilation, or other modification of, or other derogatory action in relation to, the work, that would prejudice the author's honor or reputation."

206. Hoffman, "Law for Art's Sake," 568.

207. Cynthia Esworthy, NEA Office of General Counsel, "From Monty Python to Leona Helmsley: A Guide to the Visual Artists Rights Act," *arts.community 1.7,* Microsoft Internet Explorer, page 2. Accessed March 23, 1997.

208. Hoffman, "Law for Art's Sake," 540; Costonis, *Icons and Aliens,* 80.

209. My thanks to Jean Reed Haynes for this distinction and the larger jurisprudential issues involved in the role of "activist" judges.

210. A standard work delineating this view of history can be found in Karl Popper, *Popper Selections* (New York: Harper and Row, 1977).

211. A good example of the interpretation of modern art as a series of revolutions is provided by Robert Hughes, *The Shock of the New* (New York: Alfred A. Knopf, 1981).

212. Any number of publications have documented and interpreted the end of the avant-garde. See especially Krauss, *Originality of the Avant-Garde.*

4. After *Tilted Arc*

1. A memo from Richard Andrews to Frank Hodsoll, dated March 19, 1985, acknowledges this situation and cites the examples noted in the text.

2. The attempts at removing the Serra sculpture are summarized in Susan Hegger, "But Is It Art?" *Riverfront Times,* September 4–10, 1985.

3. "Another Serra under Attack," *Art in America,* October 1985, 194. Unlike *Tilted Arc, Twain* was sponsored by a local civic group headed by Emily Rauh Pulitzer (important St. Louis arts advocate and patron) and funded with money from the NEA, the Missouri Arts

Council, thirty-five corporations, and private donors. However, many issues seemed to parallel the New York controversy. The debate also prompted articles questioning the validity of modern art and the competence of art professionals. George F. Will, in "Giving Art a Bad Name," *Newsweek,* September 16, 1985, referred to Serra's sculptures as "whims in rusty steel," and dismissed all abstract art as "anti-intellectual 'art' enveloped by ludicrous intellectualizing" (80).

4. Douglas C. McGill, "St. Louis Bid to Remove Serra Work," *New York Times,* August 21, 1985. The opening paragraph links the St. Louis action to what was happening to *Tilted Arc.* It was noted that *Twain* had been controversial since its installation in 1982 and that "a number of alderman have somewhat silently said, 'I don't like it, but who am I to judge what art is?' Now some are saying that these pieces of iron are not art, it's just causing maintenance problems, and it's a valuable piece of property that should be developed."

5. Alan Sonfist's *Time Landscape* of St. Louis (1986) fared less well. In spite of the regional arts commission's existing (but not mandatory) maintenance and deaccessioning procedures, it was destroyed in 1987, only seventeen months after its installation, without any consultation with the artist or the public. The sculpture, which consisted of plants and cobblestones evocative of the region's Indian and French history, was leveled by city bulldozers. To Evelyn O. Price, head of the parks department, who ordered the destruction of the piece, it looked like a construction site: "There were weeds there, homeless people were hanging their clothes from trees. It was as if the artist had abandoned the site, leaving it to me to use my budget and my workers to try to make it work." Emily Rauh Pulitzer speculated that the extra maintenance required by the artwork prompted employees in the parks department to sabotage it from the start. Price and Pulitzer both cited in William E. Schmidt, "After Auspicious Beginnings, Public Art Finds Itself at Odds with the Public," *New York Times,* November 2, 1987.

6. Amei Wallach, "City Sees Obstacle, Not Art," *Newsday,* February 20, 1996.

7. Conversation with the author, December 1993.

8. Art historian Yve-Alain Bois called it "the strongest and most effective public sculpture since Brancusi's vast ensemble at Tirgu Jiu and Mathias Goeritz's Satellite City Towers in Mexico City" ("The Meteorite in the Garden," *Art in America,* Summer 1984, 108–13, at 108.) The extremely positive reception was noted in Michael Brenson, "Richard Serra Works Find a Warm Welcome in France," *New York Times,* November 3, 1983. One local critic, Maiten Bouisset, observed that it was not necessary to read about the sculpture to understand it (although there was information provided at the site); one could just experience it ("Les Chateaux de Cartes de Richard Serra," *Le Matin,* November 11, 1983).

9. Interview with the author in 1983 in preparation for *Artnews* profile.

10. See Sarah King, "Serra Sculpture Defaced in Paris," *Art in America,* April 1991, 33, where she notes that Jacques Toubon, mayor of the arrondissement, was reportedly distressed over the repeated "assaults" on "one of the most important works by one of the most important sculptors of the twentieth century." The current status of the sculpture was related to me by Clara Weyergraf-Serra in a telephone interview in April 1997.

11. Serra's quotations, dated January 1989, are part of a Swiss Bank in-house publication entitled "Swiss Bank Corporation: Fine Art Program: Art News: Highlights: The Permanent Collection, Floors 11 and 12," n.d., n.p. The publication also includes discussions of work by Matt Mullican, Deborah Butterfield, and Gregoire Muller.

12. See Nancy Princenthal, "Corporate Pleasures," *Art in America,* December 1988,

38–41. As Princenthal observed, Serra's sculpture, like Jonathan Borofsky's *Man with Briefcase* (1987), "frames the corporate structures behind it and is framed by them; it is a kind of logo" (39).

13. I discuss the issue of corporate sponsorship and public art in more detail in *Contemporary Public Sculpture: Tradition, Transformation, and Controversy* (New York: Oxford University Press, 1992), chap. 6.

14. Alfred Pacquement, *Richard Serra* (Paris: Centre Georges Pompidou, 1983), 41.

15. Conversation with the author, December 1993.

16. François Barre observed that the sculpture "revives the logical pattern of a forgotten circulation of men and things ("L'espace de temps," in *Richard Serra: "Octagon for St. Eloi,"* [Chagny, France: Centre National des Arts Plastiques with Creusot-Loire Industrie, 1991], 8).

17. *Richard Serra, "Octagon for Saint Eloi."* The publication includes a major essay by Serge Lemoine entitled "Gravité," as well as shorter commentaries by Jean-Michele Pheline ("Quatre + Trois = Huit") and Alain Coulange ("Notes octagonales pour Richard Serra").

18. Pheline, "Quatre + Trois = Huit," 70, discusses the symbolism of numbers in the sculpture.

19. Other art commissions at the Holocaust Museum went to Ellsworth Kelly, Sol LeWitt, and Joel Shapiro. The art consultant for the museum was Nancy Rosen, and the selection committee included Suzanne Delehanty, then director of the Museum of Contemporary Art in Houston, who had also been on the NEA panel that recommended Serra for Federal Plaza.

20. Conversation with the author, December 1993.

21. I observed these activities in summer 1995. According to newspaper reports, Serra's gallery in Bochum had set a price far below the sculpture's market value of one million dollars, and art experts from all over the world were singing the sculpture's praises. Basel already owned one of Serra's landscape pieces, *Open Field Vertical/Horizontal Elevations: For Breughel and Martin Schwander* (1979–1980), first displayed in Werkenpark as part of a sculpture exhibition in 1980 and then permanently installed in the park in 1985 with funds from the Emanuel Hoffman Foundation. *T.W.U.* was included in the Merian Park exhibition in 1984, and in 1988 Serra made drawings, entitled *Equal Mass—Unequal Weight,* of the great skylit hall in the Kunsthalle. Early works by the artist were already in the Museum für Gengenwartskunst. Basel was thus seen as having a unique opportunity to acquire a major public piece by Serra that would round out its collection. Over time the piece continued to attract graffiti and required ongoing maintenance. See Mark Spiegler, "Rust in Peace: If *Tilted Arc* Had Lived," *New York,* January 25, 1999, 16.

22. Roberta Smith, "Richard Serra's Temporal Monument," *New York Times,* April 2, 1993.

23. Quoted in Carol Vogel, "The Art Market: The Modern's Massive Gift," *New York Times,* April 23, 1993.

24. See *Richard Serra Sculpture, 1985–1998* (Los Angeles: Museum of Contemporary Art, 1998). For a discussion of the torqued ellipses, see "Interview with David Sylvester," 187–206.

25. Patrick J. Buchanan, "In the New Kulturkampf, the First Battles Are Being Fought," *Richmond (Virginia) Times-Dispatch,* June 19, 1989. Buchanan later used this theme to threaten then President George Bush's nomination for a second term.

26. Carol Becker, "Art Thrust into the Public Sphere," in *Censorship I,* ed. Barbara Hoffman and Robert Storr, whole issue of *Art Journal,* Fall 1991, 67. See also Steven C. Dubin, *Arresting Images: Impolitic Art and Uncivil Actions* (London and New York: Routledge, 1992), 102–24.

27. The Mapplethorpe/Serrano controversies, as they came to be known, were widely covered in the national press. For a particularly acute analysis, see Dubin, *Arresting Images,* especially 96–101, 170–92.

28. For a more complete list of budget cuts, see Robert Atkins, "A Censorship Time Line," *Art Journal,* Fall 1991, 33–37.

29. See Rita Gilbert, *Living with Art,* 3rd ed. (New York: McGraw-Hill, 1992), 28; Marilyn Stokstad, *Art History* (Englewood Cliffs, N.J.: Prentice Hall and Harry Abrams, 1995), 1161; Sam Hunter and John Jacobus, *Modern Art,* 3rd ed. (Englewood Cliffs, N.J.: Prentice Hall, 1992), 374; H. H. Arnason and Marla Prather, *A History of Modern Art,* 4th ed. (Englewood Cliffs, N.J.: Prentice Hall, 1998), 596, 658–59; Daniel Wheeler, *Art since Mid-Century: 1945 to the Present* (Engelwood Cliffs, N.J.: Prentice Hall, 1991), 268; Jonathan Fineberg, *Art since 1940: Strategies of Being* (Englewood Cliffs, N.J.: Prentice Hall, 1995), 321; Edward Lucie-Smith, *Movements in Art since 1945: Issues and Concepts,* 3rd ed., rev. and expanded (London: Thames and Hudson, 1995), 171; Irving Sandler, *Art of the Postmodern Era* (New York: HarperCollins, 1996), 187–88; Robert Hughes, *American Visions: The Epic History of Art in America* (New York: Alfred A. Knopf, 1997), 568–70; Hilton Kramer, "Is Art above the Laws of Decency?" in *Public Policy and the Aesthetic Interest,* ed. Ralph A. Smith and Ronald Berman (Urbana and Chicago: University of Illinois Press, 1992), 228–35, reprinted from a *New York Times* article of July 2, 1989.

30. Margaret Jane Wyszomirski, "The Policy of Arts Policy," in *America's Commitment to Culture,* ed. Kevin Mulcahy and Margaret Jane Wyszomirski (Boulder, Colo.: Westview Press, 1995), 64; Joan Jeffri, "The Artist in an Integrated Society," in *Public Money and the Muse,* ed. Stephen Benedict (New York: W. W. Norton, 1991), 98, 101; Dubin, *Arresting Images,* 25; Dario Gamboni, *The Destruction of Art: Iconoclasm and Vandalism since the French Revolution* (London: Reaktion Books, 1997), 161.

31. All quotes are from Michael Brenson, "Public Art at New Federal Building in Queens," *New York Times,* March 24, 1989. Brenson found the artistic results in Jamaica on the whole "not worse than most other works of public art, but . . . also not better."

32. Judith Huggins Balfe, "The Process of Commissioning Public Sculpture: 'Due' or 'Duel,'" in Mulcahy and Wyszomirski, *America's Commitment to Culture,* 198, 199, 200.

33. Howard Smagula, in his *Currents: Contemporary Directions in the Visual Arts,* 2nd ed. (Englewood Cliffs, N.J.: Prentice Hall, 1989), was the only writer to address the symbolic content of the controversy: "*Tilted Arc* became, perhaps undeservedly, a tangible symbol for various social issues and psychological forces the public felt they could do without: the unremitting power of the federal government which commissioned this sculpture and controlled their daily work lives; the dehumanizing vastness and anonymity of NYC itself; and the ability of a suspect 'modern' artist to change or affect, with no prior explanation or a dialogue, where they walked and what they saw" (29–30).

34. Benjamin Buchloh, "Vandalismus von oben: Richard Serra's *Tilted Arc* in New York," in *Unerwünschte Monumente: Moderne Kunst in Stadtraum,* ed. Walter Grasskamp (Munich: Schreiber, 1992), 115. My translation.

35. Dubin, *Arresting Images,* 25.

36. Steven C. Dubin, "Impolitic Art and Uncivil Actions: Controversies in the Public Sphere," in *Paying the Piper: Causes and Consequences of Art Patronage,* ed. Judith Huggins Balfe (Chicago: University of Chicago Press, 1993), 184.

37. See, for example, Pierre Bourdieu, *Distinction: A Social Critique of the Judgement of Taste,* trans. Richard Nice (Cambridge, Mass.: Harvard University Press, 1984).

38. J. W. T. Mitchell, ed., *Art and the Public Sphere* (Chicago: University of Chicago Press, 1992), 3, 6, 11, 31, 148, 156, 253.

39. Buchloh, "Vandalismus von oben." Buchloh also abhorred the postmodern alternative of "dumbing down" by providing comfortable seating or friendly images. He admired instead public art by Hans Haacke, Dan Graham, and a few others who focused on the contradictions (or evils) of current political realities.

40. Fineberg, *Art since 1940,* 323. Lucie-Smith, *Movements in Art since 1945,* 171. Actually, I see the element of expressionism as concentrated rather than suppressed, as Lucie-Smith suggests. He also sees Serra's work as representing "a kind of transitional stage, with Minimal overtones but still some relationship to the work of David Smith" (171). In mistakenly dating *Tilted Arc* from 1989, the year it was removed, he inadvertently reveals how much its true place in history was established by its removal.

41. Hughes, *American Visions,* 568–80. Hughes discusses this fearful element in Serra's sculpture, which he defines as addressing "the body through anxiety" (568). Anna C. Chave, "Minimalism and the Rhetoric of Power," *Arts Magazine,* January 1990, 44–63.

42. Virginia Maksymowicz, "Through the Back Door: Alternative Approaches to Public Art," in *Art and the Public Sphere,* ed. Mitchell, 156. Erika Doss, *Spirit Poles and Flying Pigs: Public Art and Cultural Democracy in American Communities* (Washington, D.C.: Smithsonian Institution Press, 1995), 32.

43. Rita Gilbert, *Living with Art,* 3rd ed. (New York: McGraw-Hill, 1992), 28. Gilbert, in addition to grossly misrepresenting the process, cites the figure of 7,000 workers signing a petition against the sculpture, a figure I cannot reconstruct even if I count all the petitions and letters both pro and con. She also repeats the most prevalent misperception: that one had to walk around the sculpture to cross the plaza. Stokstad, *Art History,* 1161. *Tilted Arc* is not a minimalist work, and it was not selected by an artists' panel. Wheeler, *Art since Mid-Century,* 268.

44. Suzi Gablik, *The Reenchantment of Art* (New York: Thames and Hudson, 1991), 66.

45. Howard Smagula, *Currents: Contemporary Directions in the Visual Arts,* 2nd ed. (Englewood Cliffs, N.J.: Prentice Hall, 1989), 29–30. Rosalyn Deutsche, "Uneven Development: Public Art in New York City," *October,* Winter 1988, 19. See also Deutsche, "*Tilted Arc* and the Uses of Public Space," *Design Book Review,* Winter 1992, 22–27, and "Art and Public Space: Questions of Democracy," *Social Text* no. 33 (1992): 34–53.

46. Dale McConathy, "Serra's Unofficial Monument," in *Public Art/Public Controversy: The "Tilted Arc" on Trial,* ed. Sherrill Jordan (New York: ACA Books, 1987), 4.

47. Hughes, *American Visions,* 570. Smagula, *Currents,* 31.

48. David Antin, "Fine Furs" in Mitchell, *Art and the Public Sphere,* 253.

49. Mary Jane Jacob, Michael Brenson, and Eva M. Olson, *Culture in Action* (Seattle, Wash.: Bay Press, 1995), pp. 15, 54, 60.

50. See, for example, Barbara Hoffman and Robert Storr, eds., *Censorship I,* and *Censorship II,* whole issues of *Art Journal,* Fall 1991, Winter 1991; Dubin, *Arresting Images;*

"Censorship versus the First Amendment," *Public Art Review,* Fall/Winter 1994; Richard Burt, ed., *The Administration of Aesthetics: Censorship, Political Criticism, and the Public Sphere* (Minneapolis: University of Minnesota Press, 1994).

51. Buchloh, "Vandalismus von oben," 103–20. Damning the process that led to *Tilted Arc*'s removal as "an illegal plebescite and illegal sham proceedings" (105), Buchloh also considered "well-meaning" vandalism—the co-optation of public art by using it as civic symbol or logo—"just as hostile to and unfamiliar with art as the paranoid projections of its adversaries" (108).

52. Gamboni, *The Destruction of Art,* 154–65.

53. The controversy was variously reported in Susan Seager, "Judges Flay, Praise Federal Building's Art," *Daily Journal,* November 22, 1991; Gale Holland, "Radical Art or Simply Revolting?" *Daily Breeze,* December 2, 1991; Laurie Becklund, "Arts Rights Groups Protest Removal of Nude Sculpture," *Los Angeles Times,* December 5, 1991.

54. See Amei Wallach, "Art or Degradation? Mural Is Target of Protest," *New York Newsday,* March 27, 1992; Robert Atkins, "Antipathy/Apathy," *Village Voice,* June 23, 1992; Sonia Reyes, "A Mural Outrage, Say Hispanics," *Daily News,* March 27, 1992; Sonia Reyes, "He'll Paint Different Picture of Hispanics," *Daily News,* July 17, 1992; Yasmin Ramirez, "Protest Hits Jail Mural," *Art in America,* July 1992, 29.

55. Quoted in Daniel Grant, "Bland Art in Every Pot," *The Nation,* November 29, 1999, 46.

56. For an excellent analysis of the controversy, see Jane Kramer, "Whose Art Is It?" *The New Yorker,* December 21, 1992, 80–109, subsequently published as *Whose Art Is It?* (Durham, N.C.: Duke University Press, 1994).

57. Philip Pearlstein, "Censorship on Stylistic Grounds," *Art Journal,* Winter 1991, 65.

Conclusion

1. For the development of Kennedy's ideas, see John Wetenhall, "Camelot's Legacy to Public Art: Aesthetic Ideology in the New Frontier," *Art Journal,* Winter 1989, 303–8, subsequently published in expanded form in Harriet F. Senie and Sally Webster, eds., *Critical Issues in Public Art: Content, Context, and Controversy* (New York: HarperCollins, 1992), 142–57.

2. For a critique of political uses of modern art, see Serge Guilbaut, *How New York Stole the Idea of Modern Art: Abstract Expressionism, Freedom, and the Cold War,* trans. Arthur Goldhammer (Chicago: University of Chicago Press, 1983).

3. This was one of the chief arguments against the Vietnam Veterans Memorial when it was first installed (the same year as *Tilted Arc*). On the range and significance of responses to abstraction, see especially David Freedberg, *The Power of Images* (Chicago: University of Chicago Press, 1989), 418ff.

4. For an analysis of the political derivation of avant-garde art, see Renato Poggioli, *The Theory of the Avant-Garde* (Cambridge, Mass.: Harvard University Press, 1968).

5. For a phenomenological interpretation of Serra's work, see especially Rosalind E. Krauss, *Richard Serra/Sculpture* (New York: Museum of Modern Art, 1986), 15ff.

6. Such an offer implicitly contradicts his insistence on the site specificity of *Tilted Arc.* In a later conversation, he offered no specifics on how Federal Plaza might be changed with his approval.

7. There were public representatives in both the Richard Haas and John Ahearn controversies discussed in chapter 4, but not the public that ultimately objected. Just who may adequately represent the public continues to be a problematic issue, especially since the public at a site is always changing.

8. For the anatomy of controversies, see Steven C. Dubin, *Arresting Images: Impolitic Art and Uncivil Actions* (London and New York: Routledge, 1992), especially the introduction.

9. Quoted in William Wilson, "The Matter of Serra's 'Arc' de Trauma," *Los Angeles Times,* reprinted in *Public Art/Public Controversy: The "Tilted Arc" on Trial,* ed. Sherill Jordan (New York: ACA Books, 1987), 161.

10. Kenneth Baker suggests one symbolic aspect of lost control in "Vector of Viewer Response," *Artforum,* September 1986, 103–8: "My own guess is that, by the way it blots out building entrances visually from certain vantage points, *Tilted Arc* may remind some who staff the bureaucracies within these buildings of their own wish never to have to return to the captivity of office work. The obstacle it poses, in imagination if not in fact, reveals the coercive force of habit that underlay the plaza-users' previous comings and goings. If I'm right about this, it is easy to understand how people might make *Tilted Arc* the target of their resentment, since they may well stand more chance of dislodging it than of changing their working lives for the better" (106).

11. "Public Affairs and Education," *Art in Architecture Program Guidelines,* March 1998.

12. This expanded definition of education in art is discussed in Samuel Hope, "An Overview of the Strategic Issues in American Education," and E. Louis Lankford, "Artistic Freedom: An Art World Paradox," both in *Public Policy and the Aesthetic Interest,* ed. Ralph A. Smith and Ronald Berman (Urbana: University of Illinois Press, 1992), and more generally in David Trend, *The Crisis of Meaning in Culture and Education* (Minneapolis: University of Minnesota Press, 1995).

Index

Harriet F. Senie is director of museum studies and professor of art history at the City College and Graduate Center, City University of New York. She is the author of *Contemporary Public Sculpture: Tradition, Transformation, and Controversy* and co-editor with Sally Webster of *Critical Issues in Public Art: Content, Context, and Controversy*.